IN THE NAME OF

ALLAH

THE ALL-COMPASSIONATE, ALL-MERCIFUL

The Music Made Me Do It

*An in-depth study of music
through Islam and science*

- Title: The Music Made Me Do It — An in-depth study of music through Islam and science
- Author: Dr. Gohar Mushtaq
- English Edition 1 (2011)
- Layout Design: IIPH, Riyadh, Saudi Arabia
- Filming and Cover Design: Samo Press Group

The Music
Made Me Do It

*An in-depth study of music through
Islam and science*

وضع الموسيقي في الإسلام

دراسة علمية لتأثيراتها

Dr. Gohar Mushtaq

الدار العالمية للكتاب الإسلامي

INTERNATIONAL ISLAMIC PUBLISHING HOUSE

Copyright © 2011 International Islamic Publishing House
King Fahd National Library Cataloging-in-Publication Data

Mushtaq, Dr. Gohar
  The music made me do it / Dr. Gohar Mushtaq .- Riyadh, 2011

  288 p ; 21 cm

  ISBN Hardcover: 978-603-501-111-2

  1- Music (Islamic rulings regarding)   2- Music (scientific research
  on effects of)   I- Title

  780.953 dc   1432/5922

  Legal Deposit no. **1432/5922**
  ISBN Hardcover: **978-603-501-111-2**

International Islamic Publishing House (IIPH)
P.O. Box 55195 Riyadh 11534, Saudi Arabia
Tel: 966 1 4650818 / 4647213 — Fax: 966 1 4633489
E-mail: iiph@iiph.com.sa — iiphsa@gmail.com
www.iiph.com.sa

Table of Contents

Pronunciation and Transliteration Chart

Arabic script	Pronunciation	Transliterated form
أ	short 'a', as in *cat*	a
آ - ى	longer 'a', as in *cab* (not as in *cake*)	â
ب	/b/ as in *bell*, *rubber* and *tab*	b
ت	/t/ as in *tap*, *mustard* and *sit*	t
ة	takes the sound of the preceding diactrical mark sometimes ending in h (when in pausal form): ah, ih, or ooh; or atu(n), ati(n) or ata(n) when uninterrupted	h or t (when followed by another Arabic word)
ث	/th/ as in *thing*, *maths* and *wealth*	th
ج	/j/ as in *jam*, *ajar* and *age*	j
ح	a 'harsher' sound than the English initial /h/, and may occur medially and in word-final position as well	ḥ
خ	as in *Bach* (in German); may occur initially and medially as well	kh
د	/d/ as in *do*, *muddy* and *red*	d
ذ	as in *this*, *father*, and *smooth*	dh
ر	/r/ as in *raw*, *arid* and *war*; may also be a rolled 'r', as pronounced in Spanish	r

Arabic script	Pronunciation	Transliterated form
ز	/z/ as in *zoo*, *easy* and *gaze*	z
س	/s/ as in *so*, *messy* and *grass*	s
ش	as in *ship*, *ashes* and *rush*	sh
ص	no close equivalent in English, but may be approximated by pronouncing it as /sw/ or /s/ farther back in the mouth	ṣ
ض	no close equivalent in English, but may be approximated by pronouncing /d/ farther back in the mouth	ḍ
ط	no close equivalent in English, but may be approximated by pronouncing it as /t/ farther back in the mouth	ṭ
ظ	no close equivalent in English, but may be approximated by pronouncing 'the' farther back in the mouth	<u>dh</u>
ع	no close equivalent in English: a guttural sound in the back of the throat	'
غ	no close equivalent in English, but may be closely approximated by pronouncing it like the French /r/ in 'rouge'	gh
ف	/f/ as in *fill*, *effort* and *muff*	f

Arabic script	Pronunciation	Transliterated form
ق	no close equivalent in English, but may be approximated by pronouncing it as /k/ farther back in the mouth	q
ك	/k/ as in *king, buckle* and *tack*	k
ل	/l/ as in *lap, halo*; in the word *Allah*, it becomes velarized as in *ball*	l
م	/m/ as in *men, simple* and *ram*	m
ن	/n/ as in *net, ant* and *can*	n
ـه – ه – هـ	/h/ as in *hat*; unlike /h/ in English, in Arabic /h/ is pronounced in medial and word-final positions as well	h
و	as in *wet* and *away*	w
و	long 'u', as in *boot* and *too*	oo
ي	as in *yard* and *mayo*	y
ي	long 'e', as in *eat, beef* and *see*	ee
ء	glottal stop: may be closely approximated by pronouncing it like 't' in the Cockney English pronunciation of *butter*: *bu'er*, or the stop sound in *uh-oh!*	' (Omitted in initial position)

Diphthongs:

Arabic script	Pronunciation	Transliterated form
وَ ، أو	long 'o', as in *owe, boat* and *go*	au, aw
يَ ، أي	long 'a', as in *aid, rain* and *say*	ay, ai, ei

Diacritical marks (*tashkeel*):

Name of mark	Pronunciation	Transliterated form
ـَ fatḥah	very short 'a' or schwa (unstressed vowel)	a
ـِ kasrah	shorter version of ee or schwa (unstressed vowel)	i
ـُ Ḍammah	shorter version of oo	u
ـّ shaddah	a doubled consonant is stressed in the word, and the length of the sound is also doubled	double letter
ـْ sukoon	no vowel sound between consonants or at the end of a word	absence of vowel

Arabic honorific symbols
used in this book

(ﷻ): *Subḥânahu wa taʿâlâ* — 'The Exalted'

(ﷺ): *Ṣalla-Allâhu ʿalayhi wa sallam* — 'Blessings and peace be upon him'

(ﷺ): *'Alayhis-salâm* — 'Peace be upon him'

(﵁): *Raḍiya Allâhu ʿanhu* — 'May Allah be pleased with <u>him</u>'

(﵂): *Raḍiya Allâhu ʿanhâ* — 'May Allah be pleased with <u>her</u>'

About the word 'Lord'

$\mathcal{T}$he word *lord* in English has several related meanings. The original meaning is 'master' or 'ruler', and in this sense it is often used to refer to human beings: 'the lord of the mansion' or 'Lord So-and-So' (in the United Kingdom, for example). The word *Lord* with a capital L is used in the lexicon of Islam to refer to the One and Only God — Allah. In Islam, there is no ambiguity about the meaning of this word. While it is true that one may occasionally use the word *lord* (whether capitalized or not) to refer to a human being, in Islamic discourse the reference of this term is always clear from the context. Whereas for Christians, Hindus and other polytheists, the word *Lord* with a capital 'L' may refer to Allah, to Jesus or to some imagined deity, for Muslims, there can be no plurality of meaning. Allah alone is the Lord, and the Lord is Allah — not Jesus, not Rama, not any other being.

The Editor

When 'jihad' refers to fighting

Although jihad is often translated into English as 'holy war', it must be noted that war has never been described as 'holy' in any of Islam's primary texts or even early Islamic literature. Linguistically speaking, jihad is an Islamic term that applies to a broad spectrum of activities, ranging from daily striving to meet the day's challenges, to the striving against one's desires and self, to the struggle to provide for one's family. Its basic definition is 'the act of striving or struggling in the way of Allah'. Therefore, jihad is not limited to war; it includes struggling with one's soul, speech, body and wealth so that the message of Allah reaches all humans willing to receive it.

Islamic scholars have referred to different types of jihad, such as jihad against the self (to understand Islam, act upon it, call others to it and be patient with the difficulties of making this call), jihad against the Devil (repelling Satanic whispers, doubts and lusts), jihad against the tongue (controlling it, using it to enjoin what is good, forbid what is wrong, spread the correct teachings of Islam and answer false ideologies), jihad against aggression (with the purpose of protecting Islam and the lives, honour and property of Muslims) and other types of jihad like jihad against the hypocrites, jihad against oppressors and jihad against mischief makers.

Jihad — in the context of fighting — has specific rules and conditions that need to be met before jihad is initiated. The first rule is that people are not to be fought because of what they believe, or to coerce them to accept Islam. The second rule is to 'fight only those who fight you' and never initiate unprovoked aggression *(Qur'an 2: 190)*. That means that Muslims are only allowed to fight back, rather than initiating fighting; but 'fighting back' includes fighting against actual aggression as well as proactively addressing real threats of aggression. In both cases, Muslims are instructed to be prepared and ready to defend their nation before they actually engage in military conflict. There are additional conditions, but the above-mentioned conditions are vital for putting jihad in its broader meaning in the proper context.

Another condition of the sort of jihad which involves fighting is that it should take place only under an Islamic authority that 'raises the banner' for such jihad. It is not following the Sunnah at all for any individual or self-appointed group of Muslims to wage war on behalf of a nation. Instead, Muslims should be united under the single authority of an imam or khaleefah (caliph), except in the case where an individual needs to defend his own family and property, or to help his neighbour to do so. This is proved by the example of the early Muslims as well as texts in the Qur'an and the Sunnah:

◄When there comes to them [the hypocrites] a matter related to [public] safety or fear, they spread it about; if only they had referred it to the Messenger and to such of them as are in authority, those among them who are able to think through the matter would have understood it.►   *(Qur'an 4: 83)*

«Ḥudhayfah ibn Yaman asked the Prophet (ﷺ): What if (the Muslims) have no single leader (they are divided into disputing groups)? The Prophet (ﷺ) answered: If they have no single leader or unified group, then leave all these disputing groups, even if you have to bite on a tree until your death.» (part of a longer hadith recorded by Bukhari)

There are other conditions for jihad. In general, the rules laid out for war in Islam should be upheld unless there is some legitimate need or strategy when fighting occurs that would necessitate going against those rules. A Muslim should not kill himself or herself *(Qur'an 4: 29)* nor kill another Muslim, except by accident *(Qur'an 4: 92)*. Women, children, the elderly and other non-combatants should not be harmed. Land should not be destroyed, nor trees cut down. Corpses should not be mutilated. Islam should not be imposed upon non-believers. Rather, if combatant non-Muslims choose on their own to embrace Islam, even if only as a deceitful trick, it should be accepted by the Muslim leadership, and fighting should stop. Peace should be sought before lives are lost. Treaties and agreements should be upheld. Prisoners should be well-treated. Above all, justice must be done.

❨Fight in the path [according to the rules set by Allah] of Allah only those who fight you, but do not commit aggression [transgress limits]. Allah does not love aggressors. ...And fight them until persecution is no more, and religion is [freely embraced] for [the individual's faith in] Allah. But if they desist, then let there be no aggression except against transgressors.❩

(Qur'an 2: 190, 193)

❨Allah does not forbid you from being good, kind, just, and fair to those who have not fought you because of religion nor driven you from your homeland. Allah loves those who are just. Allah forbids you from giving allegiance to those who have fought you because of religion and have driven you from your homeland, and those who supported your expulsion...⟩   *(Qur'an 60: 8-9)*

In addition, the Muslim nation is encouraged to maintain strong military capabilities to promote justice and to deter acts of war and aggression.

⟨And make ready for them [their potential aggression] all you can of power, including steeds of war, to deter the enemy of Allah and your enemy, and others besides, whom you may not know but whom Allah knows.⟩   *(Qur'an 8: 60)*

The Editor

Publisher's Note

$\mathcal{A}$ll praise and thanks belong to Allah alone, the One, the Almighty and All-Merciful. Blessings and peace be upon Prophet Muhammad, the last of His Messengers and Prophets, and upon his family, his Companions and all those who follow in his footsteps until the end of time.

Today, with the advent of sophisticated personal electronic devices, music is available anywhere at any time, leading many Muslims to assume that it must be permissible. Although there has always been a consensus on this issue among Islamic scholars from the major schools of jurisprudence, many contemporary Muslims remain confused about the Islamic stance on music and singing.

In this groundbreaking book, Dr. Gohar Mushtaq explains why Muslims should not listen to music, by bringing together a wealth of evidence from the perspectives of both Islamic jurisprudence and modern scientific research.

We hope that this book will guide the readers to understand the authentic Islamic position on this topic, to recognize the negative effects of music on the human body and psyche, and to calm their hearts by choosing to listen to beautiful recitations of the Qur'an rather than prohibited types of songs.

May Allah accept the efforts of all those who contributed to the production of this book, and may it be acceptable to Him, *âmeen.*

Muhammad Abdul Mohsin Al-Tuwaijri

Managing Director
International Islamic Publishing House
Riyadh, Saudi Arabia

Foreword by Abdur-Raheem Green

I have finished your book, and all praise is due to Allah (ﷻ). You have written a book that should appeal to a wide range of people. In it are ample evidences from the Qur'an and Sunnah and pious scholars from a broad spectrum of schools of thought, and this should more than suffice for those who respond to Allah's commands and flee from his prohibitions. Uniquely, it also includes an analysis of the scientific evidence on the effects of music for those who seek such understandings. Questions are answered and doubts and objections that people raise are quelled, and inspiring stories are included for those whose hearts are open to repentance.

This is a book that is so much needed at this time when too many of us have forgotten that we should be making *jihad* (struggling) against our *nafs* (ego) and *hawâ* (our carnal desires), and clinging to the Qur'an and Sunnah rather than feeding our egos and desires with music, song and dance, which is indeed the Qur'an of Satan. May Allah (ﷻ) guide us all to paths of His goodness.

Foreword by Dr. Ahmed H. Sakr

This book by Dr. Gohar Mushtaq about the position of music in Islam is an excellent work for all people of the world: for Muslims and non-Muslims; for the old and the young; for the educated and for those who are seeking knowledge; for those who appreciate music and for those otherwise, and finally for those who would like to know the true position of Islam regarding music. The author was kind enough to bring information from religious, social, scientific, medical, and historical sources.

This book is really a unique work. I do encourage everyone to read it so as to correct his or her misperceptions and misunderstandings about music. Please listen and experience the recitation of the Qur'an and enjoy the melodic voice of the *Qâri'* (reciter of the Qur'an) during recitation of the Qur'an. The Qur'anic recitation touches the hearts of the believers and motivates them and inspires them to do good deeds. While listening to the recitation of the Qur'an, people do experience shivering, goose bumps and lowering of blood pressure, which has been shown in this book using scientific evidence. May Allah (ﷻ) bless you all. *Âmeen* (amen).

Foreword by Imam Tahir Anwar

𝒜 much needed book on a topic that has been greatly misunderstood. The negative ramifications of music have been explained in very practical and sensible terms. A book on the topic of the impermissibility of music was long overdue, and Dr. Mushtaq has done an extraordinary job in explaining the issue in detail.

Many individuals do not realize that music has many negative social and moral effects on a person which are intertwined with sex, drugs, and suicide, all of which have led to the downfall of societies and communities. Music has also been used to ghettoize communities, and research on all these aspects has been compiled very beautifully in this book.

Finally, all the Qur'anic verses, hadiths, and views of scholars that are found in numerous literatures have been collected into one place.

This book is a must-read for anyone who is genuinely looking for a sound view on the prohibition and ill-effects of music.

About the Author

$\mathcal{G}$ohar Mushtaq completed his high school education in Pakistan and then moved to the U.S. for higher studies. He received his Bachelors of Science degree from York College of The City University of New York in 1995, and he was the valedictorian of his graduating class. Gohar received his M.S. and PhD degrees in Chemistry (specializing in the area of biophysical chemistry) from Rutgers University in New Jersey, where he was the recipient of the Graduate Teaching Excellence Award in 2000. During his childhood, he received a thorough Islamic education from his father, and throughout his university years, he continued studying the classical Islamic sciences privately with various Islamic teachers. He frequently delivers Friday sermons and lectures at various mosques and Islamic centers in the areas of New York, New Jersey and Connecticut. He contributes articles to *Al-Jumuah* (English), *Batool* (Urdu) and *Meesâq* (Urdu) monthly magazines and is the author of the following books:

❖ Growing a Beard: In Light of Qur'an, Sunnah and Modern Science (Ta-Ha Publishers)

❖ The Intelligent Heart, The Pure Heart: An Insight into the Human Heart based on the Qur'an, Sunnah and Modern Science (Ta-Ha Publishers)

❖ Islam: Its Beauty and Wisdom (Amana Publications)

Introduction

*H*uman beings are social creatures who are affected by the environment surrounding them. Nurture plays as important a role as nature in shaping a person. Many people are not used to looking at things deeply; they take things at their face value without questioning. Their minds do not question whether the things around them are right or wrong; they simply take the 'seeing is believing' approach.

In the present age, with the unprecedented progress in scientific inventions, one of the obsessions that has spread everywhere with exponential speed is music. Today, music has become so prevalent that many Muslims listen to it without even questioning its position in Islam. Such are the Muslims who believe in whatever they see.

It is strange that such Muslims completely ignore what the *hadiths* (statements and actions) of Prophet Muhammad (*salla Allâhu 'alayhi wa sallam* — blessings and peace be upon him) say regarding music. Today Muslims ask the following questions of the Islamic scholars at just about every Islamic conference, debate, lecture or convention:

1. What are the limits of *hijab* (the veil ordained by Allah for believing women) in Islam? Do we have to cover our faces or not?

2. What is the position of music in Islam? Is it *halal* (permitted according to Islamic law) or *harâm* (forbidden according to Islamic law)?

3. Is it compulsory for men to grow the beard in Islam?

We must understand that all of these issues are the byproducts of faith. That is why Abdullah ibn Mas'ood (*radiya Allâhu 'anhu* — may Allah be pleased with him), a well-known Companion of Prophet Muhammad (ﷺ), said: "We were taught (by Prophet Muhammad) faith first, and then we were taught the Qur'an."[1]

If faith is nurtured in the heart of a Muslim, he or she will never have doubts regarding these issues. Such Muslims will not listen to music; the women will observe the hijab, and the men will grow the beard following the way of the noble Prophet (ﷺ). Today Muslims need to concentrate on strengthening our faith. Allah (ﷻ) has blessed us with the sense of right and wrong:

❨And inspired it [the soul, with discernment of] its wickedness and its righteousness.❩ *(Qur'an 91: 8)*[2]

According to the hadith below, sin is that which disturbs your heart. As we noted previously, some Muslims today keep asking the same questions of Islamic scholars even after they get, from some of the modernist and apologetic scholars, the *fatwa* (religious decision or decree) that they desire. The fact that these three issues disturb Muslims so much is in itself a sign that

---

[1] Abu Ja'far Muhammad ibn Jarir At-Tabari, *Jâmi' al-Bayan Fi Ta'wil ayi'l Qur'an* (Beirut: Dar al-Kutub al-'Ilmiyah, 1992).

[2] The translations of the meanings of the verses of the Qur'an in this book are taken (with some changes to the text) from: Saheeh International, *The Qur'an - Arabic Text with Corresponding English Meanings* (Riyadh: Abul Qasim Publishing House, 1997).

something is just not right, as indicated in the hadith narrated on the authority of Wabisa ibn Ma'bad (☺), who went to the Messenger of Allah (☺), who said: «You have come to ask about righteousness? I said: Yes. He (☺) said: Consult your heart. Righteousness is that about which the soul feels tranquil and the heart feels tranquil, and wrongdoing is that which wavers in the soul and moves back and forth in the breast (in your heart) even though people again and again have given you their opinion in its favour.» (recorded by Aḥmad and graded as reliable by al-Albâni)

An-Nawwâs ibn Sam'an narrated that the Prophet Muhammad (☺) said: «Virtue is good ethics and behaviour, and wrong action is what irritates the heart and what you do not want other people to see.» (Muslim)

It is interesting to note that the modernists among Muslims usually take a stand against the position of Prophet Muhammad (☺), his Companions and our great Imams on these three issues. They use these issues to attract a following among the Muslims. The books on Islam written by modernists and apologetics of the nineteenth and twentieth centuries bear testimony to this fact.

If we see an evil action being committed in the society, we must raise our voices against it. If we look at the lives of the prophets of Allah (peace be upon them all) throughout history, all of them raised their voices against the evil actions that were prevalent in their societies. That is one of the reasons why those prophets of Allah (peace be upon them) were disliked by the majority of the society — because they were speaking against the evils committed by that very group.

For example, if Prophet Shu'ayb (*'alayhi as-salâm* — peace be upon him) had admonished the people of Madyan against homosexuality, he might have been extremely popular among his people because homosexuality was not the evil that was prevalent among them. However, people in Madyan used to lie to their customers and cheat them in business transactions. Prophet Shu'ayb (﷽) did not beat around the bush; he raised his voice specifically about that evil which was present in his society, even though his people did not like his addressing the subject:

❨And to [the people of] Madyan [We sent] their brother Shu'ayb. He said: O my people, worship Allah; you have no deity other than Him. There has come to you clear evidence from your Lord. So fulfil the measure and weight, and do not deprive people of their due, and cause not corruption upon the earth after its reformation. That is better for you, if you should be believers.❩

(Qur'an 7: 85)

Similarly, if Prophet Loot (﷽) advised his people not to drink alcohol or gamble or backbite, he probably would have been extremely popular among his nation because those were not the most prevalent evils among the people of Sodom. The most widespread sin there was homosexuality, so Prophet Loot (﷽) chastised them about that sin:

❨And [We had sent] Loot when he said to his people: Do you commit such immorality as no one has preceded you with from among the worlds? Indeed you approach men with desire, instead of women. Rather, you are a transgressing people.❩

(Qur'an 7: 80-81)

As a consequence, the inhabitants of Sodom hated Prophet Loot (﷽). He did not fear the blame of the blamers, though; he honestly fulfilled his duty of enjoining acts of righteousness and forbidding acts of disobedience to Allah (﷽). Eventually, truth prevailed and falsehood perished, as Allah (ﷻ) tells us:

❨And say: Truth has come, and falsehood has departed. Indeed is falsehood [by nature] ever bound to depart.❩   *(Qur'an 17: 81)*

Muslims are the only torchbearers of the message of Islam and the divine message of all the prophets of Allah (peace be upon them all) who have been sent on this planet. They have been regarded as the best nation because of their duty to enjoin the acts of righteousness and forbid the acts of disobedience to Allah (ﷻ) as mentioned in the Qur'an:

❨You are the best nation produced [as an example] for mankind. You enjoin what is right and forbid what is wrong and believe in Allah...❩   *(Qur'an 3: 110)*

As the followers of Prophet Muhammad (ﷺ), we must never forget the command of our beloved Prophet (ﷺ): «Whoever among you sees an evil action, let him change it with his hand; if he is unable to do so, then let him change it by his tongue, and if he is unable to do that, let him hate it in his heart, and that is the weakest faith.» (Muslim)

Writing is one of the ways by which the hand can be used to change evil actions. This book is a humble effort to change them with my hand and a hopeful heart.

To the best of my knowledge, this is the first Islamic work of its kind to analyze the effects of music in the light of modern scientific research. The first chapter of this book presents the position of music in the light of the Qur'an and the hadiths of Prophet Muhammad (ﷺ) on this issue. The second part of the book focuses on the scientific research done by social psychologists, as well as biologists, pertaining to the effects of music on the human body. The next section deals with the behavioural and other effects of music in the society and the reasons why music is prohibited. Then, after presenting the positions of the Companions and Islamic scholars, the final verdict on music is given. The next chapter deals with answering objections that are commonly raised on this issue. The last section of this book consists of some interesting stories of individuals who not only used to listen to music but were, in fact, musical geniuses or experts in the field, yet they repented to Allah (ﷻ) and became beacons of Islam.

Some people may question the use of science to prove the harms of music, since science is always changing. In the future, they argue, science could also show that music is beneficial for us. The fact of the matter is that nothing in this world is 100 percent evil. Everything has harms and benefits associated with it, but the approach of Islamic Sharia is to weigh the benefits and harms of everything. This has been mentioned in the Qur'an clearly in the cases of drinking alcohol and gambling:

❨They ask you about wine and gambling. Say: In them is great sin and [yet, some] benefit for people. But their sin is greater than their benefit...❩   *(Qur'an 2: 219)*

Hence, in the case of alcohol and gambling, the Qur'an accepts that there are some benefits for people, but the harms of alcohol and gambling to the society more than outweigh their benefits. It is for this reason that Islamic law has prohibited them. Similarly, in the case of music, there may be slight benefits in certain types of music, such as temporarily soothing its listener, but the harms of listening to music outweigh the benefits. In addition, the soothing effect coming from music is very different than the soothing effects caused by remembering Allah (ﷻ). The former is imposed from the outside, whereas the latter is internal and deep-seated.

More importantly, the research presented in this book regarding the harms of music is not from the physical sciences alone (medicine, chemistry, biology); it is also from the social sciences. It includes surveys and statistics, and it is overwhelming. A person may find one or two scientific researchers in favour of music in the scientific literature, but hopefully, after reading this book, the reader will see that the scientific studies quoted in this book are numerous. They all support each other and definitively demonstrate that music is related to alcohol, drugs, smoking, sex and suicide.

In producing this work, I am indebted to many people who have encouraged and helped me in different ways, and they deserve special mention here. My special thanks go to Shaykh Abdur Rehman Kâshmiri who taught me the classical Arabic language, which enabled me to directly consult the Arabic sources on this subject. I am also thankful to Jamal Mâlik for his invaluable comments and suggestions on the first and then the final draft. I would like to express my special thanks to Shaykh Abdurrahman ibn Yusuf (Imam of Southern California Mosque), for his patience in reading the manuscript of my book and his deep and insightful comments and discussions about it. My indebtedness and gratitude must also be expressed to Brother Hassan Laidi (editor of *Al-Jumuah* magazine) for his valuable suggestions. I am highly grateful to my parents, Farida Mushtaq and Mushtaq Choudhry, for they are the ones who taught me Islamic sciences and who are always praying to Allah (ﷻ) for my success. Last, but by no means least — greatest, in fact — is my sincere gratitude to my wife, Sadia Gohar, because this research would have been extremely hard without her persistent support for me.

Gohar Mushtaq

U.S.A.

Chapter 1

Music from the Sharia View

Defining the problem and clarifying the point of contention

*I*n order to approach the issue of music from the point of view of Sharia (Islamic law), we first have to define the problem. The issue of listening to music and singing is a burning question for many of the Muslim youth today. The purpose of writing this book is to clarify the position of music in Islam and to specify which types of music and singing are permissible in Islam and which types are forbidden. In the modern age, with the advent of electronic devices to play and listen to music, and the advent of computer music, new dimensions have been added to an already complicated issue.

In Islamic Sharia, the correct approach to an issue is an essential element in deriving a ruling. This requires that we understand the Islamic commandments through the text of the Qur'an and the *Sunnah* (the practice and collected sayings of Prophet Muhammad that, together with the Qur'an, forms the basis of Islamic law). Then we take that understanding and apply it to the issue as it exists in reality. By combining our understanding from the Qur'an and the Sunnah and applying it to the issue, we derive the fatwa on the permissibility or impermissibility of the issue at hand. In doing so, we also look at the harms and the benefits related to the issue. The approach of the Islamic Sharia is to weigh the benefits and harms of everything, because the ultimate aim of Sharia is to benefit the society.

We can dissect the problem into three parts:

1. Musical instruments such as *duffs* (hand drums), pianos, guitars and flutes
2. Lyrics
3. Singers or composers

We will approach this issue methodologically. First, we will look at the evidence from the Qur'an and Sunnah regarding listening to music and singing. Then, we will look at the harms and the benefits related to the issue of listening to music. Next, we will look at the verdicts of the Companions and Islamic scholars. Only then we will be in a position to issue a legal ruling pertaining to music and singing.

Before we begin the discussion, it is important for us to understand that the ultimate authority for Muslims is the Qur'an and the Sunnah. Allah (ﷻ) says:

﴿وَمَا كَانَ لِمُؤْمِنٍ وَلَا مُؤْمِنَةٍ إِذَا قَضَى ٱللَّهُ وَرَسُولُهُۥٓ أَمْرًا أَن يَكُونَ لَهُمُ ٱلْخِيَرَةُ مِنْ أَمْرِهِمْ ... ﴿٣٦﴾﴾   (سورة الأحزاب : ٣٦)

﴿It is not for a believing man or a believing woman, when Allah and His Messenger have decided a matter, that they should have any choice about their affair...﴾   *(Qur'an 33: 36)*

In *soorat* (chapter) an-Noor (the Light), Allah, the Exalted, the Almighty says:

$$﴿ ... فَلْيَحْذَرِ ٱلَّذِينَ يُخَالِفُونَ عَنْ أَمْرِهِ أَن تُصِيبَهُمْ فِتْنَةٌ أَوْ يُصِيبَهُمْ عَذَابٌ أَلِيمٌ ۝ ﴾$$

(سورة النُّور: ٦٣)

❨...So let those beware who dissent from the Prophet's order, lest fitnah strike them or a painful punishment.❩ *(Qur'an 24: 63)*

The above-mentioned verses of the Qur'an tell us that we should follow the commandments of Allah (ﷻ) and His Messenger (ﷺ). We are not allowed to find loopholes in those commandments by propounding our opinions or by rationalizing our judgments simply because we are not used to seeing those as the norms in the society. When we look around us, we see that music is prevalent not only among non-Muslims but also among Muslims. However, the fact that the majority of people listen to music is not a justification to make music permissible because, as the Qur'an tells us in one instance:

$$﴿وَإِن تُطِعْ أَكْثَرَ مَن فِي ٱلْأَرْضِ يُضِلُّوكَ عَن سَبِيلِ ٱللَّهِ إِن يَتَّبِعُونَ إِلَّا ٱلظَّنَّ وَإِنْ هُمْ إِلَّا يَخْرُصُونَ ۝ ﴾$$

(سورة الأنعام: ١١٦)

❨If you follow most of those upon the earth, they will mislead you from the way of Allah. They follow nothing but assumption, and they are not but falsifying.❩ *(Qur'an 6: 116)*

Position of the Qur'an regarding music and singing

First verse from the Qur'an

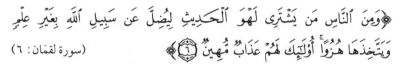

(سورة لقمان: ٦)

❰And of the people are those who purchase idle talk [*lahwal hadeeth*] in order to mislead [others] from the way of Allah without knowledge, and who throw ridicule upon it. Those will have a humiliating punishment.❱

(Qur'an 31: 6)

Abdullah ibn Mas'ood (مَسَّ) said about this verse: "I swear by the One other than Whom there is no God that it refers to *ghinâ'* (singing)," and he repeated this three times.[1] The great Companion and interpreter of the Qur'an, Ibn 'Abbâs (مَسَّ), said that it referred to 'singing and the like,' whereas according to Jâbir ibn Abdullah, it means singing and listening to songs.[2] Ibn Kathir writes in his *tafseer* (explanation of the meanings of the Qur'an) that many *tâbi'oon* (those who knew or met any of the Companions and transmitted hadiths from them) such as Mujâhid, Ikrimah, Mak'hool, Sa'eed ibn Jubayr, and Amr ibn Shu'ayb viewed it as a censure of music and song.[3] Ibn Asâkir narrates the

---

[1] Qadi Mohammad ibn Ali Shawkani, *Nayl al-Awtâr* (Lahore: Dost Associate Publishers, 2000) and aṭ-Ṭabari, *Jâmi' al-Bayan Fi Ta'wil ayi'l Qur'an*.

[2] Imam Abu Bakr Aḥmad Bayhaqi, *Sunan al-Kubrâ*, ed. Muhammad 'Abdul-Qâdir Ata (Beirut: Dar al-Kutub al-'Ilmiyah, 1423 AH/ 2003 CE) and Ḥâfidh Abul-Fida Imad ud-Deen Ibn Kathir, *Tafsir Ibn Kathir* (English translation) (Jeddah: Darussalam Publishers, 2000).

[3] Ibid.

following statement of Mak'hool:

> If a person hired a female singer so that she would play music and sing, and that person stays on that condition until his death, then I will not go to his funeral prayers because Allah has said in the Qur'an: ❨And of the people are those who purchase idle talk in order to mislead [others] from the way of Allah.❩ *(Qur'an 31: 6)* [4]

Ibn Jarir aṭ-Ṭabari, in his tafseer *Jâmi' al-Bayan*, mentioned that the meanings of the term *'lahwal ḥadeeth'* (idle talk) can be formulated into three basic categories, based on the statements of interpreters of the Qur'an. The first category defines the term *lahwal ḥadeeth*:

(a) singing and listening to songs,
(b) the hiring of male or female singers and
(c) the purchase of instruments of amusement, namely the drum. The elements of this category revolve around the reference to the blameworthy usage of instruments of idle amusement, in short, music and song. [5] Similarly, Imam Qurtubi writes in his tafseer, explaining this verse:

> Among all the explanations of the term *lahwal ḥadeeth*, the most appropriate explanation is ghinâ', and this is the position of the Companions of the Prophet Muhammad (ﷺ) and their students (tâbi'oon). [6]

---

[4] Imam Abu Muhammad al-Ḥusayn Baghawi, *Ma'alim at-Tanzeel* (Egypt: Mat'bâ Al-Minâr, 1347 AH).

[5] aṭ-Ṭabari, *Jâmi' al-Bayan Fi Ta'wil ayi'l Qur'an*.

[6] Imam Abu Abdullah Muhammad ibn Aḥmad al-Anṣâri Qurtubi, *Al-Jami li Aḥkam al-Qur'an* (Beirut and Egypt: Darul-Kutub Al-Misriyah, 1953).

It must be noted here that the orthodox Islamic scholars have deduced four ways of tafseer of the Qur'an:

1. Tafseer of Qur'an by Qur'an,
2. Tafseer of Qur'an by the Sunnah,
3. Tafseer of Qur'an by sayings of the Companions, and
4. Tafseer of Qur'an by language.[7]

The explanations of the Qur'an by the Companions of the Prophet Muhammad (ﷺ) are extremely important in terms of understanding the Qur'an. Ibn Kathir, one of the greatest commentators on the Qur'an, wrote in the preface to his tafseer:

> If we are unable to find a suitable tafseer in the Qur'an or in the Sunnah, we go to the opinions of the Ṣaḥâbah [Companions]. For verily, they knew the Qur'an better than anyone else due to their knowledge of the circumstances of its revelation, their complete and accurate understanding of it, and their righteous deeds.[8]

Second verse from the Qur'an

﴿أَفَمِنْ هَٰذَا الْحَدِيثِ تَعْجَبُونَ ۝ وَتَضْحَكُونَ وَلَا تَبْكُونَ ۝ وَأَنتُمْ سَامِدُونَ ۝ فَاسْجُدُوا لِلَّهِ وَاعْبُدُوا ۩ ۝﴾ (سورة النجم: ٥٩-٦٢)

﴿Then at this statement do you wonder? And you laugh and do not weep while you amuse yourselves [*sâmidoon*] in vanities? So prostrate to Allah and worship [Him].﴾   *(Qur'an 53: 59-62)*

---

[7] Dr. Bilal Philips, *Usool at-Tafseer: The Methodology of Quraanic Explanation* (Sharjah: Dar Al Fatah, 1997).

[8] Ibn Kathir, *Tafsir Ibn Kathir.*

According to Imam Abu Obaida, in the Yemeni dialect of the Arabic language, the word *sumood* means singing. The same position has been taken by Ikrimah.[9] Furthermore, linguist expert Ibn Manzoor writes in his *Lisânul 'Arab* (a classical Arabic dictionary) about other words that come from the same root as *sumood*:

> It is narrated by Ibn 'Abbâs that the word *sumood* means singing. In fact, this word is from the Yemeni dialect. Therefore, *Ismadee lana* means sing for us, and when it is said to a female singer *Ismadaina* then this means 'intoxicate us by singing to us.'[10]

Ibn 'Abbâs (ﷺ) also elucidated that the word *sâmidoon* in this verse refers to the pagan Arabs' habit of singing and playing music noisily whenever they heard the Qur'an being recited, in order to drown out the reciter's voice so that others would not hear it. The other possible meanings of the term *sâmidoon* from the lexical point of view include: 'idle play,' 'being indifferent' and 'negligent in their attitude.' All of these meanings are possible and are not contradictory in essence.[11]

Third verse from the Qur'an

﴿وَٱسْتَفْزِزْ مَنِ ٱسْتَطَعْتَ مِنْهُم بِصَوْتِكَ وَأَجْلِبْ عَلَيْهِم بِخَيْلِكَ وَرَجِلِكَ وَشَارِكْهُمْ فِى ٱلْأَمْوَٰلِ وَٱلْأَوْلَٰدِ وَعِدْهُمْ وَمَا يَعِدُهُمُ ٱلشَّيْطَٰنُ إِلَّا

---

[9] Maḥmood ibn Abdullah Aloosi, *Rooḥ al-Ma'âni fee Tafseer al-Qur'ân al-'Adheem was-Sab' al-Mathâni* (Beirut: Dar al-Fikr, 1983).

[10] Allama Ibn Manzoor (Al-Afriki), *Lisânul 'Arab* (Bulâq, Egypt: Mat'bâ Al-Muneeria, 1304 AH).

[11] Ibn Kathir, *Tafsir Ibn Kathir*.

(سورة الإسرَاء: ٦٤)

❦"And incite [to senselessness] whomever you can among them with your voice, and assault them with your horses and foot soldiers, and become a partner in their wealth and their children and promise them." But Satan does not promise them anything except delusion.❧   *(Qur'an 17: 64)*

Some of the tâbi'oon such as Ḍaḥḥâk, Ḥasan al-Baṣri and Mujâhid interpreted Satan's inciting humankind with his voice to mean through the use of music, song and amusement. Ḍaḥḥâk said it was the sound of wind instruments. According to Ibn 'Abbâs (رضي الله عنهما), the voice mentioned in the verse refers to every form of invitation that calls to the disobedience of Allah (ﷻ).[12] Ibn al-Qayyim writes in the commentary of this verse of Qur'an:

> Ibn Abi Hatim quoted the interpretation of Ibn 'Abbâs regarding 'your (Satan's) voice' in this verse of the Qur'an as everything which invites to sin and disobedience of Allah. And it is well known that, of all the things which invite to sin, music supersedes all of them. It is for this reason that the voice of Satan is interpreted as singing.[13]

It must also be noted that renowned Shâfi'i scholar and Sufi Shaykh Shahâb ud-Deen Suhrawardi has used the above-mentioned three verses from the Qur'an as the evidences for the prohibition of music and singing in his book *'Awârif al-Ma'ârif.*

---

[12] Aṭ-Ṭabari, *Jâmi' al-Bayan Fi Ta'wil ayi'l Qur'an.*

[13] Ibn al-Qayyim al-Jawziyah, *Ighâthat ul-Lahfân min Maṣâ'id ash-Shayṭân* (Dar Al-Bayan, 1993).

Fourth verse from the Qur'an

In describing the qualities of believers, Allah (﷿) says:

$$﴿وَٱلَّذِينَ لَا يَشۡهَدُونَ ٱلزُّورَ وَإِذَا مَرُّواْ بِٱللَّغۡوِ مَرُّواْ كِرَامًا ٧٢﴾$$

(سورة الفُرقان : ٧٢)

❨And those who do not testify to falsehood [*az-zoor*] and when they pass near ill speech, they pass by with dignity.❩

(Qur'an 25: 72)

Muhammad ibn al-Ḥanafiyah and Mujâhid interpreted *az-zoor* as singing.[14] Imam Ibn Kathir, in his tafseer, also lists one of the meanings of *az-zoor* as singing.[15] Imam Abu Bakr al-Jasâs states in the interpretation of this verse:

It is narrated by Imam Abu Ḥaneefah that *az-zoor* refers to ghinâ'.... It is possible that in this verse, *az-zoor* implies music and singing, as some scholars have considered it so. It is also possible that it could mean saying something about which the speaker does not have the knowledge. Anyway, since the word is general, both meanings could have been meant.[16]

Now we will mention the hadiths of Allah's Messenger (ﷺ) regarding music, which provide more conclusive proof for the prohibition of music. In fact, these hadiths establish the prohibition of music beyond any possibility of misunderstanding.

---

[14] Ibn Ḥajar al-Haythami al-Makki, *Kaff ar-Ra'â' 'an Muḥarramât al-Lahwa was-Samâ'* (Prohibiting People from the Forbidden Distractions and Singing) (Egypt: Shirka' Maktaba wa Mat'ba Mustafa Al-Bâbi al-Halabi wa awlâduhu, 1370 AH).

[15] Ibn Kathir, *Tafsir Ibn Kathir*.

[16] Imam Abu Bakr al-Jasâs, *Aḥkâm ul-Qur'an* (Egypt: Al-Mat'bâ Al-Bahia, 1347 AH).

Position of the Prophet regarding music and singing

Some Muslims with weak faith often argue: "If listening to music is prohibited in Islam, why was this not clearly mentioned in the Qur'an? We only obey the commandments of the Qur'an." This objection is not new, as it has been raised by many apologetic and modernist Muslims over the whole course of Islamic history. Soorah Luqmân, verse 6, provides a clear proof of the prohibition of music in Islam, but we must go to the Sunnah of the Messenger of Allah (ﷺ) for further clarification of any commandment of Islam. The Qur'an is general; it does not go into the fine details of the various commandments but directs us to follow Prophet Muhammad (ﷺ) for guidance. The Qur'an tells us clearly:

$$ ﴾ ... وَمَآ ءَاتَنكُمُ ٱلرَّسُولُ فَخُذُوهُ وَمَا نَهَىٰكُمۡ عَنۡهُ فَٱنتَهُواْ ... ﴿٧﴾ ﴾ $$

(سورة الحَشر : ٧)

❴...And whatever the Messenger has given you — take, and whatever he has forbidden you — refrain from...❵ *(Qur'an 59: 7)*

Our beloved Prophet (ﷺ) prophesized in his hadiths about the kind of people among Muslims who would raise such objections against the commandments of Islam. In one hadith narrated by al-Miqdâm ibn Ma'dikarib, Prophet Muhammad (ﷺ) warned us: «Beware! I have been given the Qur'an and something like it, yet the time is coming when a man replete on his couch will say: Keep to the Qur'an; what you find in it to be permissible, treat as permissible, and what you find in it to be prohibited, treat as prohibited.» (recorded by Abu Dâwood and graded as sound by al-Albâni)

Hadith 1

Ṣaḥeeḥ al-Bukhari, the most authentic book of Hadith, further confirms the unlawfulness of music and singing with this hadith, in which the Prophet (ﷺ) said: «There will be people of my *Ummah* (nation) who will seek to make these lawful (*yastaḥilloona*): illegal sexual intercourse, the wearing of silk [by men], the drinking of alcoholic drinks, and the use of *ma'âzif* (musical instruments).» (Bukhari)

An analysis of Bukhari's hadith:

Detailed analysis of the Arabic word 'ma'âzif' shows beyond any shadow of a doubt that it refers to musical instruments, the sounds of those musical instruments and singing with the accompaniment of instruments. Imam Qurtubi narrates that al-Jowhari (the author of the early dictionary work *aṣ-Ṣiḥaḥ*) writes about three words with the same Arabic root, asserting that *ma'âzif* signifies musical instruments, *al-'âzif* indicates one who sings, and the *'azf* of the wind is its voice. Examples of musical instruments include the violin, drum, guitar, fiddle, flute, piano, string, lute, mandolin, harmonium and others, as well as the musical sounds of such instruments generated by any other means (such as digitally-generated or computer-generated sounds).

Closer analysis of the wordings of this hadith establishes the prohibition of music for the following reasons:

1. The words 'seek to make lawful' show that music is not permissible because one can only seek to make lawful that which is not allowed.

2. If music was not prohibited, then it would not have been brought within the same context as fornication and wine drinking.

3. When we look at these four items, another element appears. They are not only ḥarâm but are mentioned with phrases such as 'an immorality and is evil as a way' *(Qur'an 17: 32)*, 'those will have a humiliating punishment' *(Qur'an 31: 6)*, and 'defilement from the work of Satan' *(Qur'an 5: 90)*. Therefore, it can be concluded that these sins are not minor sins. After all, what can be assumed about the grouping of the four together in this hadith? It shows, at the very least, that enjoying and listening to music is not a minor sin.

4. The Arabic word *yastaḥilloona* means, 'they will seek to make lawful.' This means that those people will not only commit sin but they will also consider it to be permissible in religion. This is the worst type of rebellion against religion, and it results in an increase in the intensity of the sin committed.

5. If someone claims that music is only unlawful when it is in combination with alcohol, adultery and silk, this is a false claim. The reason is that if this were the case, then why would music be the only exception? The same could also be claimed for adultery, alcohol and silk, so one could then make the case that alcohol or adultery is also permissible unless it is found in combination with the other things.

Hadith 2

«Soon there will be people from my Ummah who will drink wine, calling it by other than its real name. There will be instruments of music and singing on their heads, and they will listen to female singers. Allah (🕮) will cleave the earth under them and turn others into apes and swine.» (recorded by Ibn Mâjah and graded as sound by al-Albâni)

There are various hadiths, narrated by at least thirteen different Companions of the Prophet (ﷺ), in which the reason for Allah's punishment is attributed to the prevalence of musical instruments and singers. Some of those hadiths are authentic, others are reliable and some are weak. However, when we take a holistic look at all those hadiths, we reach the conclusion that is aptly summed up by Ibn al-Qayyim:

> It has often been mentioned in hadiths that punishment will come to this nation, and in most of these hadiths, this punishment is specifically linked to indulgence in musical instruments and drinking alcohol.[17]

Hadith 3

«Verily, Allah (ﷺ) prohibited wine, gambling and the *kuba*, and every intoxicant is prohibited. Sufyân said: I asked the narrator, 'Ali ibn Badheemah: What is the kuba? He answered: It is the drum.» (recorded by Abu Dâwood and Aḥmad, and graded as sound by al-Albâni)

Hadith 4

«Verily, Allah (ﷺ) has prohibited for my Ummah wine, gambling, a drink distilled from corn, the drum and the lute...» (recorded by Aḥmad and graded as sound by al-Albâni)

Hadith 5

«Verily, I did not prohibit weeping, but rather I forbade two voices which are imbecilic and sinfully shameless: one a voice [singing] to the accompaniment of musical amusement (*lahwa*) and Satan's [wind] instruments; the other, a voice [wailing] due to

---

[17] Ibn al-Qayyim, *Ighâthat ul-Lahfân min Maṣâ'id ash-Shayṭân*.

some calamity, accompanied by striking the face and tearing the garments. This [weeping of mine] stems from compassion, and whoever does not show compassion will not receive it.» (recorded by al-Hâkim and graded as reliable by al-Albâni)

Hadith 6

Anas ibn Mâlik (رضي الله عنه) related that the Prophet (ﷺ) said: «Two cursed sounds are that of the [wind] instrument played on the occasion of joy and grace, and woeful wailing upon the occurrence of adversity.» (recorded by Al-Haythami, who considered it sound)

Hadith 7

«Imam Nâfi' narrates that once when Abdullah ibn 'Umar (رضي الله عنه) heard the sound of a flute being played by a shepherd, he immediately put his fingers in his ears and diverted his riding animal in the other direction. Then he asked his servant Nâfi' (who had not reached adolescence yet): Can the sound still be heard? Nâfi' replied: Yes. Abdullah ibn 'Umar (رضي الله عنه) kept on walking until Nâfi' told him that the sound could no longer be heard. Abdullah (رضي الله عنه) then removed his fingers from his ears and told Nâfi' that he had seen Prophet Muhammad (ﷺ) doing the same thing when he (ﷺ) heard the sound of a flute being played by a shepherd.» (a sound hadith recorded by Abu Dâwood and Aḥmad)

Hadith 8

«'Imrân ibn Ḥusayn (رضي الله عنه) narrates that the Messenger of Allah (ﷺ) said: In my Ummah, there will be punishments of earthquakes, disfigurement of faces and showers of stones. A man from amongst the Muslims asked: O Prophet of Allah! When will that happen? He replied: When singing women and musical instruments become prevalent and drinking alcohol becomes common.» (a sound hadith recorded by Tirmidhi)

There are many more narrations of Prophet Muhammad (blessings and peace be upon him) regarding prohibition of musical instruments and unlawful singing. Only a few have been mentioned here. Imam Ibn Ḥajar al-Haythami (died 974 AH/1567 CE) gathered all these hadiths, which total approximately forty, in his excellent work, *Kaff ar-Ra'â' 'an Muḥarramât al-Lahwa was-Samâ'* (*Prohibiting People from the Forbidden Distractions and Singing*), and then concluded: "All of this is explicit and compelling textual evidence that musical instruments of all types are unlawful."[18]

An incident from the life of Prophet Muhammad (ﷺ)

'Ali ibn Abi Ṭâlib (ﷺ) said that he heard the Prophet Muhammad (ﷺ) say: «I was never attracted to the bad customs and amusements and entertainments of *jâhiliyah* (the age of spiritual darkness before the dawn of Islam) except on two nights, when Allah (ﷺ) protected me from any sin and kept me innocent.

One night, I was with a few of my young friends in Makkah, taking care of our herd of goats, when I heard the sounds of musical instruments and singing. I asked them: What is that? They told me that a marriage was taking place there. Allah, the Exalted, the Almighty, covered up my sense of hearing, and I went to sleep

---

[18] Al-Haythami, *Kaff ar-Ra'â' 'an Muḥarramât al-Lahwa was-Samâ'*.

for so long that the rays of sun on the next morning woke me up.

On the next night, I went again towards that place and heard the same sounds of music and singing that I had heard the night before. Again, Allah (ﷻ) covered up my sense of hearing. I went to sleep, and only the heat of the sun woke me up the next morning. After that, I neither intended nor was curious for such a thing until Allah (ﷻ) granted me prophethood.» (a reliable hadith recorded by Ibn Ḥajar, Ibn Is-ḥâq, Bazzâr, Bayhaqi, Abu Nu'aym and Ibn Asâkir)

Before giving the final ruling on the issue of the permissibility or impermissibility of listening to music, the harms of music in the light of modern scientific research will be discussed in the next few chapters.

Chapter 2

Scientific Research about the Effects of Music on the Body

$\mathcal{M}$usic is a highly complex sound because it not only has the characteristics of a simple sound but also has the additional element of rhythm. A rhythm means a movement or variation characterized by the regular recurrence of different sounds. The rhythm in music is time-dependent. It has effects upon the human body that can be measured and recorded. When combined with singing, the effects of music upon its listeners become even more powerful. Because people tend to consciously ignore auditory (listening) experiences, or they consider them insignificant, there is little indication that they are aware of either the power or the pervasiveness of music.

Several scientific studies have been done to show that music and singing affect both our bodies and our brains. Our responses to musical tempo could be due to our body's own rhythms. Human hearts normally beat at a rhythm of about seventy to eighty beats every minute, and interestingly, most Western music is paced at that same tempo.[1]

---

[1] Anne H. Rosenfeld, "Music, The Beautiful Disturber," *Psychology Today*, December 1985.

According to musical composer Roger Sessions, music is controlled movement of sound in time. Elaborating on this definition, Anne H. Rosenfeld, a psychologist and musician, explains:

> The notion of control in music is important. Music is rarely the spontaneous outpouring of whatever sounds someone happens to be moved to make. It is highly patterned sound, chosen and shaped, consciously or not, in quite logical ways that often follow rigid rules.[2]

Hence, music is a powerful force that has profound effects on its listeners. It is not simply an innocent entertainment or a haphazard mixture of sounds. In fact, music is composed of highly structured and carefully chosen sounds, as psychologist Rosenfeld pointed out. Therefore, listening to music is not an issue of merely seeking entertainment; listening to music has deep consequences on our bodies and our behaviours. It is for this reason that the matter of listening to music has been taken seriously in the teachings of the Qur'an and the Sunnah. In this chapter, we will discuss the effects of music on the human body and brain in light of modern scientific research.

Scientific relationship between music and emotions

In the past, scientists thought that reason and emotions were completely separate from each other, but that view has been changing recently. It has been shown that our emotions are much

---

[2] Rosenfeld, "Music, The Beautiful Disturber."

faster than our thought process, and they can hijack the linear reasoning process of the brain due to their speed.[3] Antonio Damasio, head of neurology at the University of Iowa and a prominent researcher on human brain function, has recently challenged the traditional view in his book *Descartes' Error: Emotion, Reason and the Human Brain*. He argues that psychology's conventional idea of a separation of reason from emotion is wrong, and that emotions actually play a central role in human decision-making. Damasio shows that rational decisions are not the result of logic alone but are profoundly affected by emotions and feelings.[4]

There are scientific studies which provide evidence that people experience emotions while listening to music. For example, Pike's analysis of music experience, published in the *Journal of Research in Music Education* in 1972, concerned an experiment carried out on a number of participants with no musical training who were asked to listen to different pieces of music. The results of that study showed that 96% of participants experienced a feeling of pleasure, 83% experienced a feeling of oneness with the music, 72% felt transient mood states, and 65% had the feeling of movement. The findings of this study provided evidence that listeners do experience emotions in relation to music.[5]

Researchers have also shown evidence of expressive behaviour in responses to music. In 1991, there were two separate

---

[3] J.T. Cacioppo and W. L. Gardner, "Emotion," *Annual Review of Psychology* 50 (1999): 191-214.

[4] Antonio Damasio, *Descartes' Error: Emotion, Reason and the Human Brain* (New York: Quill Publishers, 1994).

[5] Alfred Pike, "A Phenomenological Analysis of Emotional Experience in Music," *Journal of Research in Music Education* 20 (1972): 262-267.

studies, one by John A. Sloboda of the University of Keele (UK)[6] and another by A. Gabrielsson (a Canadian researcher),[7] which showed that people cried when they listened to certain kinds of music. In addition, studies using facial electromyography (EMG) have demonstrated that facial expressions change while people listen to expressive music, and the listeners are sometimes not even aware of this.[8] In the same vein, researchers Nyklicek, Thayer and van Doornen have reported evidence that, depending on the type of music (happy, sad, agitated, or calming), there are cardio-respiratory effects (such as increasing or slowing down of the heartbeat, breathing, or pulse rate) on individuals listening to music.[9]

In discussing human responses to music, Pennsylvania State University psychologist Julian Thayer argues that music "may have innate, universal underpinnings directly related to certain elements of sound, in general, and music, in particular."[10] For instance, the mood of high-pitched music is understood to be happy and playful, while the mood of low-pitched music is regarded as sad and serious. All this discussion provides evidence that there is a profound relationship between music and emotions.

---

[6] John A. Sloboda, "Music Structure and Emotional Response: Some Empirical Findings," *Psychology of Music* 19 (1991): 110-120.

[7] A. Gabrielsson, "Experiencing Music," *Canadian Journal of Research in Music Education* 33 (1991): 21-26.

[8] Witvliet and Vrana (1996), quoted in John A. Sloboda and Patrik N. Juslin, "Psychological Perspectives on Music and Emotion," in *Music and Emotion: Theory and Research*, edited by John A. Sloboda and Patrik N. Juslin (New York: Oxford University Press, 2001), 71-104.

[9] I. Nyklicek, J.F. Thayer and L.J.P. van Doornen, "Cardiorespiratory Differentiation of Musically-induced Emotions," *Journal of Psychophysiology* 11 (1997): 304-321.

[10] Rosenfeld, "Music, The Beautiful Disturber."

This is because music affects the limbic system, which is the region of the brain that regulates our emotions, as will be discussed later.

Biological effects of music on the body

A few studies have explored a special kind of intense biological response of the human body to music, known as 'thrills.' According to the Oxford English Dictionary (1933), a thrill is defined as 'a subtle nervous tremor caused by intense emotion or excitement (as pleasure, fear, etc.), producing a slight shudder or tingling through the body...'

These reports suggest that such bodily responses to music are quite common. One such study was carried out at Stanford University (California) by Avram Goldstein, a scientist who studied the phenomenon of the spine-tingling chill that often results in goose bumps, tears, or a lump in the throat. Since music affects our emotions, Goldstein tested to see if music has the ability to cause thrills in its listeners. He found (as shown in the table below) that 96% of his subjects reported such thrills in response to music, as compared to much lower rates for physical exercise (36%), problem solving (57%), spectator sports (52%) or even sexual activity (70%).[11] Moreover, a comparison of the physiological responses of the individuals indicated that listening to music caused more physical arousal than being enthralled by a novel or mesmerized by a beautiful picture.

---

[11] Avram Goldstein, "Thrills in Response to Music and Other Stimuli," *Physiological Psychology* 8, no. 1 (1980): 126-129.

After analyzing 250 participants in his study, Goldstein found that the most frequently mentioned thrills occurred in response to music. A typical thrill is described as a tingling sensation, a shudder or a chill which emanates from the back of the neck and spreads to the front of the face and over the scalp, as well as downward along the spine and forward over the chest, thighs and legs. It may also be accompanied by palpitation, tension of facial muscles and incipient weeping. Goldstein observed that there was no difference between men and women in regard to the thrills caused by music.

Goldstein did another experiment to prove that the thrills caused by music are due to endorphins (natural painkillers in our body), as is the case with other emotional responses. One group of people listening to music was injected with naloxane (a chemical that prevents the occurrence of thrills in our body) while the other group was injected with only salt water, but the participants were not told what they had received. The findings clearly demonstrated that thrills became very weak or did not occur in the listeners who were injected with naloxane.[12] This study provides scientific evidence that something powerful happens to many people emotionally when they listen to music. It was found that the most powerful stimulus for evoking thrill-like sensations in the human subjects was music. Hence, music causes arousal in the subjects; in other words, it can increase the heart rate, alter the respiratory rate, raise the pulse rate and dilate the pupils.

---

[12] Avram Goldstein, "Thrills in Response to Music and Other Stimuli."

Table: Different types of stimuli that gives us "Thrills"

Item	% of people who experienced thrills
Musical passages	96
Scene in a movie, play, ballet or book	92
Great beauty in nature or art	87
Physical contact with another person	78
Climactic moments in opera	72
Sexual activity	70
Sudden insight or solution to a problem	57
Particular moments at a sports event	52
Particular fragrances	39
Physical exercise	36

Summarized from: "Thrills in Response to Music and Other Stimuli" *Physical Psychology*, (1980) Vol. 8, No. 1, pp. 126-129

Electroencephalography (EEG) is a medical procedure used to measure the brain's electrical activity. In order to estimate the effects of music on the human brain, scientists have employed EEG and placed electrodes on the scalps of the subjects while music was played to them. In one such study by Schmidt and Trainor, it was observed that while a person is listening to the music, various areas in the brain become activated (which could be due to changes in blood flow pattern in those brain areas). They also noted that there was comparatively greater activity in the left (frontal) portion of the brain when the music expressed joy and happiness, whereas greater activity was noticed in the right portion of the brain with music expressing fear and sadness.[13] This could be because the right and left sides of the brain control different emotions.

When singing is accompanied by musical instruments, it becomes extremely powerful in terms of affecting the emotional responses of the subjects. In a study published in the *Journal of Applied Social Psychology* in 1972, researchers Galizio and Hendrick demonstrated that the subjects who listened to a song became more aroused, were easier to persuade and were more likely to accept the message of a song when it was accompanied by a guitar, as compared to the song without a guitar.[14]

Biological effects of music on the brain

When music is played, it acts much like an intoxicant, in that it makes a person forget about his or her surroundings. It takes the mind into a delusional state. In the realm of the mind, there is mounting evidence that certain types of music have a negative effect on one's ability to think and learn, especially at the time he or she is listening to the music. Studies at two separate universities, for example, have found that rats have a much more difficult time learning to pass through a maze if they are subjected to rock music, as noted in an *Insight* magazine article on April 27,

[13] L. Schmidt and L. Trainor, quoted in Isabelle Peretz, "Listen to the Brain: A Biological Perspective on Musical Emotions," in *Music and Emotion: Theory and Research,* edited by Patrik N. Juslin and John A. Sloboda (New York: Oxford University Press, 2001), 105-133.

[14] M. Galizio and C. Hendrick, "Effect of Musical Accompaniment on Attitude: The Guitar as a Prop for Persuasion," *Journal of Applied Social Psychology* 2 (1972): 350-359.

1987. In other words, the learning abilities of rats deteriorated temporarily due to the influence of music. Music blurs the critical judgment abilities of the brain.

The human brain is the organ of thought, speech and emotions; it acts as the body's control center. The brain consists of many parts, such as the brain stem (an extension of the spinal cord), the cerebrum and, above the brain stem, the large forebrain known as the cerebellum. The cerebellum consists of left and right brain hemispheres. Deep within the forebrain is the region comprising the limbic system, which includes structures such as the amygdale, hippocampus and hypothalamus. The limbic system in our body has the following functions:

- ❖ control of emotions
- ❖ emotional responses (including sexual response)
- ❖ hormonal (chemical) secretions
- ❖ mood
- ❖ pain and pleasure sensations
- ❖ long-term memory

Emotions and feelings like aggression, fright, passion, love, hate, joy and sadness all originate in the limbic system. This system is also responsible for some aspects of personal identity and for important functions related to memory. If damage occurs to the limbic area of the brain (due to disease or an accident), the most commonly observed effects are abnormalities of emotional response, such as inappropriate crying or laughing, easily provoked rage, anxiety and depression, and excessive sexual interest.[15]

---

[15] Charles B. Clayman, MD, ed., *The American Medical Association Home=*

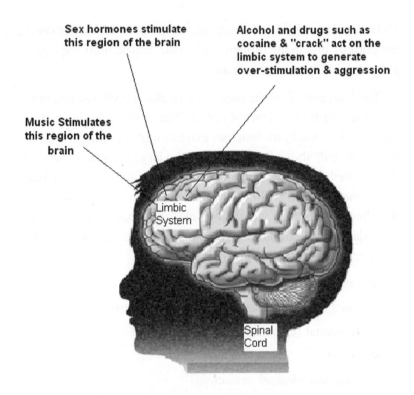

Sex hormones stimulate this region of the brain

Alcohol and drugs such as cocaine & "crack" act on the limbic system to generate over-stimulation & aggression

Music Stimulates this region of the brain

Limbic System

Spinal Cord

Figure: Music affects the same region of the brain
that is stimulated by the sex hormones, alcohol and drugs

It seems that sex, drugs and rock and roll are so strongly connected to one other that they even stimulate the same region of the human brain, that is, the limbic system, as shown in the figure. Among human beings, youth is already a period of great stress. In male adolescents, the production of the male hormone testosterone is increased to twenty times the normal level, and the production of female hormones increases similarly in adolescent

---

=*Medical Encyclopedia: An A-Z Reference Guide to over 5000 Medical Terms* (New York: Random House, 1989).

girls. At puberty, the limbic system of the brain is stimulated by the surge of these sex hormones, which may be a significant factor in acts of aggression among the youth.[16]

Teenagers enjoy the pounding music that stimulates the limbic system of the brain, which is the same region of the brain that is activated by sex hormones. Interestingly, alcohol also acts on the limbic system, stimulating it and causing aggression.[17] Drugs such as cocaine and crack also act on the brain's limbic system (especially the hypothalamus) to generate over-stimulation, aggression, loss of appetite and nervousness. In fact, many people take drugs like cocaine in order to boost their sex drives. It is little wonder that the incidence of violent crimes is highest among persons between the ages of 15 and 24.[18]

Similarly, of 130 suicide cases studied at the University of San Diego, the use of alcohol and other drugs was the major factor in 66% of those cases.[19] Dr. Paul King is assistant professor of child and adolescent psychiatry at the Medical School of the University of Tennessee, Memphis. He notes, "Music that speaks directly to young people about sex, violence, and suicide may be a serious public health problem."[20]

In addition, the hippocampus, which is part of the brain's limbic system, is involved in the formation of long-term memory

---

[16] B. Geller and D.E. Greydanus, "Aggression in Adolescents: Aspects of Pathogenesis," *Journal of Adolescent Health Care* 1, no. 3 (1981): 236-243.

[17] Paul King, M.D., "Heavy Metal Music and Drug Abuse in Adolescents," *Postgraduate Medicine* 83, no. 5 (April 1988): 295-301, 304.

[18] S.B. Guze, *Criminality and Psychiatric Disorders* (New York: Oxford University Press, 1976).

[19] C.L. Rich, D. Young and R.C. Fowler, "San Diego Suicide Study. I. Young vs. Old Subjects," *Archives of General Psychiatry* 43, no. 6 (1986): 577-582.

[20] King, "Heavy Metal Music and Drug Abuse in Adolescents."

(memory that sometimes lasts forever). When people listen to music that acts on the limbic system of the brain, the sexual or aggressive messages of the songs become part of their character for the rest of their lives.

Role of music and singing in arousing sexual feelings

In 1871, Charles Darwin took note of the role of music in arousing sexual feelings by proposing that music serves to attract sexual partners.[21] One does not need to emphasize that whether in the East or the West, the most prevalent theme of music and singing is sex. The sexual element has always been present in most of the world's dancing accompanied by music. In many preliterate cultures, music and dancing served as preliminaries to mating and were closely connected with the choice of a marriage partner. This is similar to the dancing seen in animals during courtship. For example, a peacock dances with its beautiful feathers displayed before mating with a peahen,[22] and it even produces sounds while dancing.

The reason for the widespread prevalence of — and addiction to — music, singing and dancing is their appeal to the inborn sensual desires of most people. In this context, this statement of Plato's about music can be easily understood: "Rhythm and melody, accompanied by dance, are the barbarous expression of

---

[21] Charles Darwin, *The Descent of Man, and Selection in Relation to Sex* (London: John Murray, 1871).

[22] A. Loyau, M. Saint Jalme and C. Cagniant, "Multiple Sexual Advertisements Honestly Reflect Health Status in Peacocks (*Pavo cristatus*)," *Behavioral Ecology and Sociobiology* 58, no. 6 (2005): 552-557.

the soul." [23] In fact, in his famous book *The Republic,* Plato demanded strict censorship over popular music. He feared that citizens "would be tempted and corrupted by weak and voluptuous airs and led to indulge in demoralizing emotions." The spirit of music has been better summed up in a very laconic and precise saying of the early Muslim scholar al-Fudayl ibn Iyâd:[24] "Ghinâ' is a prelude to *zinâ* (adultery or fornication)."[25]

Accordingly, we cannot overemphasize the observation that teenagers are even more prone to the pernicious effects of music than people in other age groups. The relationship between music and sexuality can also be understood by the observation that when teenagers reach the age of puberty, they tend to receive inspiration from the prevalent themes of music and singing, as noted by Elizabeth Brown and William Hendee:

> Music is important to adolescents in many ways. For example, music plays a large role in adolescent socialization. As adolescents gain independence, they turn to music as an information source about sexuality and alternative lifestyles, subjects that are largely taboo in both home and school.[26]

---

[23] Allan Bloom, *The Closing of the American Mind* (New York: Simon and Schuster, 1987).

[24] Al-Fudayl ibn Iyâd was the great Islamic scholar of the science of tazkiyah (purification of the self). He was regarded as one of the *shuyukh as-salaf* (scholars of the early generations) by Shaykh al-Islam Ibn Taymiyah in his *Majmoo'ul Fatâwa* (vol. 10) under his commentary of 'Abdul-Qâdir Jilâni's *Futooh al-Ghayb*. He died in 187 AH.

[25] Shaykh Shahâb ud-Deen Suhrawardi, *'Awârif al-Ma'ârif* (Beirut: Darul Kitâb Al-'Arabi, 1966).

[26] E.F. Brown and W.R. Hendee, "Adolescents and their Music: Insights into the Health of Adolescents," *The Journal of the American Medical Association* 262 (1989): 1659-1663.

In research published in 1971, social scientist R. Cole reported that nearly three-fourths of the lyrics of the top songs of the 1960s used love and sex as their predominant theme.[27] The trend did not change over later years. In more recent research published in the *Journal of Communication* in 1986, researchers Sherman and Dominick found that song lyrics did not become less sexually oriented in the 1970s and 1980s.[28] In the same vein, Christenson and DeBenedittis noted in their study published in 1986 that popular music lyrics contain references — explicit and metaphorical — to sexual activity.[29] These results show that much of the popular music focuses on sexual themes.

The research conducted on the biological effects of music on the human body, which was cited previously, shows how music has a powerful emotional and physical effect on the listeners. One can easily understand what the consequences of listening to such music and singing can be. The results of these scientific studies clearly suggest that when singing is accompanied by musical instruments, this increases its power and influence in persuading the listeners to the path of corruption and lewdness.

Research on endorphins and self-delusion

Endorphins are natural painkillers in our bodies that are released in times of massive stress or trauma. This is a natural

---

[27] R. Cole, "Top Songs in the Sixties," in *Mass Communication and Youth: Some Cultural Perspectives*, edited by F. Gerald Kline and P. Clarke (Beverly Hills, CA: Sage Publications, 1971).

[28] B. Sherman and J. Dominick, "Violence and Sex in Music Videos: TV and Rock 'n' Roll," *Journal of Communication* 36, no. 1 (1986): 79-93.

[29] P. Christenson and P. DeBenedittis, "Eavesdropping on the FM Band: Children's Use of Radio." *Journal of Communication* 36, no. 2 (1986): 27-38.

mechanism that takes place in our bodies, at the time of an accident or injury, to reduce the intensity of pain. There is a trade-off, though, in that we lose alertness and attentiveness, moving into a state of self-delusion where we lose the sensation of pain. Simply stated, endorphins have pain-relieving properties similar to drugs such as morphine and codeine, which also cause loss of attentiveness.

Music has the same effect in the psychological realm. The limbic system of the brain plays a major role in the reaction to music. That portion of the brain has regions called opioid receptors that are highly sensitive to the presence of endorphins, which blunt the feeling of pain. The fact that music affects the emotions so profoundly could be due to the involvement of music in the release of endorphins, which cause the emotional responses that we feel. Due to the lessening of the pain, listening to music may make a person feel better. However, this is a very short-term effect, which lasts only while the music is being played. This unfortunately may lead a person to play music all the time to get that feeling, leading to addiction. This is how drugs work, too.

People try to alleviate the anxiety of the self through intermediates that in reality are shallow. They are like food, which satiates the hunger, but only temporarily. This is true of the spiritual hunger as well, in that music satiates the soul only temporarily. In addition, music is not even a pure food; it is what Professor Allan Bloom calls 'junk food for the soul.'[30] Such a food is more like the saltiest water of the sea; the more a person drinks it, the thirstier he or she gets. Such a food is actually detrimental to our spiritual health because it grinds down our spiritual strength and puts us into a state of spiritual self-delusion.

---

[30] Bloom, *The Closing of the American Mind.*

Healthful food is constructive for our physical body; it builds it up. On the other hand, when junk food enters into our body, it feels tasty to the tongue, but it is unhealthy for our body. In the same way, listening to music is not spiritually beneficial, and it causes spiritual diseases of the heart in its listener.

The diseases of the heart, according to the great Muslim scholar Ibn al-Qayyim al-Jawziyah,[31] can be divided into two major categories: diseases of doubts and diseases of desires.[32]

Diseases of doubts creep into the heart when the level of faith is reduced. This happens when hypocrisy is nurtured in the heart due to listening to music. There is a profound link between listening to music and the disease of hypocrisy, as will be shown in detail later in this book. Diseases of desires arise when the heart succumbs to the lowly desires of the self and wants to go into a state of self-delusion. Music ignites sexual passions in its listeners and acts as a drug, as will be shown in detail in the next chapter of this book. A diseased heart will bring about the wrath of Allah (ﷻ) on the Day of Judgment. Only spiritually sound hearts, free from spiritual diseases, will be successful on that day, as mentioned in the Qur'an:

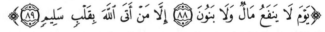

﴿يَوْمَ لَا يَنفَعُ مَالٌ وَلَا بَنُونَ ۝ إِلَّا مَنْ أَتَى ٱللَّهَ بِقَلْبٍ سَلِيمٍ ۝﴾

(سورة الشُّعَرَاء : ٨٨–٨٩)

---

[31] Ibn al-Qayyim al-Jawziyah was one of the greatest Islamic scholars of all times. A devoted disciple of Ibn Taymiyah, he was a prolific writer who wrote original and well-researched books on various Islamic subjects including tafseer, jurisprudence, hadith, music, psychology, and many others. He died in 751 AH/ 1350 CE.

[32] Aḥmad Farid, comp., *The Purification of the Soul* (London: Al-Firdous Publications Ltd., 1989).

❨The Day when there will not benefit [anyone] wealth or children but only one who comes to Allah with a sound heart.❩

(Qur'an 26: 88-89)

The heartbeat rhythms and the musical rhythms

Rhythm is a physical force that exists in nature, in the beating of our hearts, our walking, and our breathing, for example. Our bodies readily respond to strong, external rhythmic stimuli from drums, pulsating beats, hypnotic lighting effects and the like. It is little wonder that the most soothing music usually beats at about seventy to eighty tones per minute, which resembles the natural rhythm of a heartbeat. The defining characteristic of jazz is its pulsating rhythm, and its drumbeat resembles the heartbeat in that both involve beats of about seventy-two times per minute.

Due to the intoxicating rhythms of music, people can be 'possessed' by music and surrender themselves to the music in the process. Music can hypnotize people and, hence, capture their minds. The basic feature of hypnosis is repetition, just as the main ingredient of any music is repetition. A repetitive beat, ideally in the range of seventy-two beats per minute (as we said, close to the beat of the human heart) is very hypnotic, and prolonged exposure to such a rhythm can be trance-inducing. The steady, repetitive drumbeat can generate an altered state of consciousness, and it can place the listener's mind into a dangerous state of suggestive hypnosis. In such a hypnotic state, the messages of the songs become imprinted on the minds of their listeners without any critical analysis; their minds passively absorb what the songs tell them. Renowned American composer, electric guitarist and record producer Frank Vincent Zappa wrote in *Life* magazine on

June 28, 1968: "The ways in which sound affects the human organism are myriad and subtle... the loud sounds and bright lights of today are tremendous indoctrination tools."

Musicologist Leonard Meyer, in his famous book *Emotion and Meaning in Music*, describes the same rhythmic quality of music. According to Meyer, music is generally arranged in such a way that certain melodies or themes of a song are presented, repeated and modified with other themes. Then the original melodies or themes eventually come back in the song, and this gives us a feeling of comfort and relief. This occurs not only in a classical symphony but also in folk or pop music, since the chorus and verses in the song alternate, but the song always ends with a familiar phrase or verse.[33]

Rhythm was the main ingredient in the prolonged periods of singing, dancing, chanting, and drumming of primitive peoples. The purpose of such rhythmic exercises was to induce altered states of consciousness such as trances. Indeed, certain kinds of drumming may produce these trance-like states by driving the brain's electrical rhythms, as has been proposed by psychological anthropologist Ralph G. Locke and experimental psychologist Edward F. Kelly of the Spring Creek Institute, Durham, North Carolina.

Corruption of the heart through the ears

At the School of Behavioural Sciences in New South Wales, researcher Roderick Power demonstrated that sight and sound are

---

[33] Leonard Meyer, *Emotion and Meaning in Music* (Chicago: University of Chicago Press, 1961) quoted in Rosenfeld, "Music, The Beautiful Disturber."

the major senses in our body, while the senses of taste, touch and smell hold secondary importance and may depend on cues furnished by those major senses.[34] All sounds impact us, and they can nourish or debilitate. For this reason, ears are the major inroad to the corruption of the heart. Satan knows how to exploit this weakness in human beings, which is why Allah (ﷻ) says regarding him:

﴾وَٱسْتَفْزِزْ مَنِ ٱسْتَطَعْتَ مِنْهُم بِصَوْتِكَ وَأَجْلِبْ عَلَيْهِم بِخَيْلِكَ وَرَجِلِكَ وَشَارِكْهُمْ فِى ٱلْأَمْوَٰلِ وَٱلْأَوْلَٰدِ وَعِدْهُمْ وَمَا يَعِدُهُمُ ٱلشَّيْطَٰنُ إِلَّا غُرُورًا ۝﴿

(سورة الإِسْرَاء: ٦٤)

❴"And incite [to senselessness] whomever you can among them with your voice, and assault them with your horses and foot soldiers, and become a partner in their wealth and their children and promise them." But Satan does not promise them anything except delusion.❵ *(Qur'an 17: 64)*

Satan leads human beings astray by his voice — that is, by music and singing. Music is part of his grand plan to lead human beings to the path of disobedience to Allah (ﷻ). Satan corrupts the human heart (which is both the physical and spiritual organ of cognition in human beings)[35] through the ears. It is true that it is hard to protect our ears, more so even than our eyes. That is why, in the Qur'an, the sense of hearing is mentioned before the sense of sight. For example, Allah (ﷻ) says:

---

[34] Roderick Power, "The Dominance of Touch by Vision: Occurs with Familiar Objects," *Perception* 10 (1981): 29-33.

[35] Gohar Mushtaq, PhD, *The Intelligent Heart, The Pure Heart: An Insight into the Heart based on Qur'an, Sunnah and Modern Science* (London: Ta-Ha Publishers, 2006).

﴿ ... إِنَّ ٱلسَّمْعَ وَٱلْبَصَرَ وَٱلْفُؤَادَ كُلُّ أُوْلَٰئِكَ كَانَ عَنْهُ مَسْـُٔولًا ٣٦ ﴾

(سورة الإسْرَاء: ٣٦)

❨...Indeed, the hearing, the sight, and the heart — about all those [one] will be questioned [by Allah].❩   *(Qur'an 17: 36)*

At the time of birth, the newborn's sense of hearing is fully functional, whereas a baby cannot see or recognize objects beyond a certain distance. It takes infants a few weeks before they can recognize the faces of different people. In the Qur'an, Allah (ﷻ) tells us in different places:

﴿وَٱللَّهُ أَخْرَجَكُم مِّنۢ بُطُونِ أُمَّهَٰتِكُمْ لَا تَعْلَمُونَ شَيْـًٔا وَجَعَلَ لَكُمُ ٱلسَّمْعَ وَٱلْأَبْصَٰرَ وَٱلْأَفْـِٔدَةَ لَعَلَّكُمْ تَشْكُرُونَ ٧٨ ﴾   (سورة النّحل: ٧٨)

❨And Allah has extracted you from the wombs of your mothers not knowing a thing, and He made for you hearing and vision and hearts that perhaps you would be grateful.❩   *(Qur'an 16: 78)*

﴿قُلْ هُوَ ٱلَّذِىٓ أَنشَأَكُمْ وَجَعَلَ لَكُمُ ٱلسَّمْعَ وَٱلْأَبْصَٰرَ وَٱلْأَفْـِٔدَةَ قَلِيلًا مَّا تَشْكُرُونَ ٢٣ ﴾   (سورة المُلك: ٢٣)

❨Say: It is He who has produced you and made for you hearing and vision and hearts; little are you grateful.❩   *(Qur'an 67: 23)*

Hence, in the Qur'an, the reference to the sense of hearing is made first, and then the sense of sight is mentioned. This is because the sense of hearing is developed first in the child (a fact that has been only recently discovered by scientists). Also, it is a common observation that children listen for a long time before they begin to speak.

Moreover, Prophet Muhammad (ﷺ) used to make the following supplication to Allah (ﷻ) in the morning and in the evening, in which he mentioned the sense of hearing before the sense of seeing: «O Allah, grant my body health, O Allah, grant my hearing health, O Allah, grant my sight health. None has the right to be worshipped except You.» (Bukhari, Abu Dâwood and Nisâ'i)

The importance of the sense of hearing can also be understood by the fact that this sense has been mentioned along with intellect in the Qur'an:

﴿وَقَالُوا لَوْ كُنَّا نَسْمَعُ أَوْ نَعْقِلُ مَا كُنَّا فِى أَصْحَـٰبِ ٱلسَّعِيرِ ۝﴾ (سورة المُلك: ١٠)

(And they will say: If only we had been listening or reasoning, we would not be among the companions of the blaze.) *(Qur'an 67: 10)*

Similarly, at another place in the Qur'an, the sense of hearing is associated with understanding:

﴿رَّبَّنَآ إِنَّنَا سَمِعْنَا مُنَادِيًا يُنَادِى لِلْإِيمَـٰنِ أَنْ ءَامِنُوا بِرَبِّكُمْ فَـَٔامَنَّا ... ۝﴾
(سورة آل عِمرَان: ١٩٣)

(Our Lord, indeed we have heard a caller [Muhammad] calling to faith: Believe in your Lord; and we have believed...)
(Qur'an 3: 193)

Also, the relationship of the heart and the ears is described in the Qur'an as follows:

﴿إِنَّ فِى ذَٰلِكَ لَذِكْرَىٰ لِمَن كَانَ لَهُ قَلْبٌ أَوْ أَلْقَى ٱلسَّمْعَ وَهُوَ شَهِيدٌ ۝﴾
(سورة قۤ: ٣٧)

❨Indeed, in that is indeed a reminder for whoever has a heart or who listens while he is present [in mind].❩   *(Qur'an 50: 37)*

If we look at the sense of hearing, it is circular, in contrast to the sense of sight, which is linear. In other words, we can hear from all directions, but we can see only what is in front of us. In fact, psychoacoustician Reinier Plomp has argued that the "most striking property of the hearing system is its ability to *analyze* the world of superimposed sounds and to separate them according to their various sources."[36] If there is an act of disobedience to Allah (ﷻ) happening in front of us, we can close our eyes or turn our faces away very easily, but to protect our ears, we have to physically leave that place.

Furthermore, the sense of hearing can work in the dark as well as in the light, whereas eyes cannot see in the dark; they can only see in the presence of light. Similarly, the sense of hearing stays active even when we are asleep, whereas the sense of seeing stops operating when a person goes to sleep.[37] A loud sound can wake a sleeping person. For this reason, smoke detectors produce a loud sound, not a bright light, because if there is a fire while people are sleeping, they can be awakened by hearing a loud sound. In the story of the cave dwellers, Allah (ﷻ) tells us that He covered their sense of hearing so that their sleep would not be disturbed:

﴿فَضَرَبْنَا عَلَىٰٓ ءَاذَانِهِمْ فِى ٱلْكَهْفِ سِنِينَ عَدَدًا ۝﴾ (سورة الكهف: ١١)

❨So We cast [a cover of sleep] over their ears within the cave for a number of years.❩   *(Qur'an 18: 11)*

---

[36] Reinier Plomp, *The Intelligent Ear: On the Nature of Sound Perception* (Mahwah, New Jersey: Lawrence Erlbaum Associates, 2002).

[37] Ibid.

Hence, it is harder to protect the ears from sins than it is to protect the eyes. Music destroys our spiritual heart through the ears. The fact that our ears are the easiest inroad to the corruption of the heart can be understood by the scientific findings indicating that auditory nerves are some of the predominant nerves in the body. This is why our ears are very sensitive, and there is plenty of evidence for this.

Our brains comprise left and right hemispheres, which perform different functions. Consequently, our left and right ears have different ways of processing information obtained from music and singing. In other words, one ear processes the emotional tone of the singer, and the actual content of the song, differently from the other ear. British neurologist John Hughlings Jackson was the first to notice that difference between the two ears.[38] Later on, 'dichotic listening' experiments were done in this area. In dichotic studies, different sounds or sound patterns (in this case, music and songs) are presented to the two ears through earphones. By studying which ear's signals are better discriminated, researchers can tell which ear processes which type of music.

For example, in 1982, Ley and Bryden discovered, by conducting dichotic studies with normal adults, that the left ear is better at recognizing the emotional tone of the singer's voice, while the right ear does a better job of recognizing the actual content of the words in the same sentences of a song.[39] It seems that our ears are very sensitive to the type of information entered

---

[38] John H. Jackson, "On Affections of Speech from Disease of the Brain," *Brain* 1 (1878): 304-330.

[39] P. Bryden, R. Ley and J. Sugerman, "A Left-ear Advantage for Identifying the Emotional Quality of Tonal Sequences," *Neuropsychologia* 20 (1982): 83-87.

because that information will eventually have effects on our actions. It is a fact, as we have seen in the evidence from the Qur'an, from the traditions of Prophet Muhammad (ﷺ), from his Companions and from the scholars of Islam, that singing and music go together. It is no wonder that by combining singing and music, Satan exploits both the left and the right ear in order to cause sickening of the spiritual heart.

Chapter 3

Sex, Drugs and Rock and Roll

$\mathcal{I}$n one hadith, the Prophet Muhammad (ﷺ) said: «There will be people of my Ummah who will seek to make these lawful: illegal sexual intercourse, the wearing of silk [by men], the drinking of alcoholic drinks, and the use of ma'âzif.» (Bukhari)

Based on this hadith, there are three things that can be regarded as three corners of a vicious triangle, namely: drinking alcohol, listening to music and illicit sexual relations. If we look at the history of fine arts in Europe and the paintings produced by the European artists during the periods of Romanticism, Realism, Impressionism and Post-Impressionism, we see that the pleasures of wine, women and musical instruments are depicted together in many of those paintings. Even today, in American and European nightclubs, there is alcohol, music and dancing, and sometimes the presence of prostitutes.

The phrase 'rock and roll' itself has strong sexual connotations. Music, alcohol and illicit sex grievously affect the society, and these three things always go together. It must be noted that in Islamic teachings, every form of music is ḥarâm, whether it be religious, classical, traditional, country, pop, rock and roll, jazz, heavy metal, or rap. In this chapter, the relationship of music and singing to sex and drugs will be discussed in detail.

Relationship of ghinâ' to zinâ

There is a profound relationship between music and fornication, as was noted by the Prophet Muhammad (ﷺ) in the hadith above. In a similar hadith narrated by the Prophet's Companion 'Imrân bin Ḥusayn (رضي الله عنه), Prophet Muhammad (ﷺ) mentioned about the period towards the end of time: «...When singing women and musical instruments become prevalent and drinking alcohol becomes common.» (a sound hadith recorded by Tirmidhi)

As stated earlier, al-Fudayl ibn Iyâd summarized this relationship in this eloquent saying: "Ghinâ' is a prelude to zinâ." (*'Awârif al-Ma'ârif*)

Singing can act as a ladder to adultery. Music and singing ignite the sensual desires of a person, and this can ultimately end with bad consequences. Most songs speak of premarital relationships as a norm. As mentioned previously, if we go through the history of Western fine arts and look at the paintings of any period of art, we will see musical instruments, women and alcohol depicted together because music, fornication and drugs are related to each other. Abdur-Raḥman Ibn al-Jawzi (who died in 597 AH) wrote:

There are two harms added together in singing. On the one hand, it diverts the heart from the remembrance of the Greatness of Allah (ﷻ); on the other hand, it persuades the heart towards material pleasures. It is known that among all the material pleasures, the strongest one is the pleasure of intimacy of man and woman. However, this pleasure is completed only when there is continuous novelty and uniqueness in it, and it is obvious that it is not possible to get such novelty in a halal way. Therefore, singing persuades the person towards fornication and adultery. There is a deep connection between singing and fornication. Singing is a temptation for the soul, whereas fornication is the biggest pleasure of the body.[1]

Renowned U.S. psychologist M. Scott Peck reiterates the same argument in his book *The Road Less Traveled* — that sex remains charming as long as we find novelty in it.[2] Music and singing encourage people to seek such novelty.

It must be clarified here that Muslims are not puritanical in their attitudes towards sex. According to Islamic teachings, while procreation is the primary purpose of marriage, permitted forms of sex are encouraged between lawfully married husbands and wives. For example, Islam not only permits but encourages sexual foreplay between the spouses. Other purposes of marriage include companionship, fulfilment of the natural urge, comfort and relief to the soul and enjoyment of the spouse. Islam teaches us that if one cohabits with one's own spouse, it is an act of piety and devotion, meriting the pleasure and reward from God, as mentioned in hadiths.

The Qur'an clearly asserts that Allah (ﷻ) created spouses for both sexes to provide them with love, mercy and tranquility, and this is regarded as one of the signs of Allah (ﷻ).

وَمِنْ ءَايَٰتِهِۦٓ أَنْ خَلَقَ لَكُم مِّنْ أَنفُسِكُمْ أَزْوَٰجًا لِّتَسْكُنُوٓا۟ إِلَيْهَا وَجَعَلَ

---

[1] Imam 'Abdur-Raḥman Ibn al-Jawzi, *Talbees Iblees* (The Devil's Deception) (Multan: Kutab Khana Majeedia, 1991).

[2] M. Scott Peck, *The Road Less Traveled* (New York: Simon and Schuster, 1998).

بَيۡنَكُم مَّوَدَّةً وَرَحۡمَةً إِنَّ فِى ذَٰلِكَ لَأَيَٰتٍ لِّقَوۡمٍ يَتَفَكَّرُونَ ۞

(سورة الرُّوم: ٢١)

❨And of His signs is that He created for you from yourselves
mates that you may find tranquility in them; and He placed
between you affection and mercy. Indeed in that are signs for a
people who give thought.❩   *(Qur'an 30: 21)*

In a study published in the *Journal of Broadcasting and
Electronic Media* in 1985, Baxter and his associates analyzed the
content of music videos and concluded that 60% of them portray
sexual feelings and impulses. A substantial minority of those
music videos also display provocative clothing and sexually
suggestive body movements.[3]

In another study, researcher Durant and his colleagues
analyzed 518 music videos from MTV, CMT, and VH1[4] for
portrayals of alcohol and tobacco use. They found that portrayals
of drug use differed among various networks and by music type,
with MTV having the highest percentage of videos that portrayed
alcohol and tobacco use. One of the striking findings from this
study was that alcohol use was found in a higher proportion in
music videos that had sexual content, as compared to those videos
that did not have any sexual content in them.[5] This study shows

---

[3] R.L. Baxter, C. De Riemer, A. Landani, "A Content Analysis of Music
Videos," *Journal of Broadcasting and Electronic Media* 29 (1985): 333-340.

[4] MTV (originally 'Music Television'), CMT (Country Music Television) and
VH1 (originally 'Video Hits 1') are popular American television networks
devoted to broadcasting music videos. [Editor]

[5] R.H. DuRant et al., "Tobacco and Alcohol Use Behaviors Portrayed in
Music Videos: A Content Analysis," *American Journal of Public Health* 87
(1997): 1131-1135.

that sex, drugs and music tend to coexist, as mentioned in the hadith at the beginning of this chapter.

In a recent study, the content of six different types of media was analyzed in terms of its exposure and its outcome on the young people. These media included movies, television shows, newspapers, magazines and popular music. Researcher Pardun and associates found in this study that sexual content is much more prevalent in popular music lyrics than in any other medium.[6]

Just as promiscuity and free love destroy the physical health of a person, similarly they destroy the moral health of the whole society. One of the most important themes of music is premarital love and promiscuity; as a result, millions of young boys and girls commit 'moral suicide.' These young people destroy their modesty and chastity under the intoxicating influence of music that fires up their sexual desires.

American intellectual and professor at the University of Chicago, Allan Bloom, is quite correct when he asserts in his book *The Closing of the American Mind* that the present-age music has one appeal only:

> a barbaric appeal, to sexual desire — not love... but sexual desire undeveloped and untutored... rock [music] gives children, on a silver plate, with all the public authority of the entertainment industry, everything their parents always used to tell them they had to wait for until they grew up.... This has a much more powerful effect than does pornography on youngsters.[7]

---

[6] Carol J.Pardun, Kelly Ladin L'Engle and Jane D. Brown, "Linking Exposure to Outcome: Early Adolescents' Consumption of Sexual Content in Six Media," *Mass Communication and Society* 8 (May 2005): 75-91.

[7] Bloom, *The Closing of the American Mind.*

There are plenty of examples, but owing to the length of this section, a look at a few recent top songs and their titles will suffice. At the end of 2009, AOL Radio Blog published its list of the year's top ten songs, as rated by AOL Radio listeners. Even by looking at the titles of these songs, it is obvious that the focal point of their message is free love. Here are the titles and brief descriptions of a few of those songs:

"You Belong With Me" by Taylor Swift

In this song, the singer is in love with a friend, so she tries to convince him that she loves him more than his other girlfriend.

"Replay" by Iyaz

This song is about a girl that the singer cannot get out of his head. As a result, both of them are singing continuously while their 'iPod's stuck on replay.'

"Poker Face" by Lady GaGa

The main themes of this song are sex, gambling, and bisexuality.

"Use Somebody" by Kings of Leon

The lyrics of this song talk about feeling lonely on the road.

"My Life Would Suck Without You" by Kelly Clarkson

In this song, Clarkson sings that although she and her boyfriend often fight with each other, she cannot let him go because somehow he makes her life better.

"Right Round" by Flo Rida

This song is about a night that the singer spent at a strip club.

"Whatcha Say" by Jason Derulo

The lyrics of this song focus on a situation in which a girlfriend catches her boyfriend having an affair with another woman.

In October 1987, a conference was held in Washington, D.C. on the topic "Raised on Rock and Roll — The Sound and the Fury." In that conference, United States Surgeon General Dr. C. Everett Koop indicated that this type of music appears to be 'a close relative of pornography.'[8] Hence, the U.S. Surgeon General accepted the fact that music and pornography are close relatives. It seems that he understood the wisdom of the saying of the Prophet, uttered about fourteen centuries ago, in which he (ﷺ) described music along with fornication, to show that they are closely related.

Relationship of ghinâ' to hypocrisy

Abdullah Ibn Mas'ood (رضي الله عنه), the distinguished Companion of Prophet Muhammad (ﷺ), said, "Singing fosters hypocrisy in the heart."[9]

Similarly, Imam Aḥmad ibn Ḥanbal, when asked about his position regarding music, replied: "Singing sprouts hypocrisy in the heart; it does not please me."[10] There exists a subtle link between singing and hypocrisy. Both fornication and hypocrisy are signs of a diseased heart. When we look in the Qur'an, we will notice that in soorat an-Noor (the Light), the punishment for fornication and the rulings of covering modestly and Islamic dress

---

[8] King, "Heavy Metal Music and Drug Abuse in Adolescents."

[9] Ibn al-Qayyim, *Ighâthat ul-Lahfân min Maṣâ'id ash-Shayṭân.*

[10] Ibn al-Jawzi, *Talbees Iblees.*

are mentioned, and right after that, the defects or traits of hypocrisy and the hypocrites are described.

In soorat al-Aḥzâb (the Combined Forces), the subject of hypocrites is discussed along with the rulings of hijab. It is obvious that singing is a prelude and impetus to fornication.

In this quote from Ibn Mas'ood, singing and hypocrisy have been brought together. The hypocrisy of Muslim singers who use musical instruments in their songs can be seen from their press releases, in which they are often thanking God for selling so many records or winning awards. They do not understand that they cannot serve two masters; a person cannot dance with the devil and praise the Lord at the same time. The condition of hypocrites is described in the Qur'an:

﴿وَمِنَ ٱلنَّاسِ مَن يَقُولُ ءَامَنَّا بِٱللَّهِ وَبِٱلۡيَوۡمِ ٱلۡأٓخِرِ وَمَا هُم بِمُؤۡمِنِينَ ۝ يُخَٰدِعُونَ ٱللَّهَ وَٱلَّذِينَ ءَامَنُواْ وَمَا يَخۡدَعُونَ إِلَّآ أَنفُسَهُمۡ وَمَا يَشۡعُرُونَ ۝ فِى قُلُوبِهِم مَّرَضٞ فَزَادَهُمُ ٱللَّهُ مَرَضٗاۖ وَلَهُمۡ عَذَابٌ أَلِيمُۢ بِمَا كَانُواْ يَكۡذِبُونَ ۝﴾ (سورة البَقَرَة: ٨-١٠)

❨And of the people are some who say: We believe in Allah and the last day; but they are not believers. They [think to] deceive Allah and those who believe, but they deceive not except themselves and perceive [it] not. In their hearts is disease, so Allah has increased their disease...❩   *(Qur'an 2: 8-10)*

In his book *Ighâthat ul-Lahfân min Maṣâ'id ash-Shayṭân*, the great Islamic scholar Ibn al-Qayyim sheds light on other aspects of the relationship between singing and hypocrisy:

It must be known that singing has specific characteristics that weaken the heart, causing hypocrisy to spring therein, just as water sprouts plants. Among its characteristics is that it distracts the heart and prevents it from contemplation of the Qur'an and from applying it to ourselves. This is so because the Qur'an and songs can never coexist in the heart, since they are mutually conflicting. There is no doubt that the Qur'an forbids the pursuit of frivolous matters and commands restraint of the passions of the soul and temptations to evil. On the other hand, singing encourages the exact opposite of these qualities, as it incites the hidden inner self and entices the soul to injustice by driving it towards every shameful desire... In addition, hypocrisy is based on falsehood, and singing contains many false lyrics. It attempts to beautify the ugly and to encourage it, while seeking to make ugly and to discourage that which is good. This is the nature of hypocrisy. A person's addiction to songs noticeably makes listening to the Qur'an a heavy burden upon his heart and hateful to his ears. If this is not hypocrisy, then what is hypocrisy?[11]

Relationship of ghinâ' to alcohol and drug use

The Prophet Muhammad (ﷺ) said (as mentioned previously): «There will be people of my Ummah who will seek to make these lawful: illegal sexual intercourse, the wearing of silk [by men], the drinking of alcoholic drinks, and the use of ma'âzif.» (Bukhari)

---

[11] Ibn al-Qayyim, *Ighâthat ul-Lahfân min Maṣâ'id ash-Shayṭân.*

In this hadith, music has been described along with alcohol. By analogy, it applies to drugs as well because they also cause intoxication. In the Islamic teachings, everything that causes intoxication is treated like alcohol. The Prophet's Companion Ibn 'Umar (ﷺ) narrated this hadith in which Allah's Messenger (ﷺ) said: «Every intoxicant is *khamr* (alcohol), and all alcohol is unlawful. He who drinks alcohol in this world and dies while he is addicted to it, not having repented, will not drink it in the hereafter.» (Muslim)

Indeed, there is a profound relationship between music and drugs. Music temporarily paralyzes and hypnotizes our minds just like narcotics such as alcohol, opium, heroin and cocaine, as well as other addictive substances such as tobacco. In fact, they act on the same region of the brain (the limbic system), as discussed in Chapter 2. The late American guitarist, singer and songwriter James Marshall 'Jimi' Hendrix is considered by many people to be one of the most influential musicians of his era. Jimi Hendrix said the following about the power of music in an interview with *Life* magazine published on October 3, 1969:

> I can explain everything better through music. You hypnotize people to where they go right back to their natural state, and when you get people at their weakest point, you can preach into their subconscious what you want to say.

There is no doubt that music and drugs are closely related. Through a study in the field of social psychology, researcher R. E. Milliman showed that the tempo of background music in a restaurant affects the customers in the restaurant with respect to the duration of their meals and the amount of money they spend. In addition, the background music played in the restaurant significantly influences the consumption of alcoholic beverages by regular customers during their meals. More importantly, the dining customers stay longer and consume more alcohol when slow tempo instrumental background music (such as classical music) is playing than when fast tempo instrumental music (such as pop music) is used.[12]

Similarly, Dr. Adam Knieste, a musicologist who studies the effects of music upon people, was quoted in a *Family Weekly* article on Jan. 30, 1983 as saying: "It's really a powerful drug. Music can poison you, lift your spirits, or make you sick without knowing why."

Music has been identified as a source through which young people learn about alcohol, tobacco and drugs. Alcohol has always occupied a central role in American popular music. In one study conducted for the Office of National Drug Control Policy, researchers Donald F. Roberts, Lisa Henriksen and Peter G. Christenson examined one thousand of the most popular songs from 1996 to 1997. The music samples came from rankings compiled by *Billboard*, *Radio and Records* magazine and the *College Music Journal*. They found that about one-fifth of those songs contained references to alcohol. When alcohol was portrayed, no adverse consequences were associated with consumption in 91% of the songs. In other words, in 91% of the songs referring to alcohol, alcohol use was portrayed in a positive way. Commenting on the findings of this study, researcher Roberts noted that the extent of alcohol and tobacco use in music 'was the single most striking finding' and said, "This is a world

---

[12] R.E. Milliman, "The Influence of Background Music on the Behavior of Restaurant Patrons," *Journal of Consumer Research* 13 (1986): 286-289.

where alcohol and tobacco are similar to the air we breathe. It's all around us all the time." [13]

In his book *Popular Music Perspectives: Ideas, Themes and Patterns in Contemporary Lyrics*, author Lee B. Cooper discusses the predominant themes in the history of popular songs. He lists a myriad of songs over the years that focus primarily on drinking alcohol. They include such titles as: "Red, Red Wine" (Neil Diamond, 1968), "Chug-a-lug" (recorded by Roger Miller in 1964), "Margaritaville" (Jimmy Buffett, 1977) and "Scotch and Soda" (Ray Price, 1983).[14] Many more examples could be easily compiled, ranging from early blues to contemporary rap, rock and country music, and this is only considering the songs which have drinking alcohol as their major theme. Many other songs talk about drinking in the context of other subject matter. For instance, the Mavericks sang of the sadness of lost love with these lines in their 1997 country hit song:

I can't sleep a wink anymore,
Ever since you walked out of the door
And I just started drinkin' to forget.[15]

References to tobacco use are also found in popular music, although not as frequently as references to alcohol and drugs. Tex Williams' 1947 recording of "Smoke! Smoke! Smoke! (That Cigarette)" adopted tobacco use as a central theme. However, in

---

[13] Donald F. Roberts, L. Henriksen and Peter G. Christenson, *Substance Use in Popular Movies and Music* (Washington, DC: Office of National Drug Control Policy, 1999).

[14] Donald F. Roberts and Peter G. Christenson, *"Here's Looking at You, Kid"*: *Alcohol, Drugs and Tobacco in Entertainment Media* (New York: Kaiser Family Foundation, 2000).

[15] Ibid.

most of the songs, tobacco use is mentioned in passing, as in the following lines from the song "What I Got" (1996) by the alternative rock group Sublime:

Early in the morning
Rising to the street
Light me up that cigarette
And strap shoes on my feet.[16]

In the content analysis of one thousand of the most popular songs from 1996 to 1997 (which was the first scientific study to provide a quantitative measure of the frequency of tobacco references in popular music), it was found that 3% of those songs mentioned smoking or chewing tobacco, although 64% of rap/ hip-hop songs contained such references.[17] However, smoking appears more frequently in music videos than in the lyrics themselves. DuRant and his colleagues found that smoking was portrayed most frequently in rap music videos, in which 30% of the characters were shown smoking. In country and R&B (rhythm and blues) music, the figure was 10%, and in rock and adult contemporary music 22%. The authors of this study note:

> This positive portrayal of tobacco and alcohol use in music videos is likely to have a considerable impact on adolescent's normative expectations and subsequent behaviours.[18]

Many youth have a tendency to adopt musicians as their role models; hence, actual drug use by musicians is also a matter of

---

[16] Ibid.

[17] Roberts, *Substance Use in Popular Movies and Music.*

[18] DuRant et al., "Tobacco and Alcohol Use Behaviors Portrayed in Music Videos: A Content Analysis."

concern.[19] The September 26, 1969 issue of *Time* magazine noted that: "Rock musicians use drugs frequently and openly, and their compositions are riddled with references to drugs."

For example, John Cale writes in the May 1990 issue of *Spin* magazine that songs such as Velvet Underground's "Heroin" encouraged young people to experiment with drugs, leading to tragic ends in many cases. Similarly, Wilson Bryan Key states the following about the Beatles:

> The Beatles popularized and culturally legitimized hallucinatory drug usage among teen-agers throughout the world. The Beatles became the super drug culture prophets and pushers of all time.[20]

For instance, one of the most popular recordings of 1968 was the Beatles' single "Hey Jude." In this song, Paul McCartney sang "Hey Jude," providing to the listeners spiritual advice in the form of drugs as an escape route from the bitter experiences of life. Likewise, *Sergeant Pepper's Lonely Hearts Club Band* was the Beatles' most successful album, released by Capitol Records. This album sold in the millions, and its music and songs were listened to repeatedly by innumerable people of all ages. References to psychedelic drugs such as LSD were allegedly made in the songs in this album such as "Fixing a Hole" and "Lucy in the Sky with Diamonds" (or LSD for short).[21] More recent examples of drug references are just as easy to find. For example:

---

[19] Peter G. Christenson and Donald F. Roberts, *It's Not Only Rock and Roll: Popular Music in the Lives of Adolescents* (Cresskill, NJ: Hampton Press, 1998).

[20] Wilson Bryan Key, *Media Sexploitation* (New York: Signet Books, 1976).

[21] Ibid.

I don't get angry when my mom smokes pot,
Hits that bottle and goes back to the rock.
(Sublime, "What I Got," 1996)
Pass the hay (marijuana) you silly slut,
Blaze it up so I can hit that bud,
Get me zoned and I'll be on,
Cuz I love to smoke upon hay.
(Crucial Conflict, "Hay," 1997)
I'm a thug, I'm a die high,
I be out in Jersey, puffin' Hershey.

(Puff Daddy, "Can't Nobody Hold Me Down," 1997)[22]

Among the contemporary music stars who died because of drug abuse are Brian Jones of the Rolling Stones, Dennis Wilson of the Beach Boys, Sid Vicious of the Sex Pistols, Elvis Presley, Jimi Hendrix, Jim Morrison of The Doors, folk singer and songwriter Tim Hardin and R&B singer Frankie Lymon. Recently, David Ruffin of the Temptations died from a cocaine overdose.[23] Similarly, many prominent singers of traditional music in Muslim countries have died due to alcohol overdose or alcohol abuse.

Dr. Paul King did a scientific study on the relationship of music and drugs.[24] Over a three-year period, he studied 470 adolescent patients (242 boys and 228 girls) who were admitted to Charter Lakeside Hospital in Memphis, Tennessee. The patients, most of whom were white, were between 13 and 18 years old;

---

[22] Roberts and Christenson, *"Here's Looking at You, Kid": Alcohol, Drugs and Tobacco in Entertainment Media.*

[23] Frank Ankenberg and John Weldon, *The Facts on Rock Music* (Eugene, Oregon: Harvest House Publishers, 1992).

[24] King, Paul M.D., "Heavy Metal Music and Drug Abuse in Adolescents."

they came from a wide range of socio-economic backgrounds, from cities or rural areas of Mississippi, Arkansas or Tennessee. The results of this study revealed that nearly 60% of the patients who were involved in drug abuse designated heavy metal music as their music of choice. Dr. King notes:

> Those who work with adolescents who have significant drug problems find that these youngsters not only are involved in antisocial behaviour and precocious sexual activity but also are preoccupied with heavy metal music. In fact, young people using drugs extensively enough to warrant treatment know the lyrics of a great many songs. Clearly, 'their music' is very important to them, and attempts to remove heavy metal music from the home environment may be met with extreme resistance and even aggressive behaviour.[25]

According to Dr. King, a teenager who is already saturated with negative feelings can get inspiration from music that promotes antisocial, drug-addictive behaviour. In another study conducted to study the effects of media on behaviour, researchers Grube and Wallack found that simple exposure to alcohol advertisements does not affect alcohol use. Instead, the effects of alcohol advertisements depend largely on the extent to which young people like and attend to them. Consequently, music and humor were used in advertisements promoting alcohol use among adolescents. The results of this study (which used statistical modeling) showed that attention to alcohol advertising resulted in increased adolescent drinking.[26] Hence, music and humor were

---

[25] Ibid.

[26] J.W. Grube and L. Wallack, "Televised Beer Advertisement and Drinking Knowledge, Beliefs, and Intentions among School Children," *American Journal of Public Health* 84 (1994): 254-259.

the key elements in those advertisements encouraging alcohol use.

It must be noted that not only heavy metal music but also other kinds of music are related to alcohol and drugs. Many researchers have emphasized this point. Similarly, field research on alcohol drinking behaviour has shown that an increased level of consumption of alcohol is directly linked to exposure and listening to country music.[27] In a report published in the *Journal of Studies on Alcohol*, Paul Chalfant and Robert Beckley analyzed the thirty most popular country songs and noted that the lyrics of country music[28] often depict drinking alcohol as an essential and normal method of dealing with life's problems. Those songs suggest that "life is hard, and that drinking is the only way to face what cannot be dealt with any other manner."[29]

In 25% of those country songs, alcohol use was shown as contributing to illicit sex. For example, in a song entitled: "After the Fire is Gone," alcohol is seen as emboldening the characters to seek extramarital relations when "the fire's gone out at home." The man and woman in "Third Rat Romance" check into a cheap motel after they have been drinking at a bar. In the song entitled "Take Me Home to Somewhere," the singer shows that in bars he has "had my share of good times and a lot of good women..." The

---

[27] James M. Schaefer, "Slow Country Music and Drinking" (paper presented at the annual meeting for the American Anthropological Association, Phoenix, Arizona, 1988).

[28] Country music refers to a simple style of folk music heard mostly in the Southern United States but also popular in other countries. It is usually played on stringed instruments.

[29] Paul Chalfant and Robert Beckley, "Beguiling and Betraying: The Image of Alcohol Use in Country Music," *Journal of Studies on Alcohol* 38 (1977): 1428-1433.

same theme of illicit sex and alcohol is promoted in songs entitled "City Lights," "Western Man" and "Here I am in Dallas."[30] All this research confirms that there is a close relationship among music, drugs and sex and that they tend to coexist, as this relationship was mentioned by Prophet Muhammad (ﷺ) about fourteen hundred years ago.

Professor Allan Bloom of the University of Chicago, who also has experience teaching students at Yale University, the University of Paris, the University of Toronto and Cornell University, describes another similarity between music and drugs in the sense that both of them tend to have the same after-effects and both destroy future enthusiasm in people who are involved in them: "Rock music provides premature ecstasy and, in this respect, is like the drugs with which it is allied."[31]

Professor Bloom noted, based on his decades of experience in dealing with youth, that students who had indulged in drugs in their early years and then got over it later on, had difficulty finding passion and enthusiasm in their life. It appeared as if all the colour of life had been drained out of their bodies, and now they viewed life as black and white only. The pleasure they received while experimenting with drugs was so intense that afterwards, they did not feel pleasure in anything in their life. Professor Bloom points out that in this respect, rock music is very similar to drugs in its effects on the youth.[32]

---

[30] Ibid.

[31] Bloom, *The Closing of the American Mind.*

[32] Ibid.

Importance of Music in Mass Deception

We have to protect our body from sins because we will be responsible for our actions on the Day of Judgment. Satan does not have access to the thoughts that come into our hearts. However, he has the ability to whisper into our hearts:

(سورة النَّاس: ٥)   ﴿ٱلَّذِى يُوَسْوِسُ فِ صُدُورِ ٱلنَّاسِ ۝﴾

﴿[Satan] who whispers [evil] into the breasts of mankind.﴾
(Qur'an 114: 5)

The result may be a sinful action afterwards. If the heart is spiritually very healthy, the whisper of Satan is weak. On the other hand, if the heart is spiritually weak, the whisper of Satan is very strong and effective.

One of the interesting things about Satan is that he lacks originality. He keeps on using the same old tricks on humans, possibly because he knows that they work. Satan uses and abuses the weaknesses of human beings to cause disease in their hearts. Maryam Jameelah wrote about human nature:

> Man's disposition, his biological and psychological needs, his physical and mental capacities, the temptations which make him succumb to evil and his eternal quest for the moral and spiritual values that give human life its meaning and purpose and distinguishes him from the lower animals, have not changed at all since the emergence of human beings.[33]

---

[33] Maryam Jameelah, *The Generation Gap: Its Causes and Consequences* (Lahore: Mohammad Yusuf Khan and Sons, 1981).

Because of the lack of originality on the part of Satan in manipulating and exploiting human nature, it becomes somewhat easy to understand the ways he deceives humans into falling into his trap. It is a fact that music deludes a person and creates negligence in its listener about his or her relationship with Allah (ﷻ). Music is an old trick of Satan that is used to make human beings negligent of the lofty purpose of their creation, which is worship of Allah (ﷻ). In soorah Luqmân, Allah (ﷻ) has said:

﴿وَمِنَ ٱلنَّاسِ مَن يَشْتَرِى لَهْوَ ٱلْحَدِيثِ لِيُضِلَّ عَن سَبِيلِ ٱللَّهِ بِغَيْرِ عِلْمٍ وَيَتَّخِذَهَا هُزُوًا أُوْلَٰئِكَ لَهُمْ عَذَابٌ مُّهِينٌ ٦﴾   (سورة لقمَان : ٦)

{And of the people is he who purchases idle talk [*lahwal ḥadeeth*] to mislead [others] from the way of Allah without knowledge and who takes it in ridicule. Those will have a humiliating punishment.}   *(Qur'an 31: 6)*

In this verse, the term '*lahwal ḥadeeth,*' or idle talk, means music and singing, as it was explained by the Companions of the Prophet (ﷺ) like Ibn Mas'ood, Jâbir and Ibn 'Abbâs (may Allah be pleased with them) and by many of the tâbi'oon such as Ikrimah, Mujâhid and Makhool.[34] The scholars of Hadith narrate the following incident in explaining the reason that this verse was revealed:

When Prophet Muhammad (ﷺ) was spreading his message in Makkah, there was a rich merchant there named Naḍr Ibn Ḥârith who was using various methods to distract people from the message of Islam. One of the things he did was to buy some slave girls as songstresses. Whenever he found that a person

---

[34] Abu Bilal Mustafa Al-Kanadi, *The Islamic Ruling on Music and Singing* (Jeddah: Abul-Qasim Bookstore, 1986).

was taking interest in the Qur'an or in accepting Islam, Naḍr would go to him and appoint one of his slave girls to feed the person excessively with food and wine and sing beautiful songs to him. After a few days, he would visit the person and ask: "Tell me, is that drinking alcohol and eating delicious foods and listening to music and singing better, or the message that Muhammad (ﷺ) has brought, jihad, prayers, fasting and the like?" In this way, Naḍr was able to divert many would-be Muslims or Muslims with weak faith, back to the religion of paganism.[35]

In addition, according to the Arab historian al-Mas'oodi, it was Naḍr ibn Ḥârith who first introduced playing the *'oud* (a Middle Eastern stringed instrument) in Arabia after he learned how to play it and sing with it during his trip to Persia.[36]

The rulers, politicians and capitalists of the present age still hold the same mentality as that of Naḍr ibn Ḥârith, and they employ the same methods of seduction that he used. In fact, the modern methods of seduction are much more refined and subtle because now they are backed up by modern technology and media. They have become weapons of mass deception. In almost all Muslim countries, the governments have devoted separate TV channels for musical entertainment shows. They indulge their people in every kind of *lahwal ḥadeeth* (idle talk) so that they can rule their subjects easily. Roman rulers used to keep their public occupied with trivial entertainments that came to be called 'bread and circuses.'

---

[35] Aloosi, *Rooḥ al-Ma'âni.*

[36] Maḥmood ibn Abdullah al-Mas'oodi, "The First Ghinâ' among the Arabs," in *Murooj adh-Dhahab* (Beirut: Dar El-Marefah, 2005).

It is the same method of rulers in every age: amusing their subjects to death. The rulers, who manipulate the media, deliberately want to keep the public in the dark. They want their subjects to be drugged by any activity that keeps them away from proper contemplation of their life. People become so busy trying to join in on the media-created activities (such as music and singing, sports and the like) so that they can have fun, that they miss the really obvious questions about their very being. People become addicted to 'bread and circuses' so much that they waste their time in frivolous pastimes. In fact, this is the timeless art of seduction.

Hollywood is the biggest 'Naḍr ibn Ḥârith' of this century. People spend an enormous amount of money on films, which are in fact the *lahwal ḥadeeth* on a grand scale. The film *Titanic* is one of the most expensive films of this era, costing approximately 285 million U.S. dollars. The theme of this movie is a love story; that is, if you indulge in love before marriage, you become a hero. Music played a central and very crucial role in conveying this message in the movie. It is little wonder that the Celine Dion song from *Titanic,* "My Heart Will Go On", won many musical awards. In recognition of this manipulative power of music, contemporary writer David Chagall warned in an article in *Family Weekly* on Jan. 30, 1983:

> Music is used everywhere to condition the human mind. It can be just as powerful as a drug and much more dangerous, because nobody takes musical manipulation very seriously.

Those who control the media are well aware of the power of music to bring about mental disturbances. They know that music can be used as an indoctrination tool by penetrating minds and controlling mental faculties.

Denise Winn, a British journalist specializing in the area of psychology and medicine, writes in her book *The Manipulated Mind: Brainwashing, Conditioning, and Indoctrination* that there are three elements needed for a successful brainwashing program: physical and mental exhaustion, repetition, and reducing the desired messages to slogans.[37] When we look at music and singing, all three elements are there. People consider music to be entertainment, and hence, they often listen to music when they are physically and mentally exhausted. There is repetition in the lyrics of a song, and the messages are presented in a very concise form, which is quite similar to slogans. Therefore, music can successfully brainwash and condition its listener, without the person even being aware of it. Renowned psychologist John Kappas noted that people:

> are truly susceptible to conscious messages on a record and that excitation and melancholy can be created by music/ sensory overload... Any time you overload the mind, the person becomes very suggestible. They will take in anything that you suggest at that time because they have no defenses against it. People can walk out of concerts in a hyper-suggestible state... Music has a tendency to defuse thinking and create moods. And in turn, the messages seep in.[38]

---

[37] Denise Winn, *The Manipulated Mind: Brainwashing, Conditioning, and Indoctrination* (Cambridge, MA: Marlor Books, 2000).

[38] Ted Schwartz and Duane Empey, *Satanism: Is Your Family Safe?* (Grand Rapids, MI: Zondervan, 1989).

Importance of Music in the Film Industry

Music is one of the strongest sources of emotions in the movies. If we take music out of the 'picture', the whole film industry will collapse because music is the strongest weapon through which they seduce the audience. The fact of the matter is that all the scenes in a movie, whether they are scenes of suspense, mystery, comedy or romance, depend primarily upon music, which is present during a major portion of the duration of the films. The sound tracks of movies and television series have music as their main ingredient. Music can transform a trivial and silly story in a movie into something significant. Music animates the love scenes in a movie.

To put it simply, the seductive power of the movies and dramas is enhanced dramatically with the use of music. Every film industry in the world relies heavily on the use of music, whether it is Hollywood, U.S.A., India's Bollywood or Arabic dramas and movies. Music has the capability to express emotions in the movies in a far better way than the picture alone. This is due to the ability of music to simultaneously carry various types of emotional information in its harmony, melody, timbre and rhythm.

The importance of music in the film industry can be understood from the fact that when silent movies were first introduced in the beginning of the twentieth century, music was used in the theatres to illustrate and explain the actions.[39] Harvard

---

[39] Annabel J. Cohen, "Music as a Source of Emotion in Film," in *Music and Emotion: Theory and Research,* edited by Patrik N. Juslin and John A. Sloboda, 249-272 (New York: Oxford University Press, 2001).

University psychologist Hugo Münsterberg was a pioneer in the area of film theory. One of his last books was *The Photoplay: A Psychological Study*, originally published in 1916, which can be considered the first book on film theory. In this book, Münsterberg stressed that there should be music in films because, according to him, music relieves tension, maintains interest, gives comfort, arouses emotions and provides the aesthetic experience. He argued that cinema is more similar to music than it is to photography and drama because in the area of aesthetics, the art of musical tones has:

> overcome the outer world and social world entirely, they unfold our inner life, our mental play, with its feelings and emotions, its memories and fancies, in a material which seems exempt from the laws of the world of substance and material, [musical] tones which are fluttering and fleeting like our own mental states.[40]

Münsterberg died in 1916, the same year his book *The Photoplay* was published, and the film industry did not initially realize the significance of his ideas. In 1927, when talking movies became possible, music was taken out of the films. It was thought that with real voices and sound effects, music was no longer needed in order to elicit emotions and mood. Within a few years, people lost interest in films. They felt that there was no life in the film screen without music. Hence, the film industry learned the bitter lesson that emotions could not be expressed in a film without the presence of music.[41] In the words of Kalinak:

---

[40] Hugo Münsterberg, *The Photoplay: A Psychological Study* (New York: Arno, 1970).

[41] Cohen, "Music as a Source of Emotion in Film."

When the possibility of synchronized speech and sound effects released sound film from its reliance upon continuous musical accompaniment, it initially rejected music entirely. But the life span of the all-talking picture [with no music in it] was brief, the need that music filled quickly reasserting itself.[42]

For this reason, it has been proposed that music adds a third dimension to the two-dimensional film screen.[43]

In one study reported by Bullerjahn and Guldenring in 1994, top professional composers of film music created a total of five different background music tracks (for example, crime or melodrama) for the same ten-minute film segment.[44] The results of the study revealed that depending on the musical soundtrack, the viewers made different judgments regarding the appropriateness of emotional categories (such as sad, sentimental, thrilling, or vivid), choice of movie scene (crime, horror, comedy, thriller), reasons for the actions of the leading character and expectations about the end of the movie. Hence, music alters the meanings of any particular aspect of the film. In discussing the paramount role of music in films, Annabel J. Cohen writes:

Music does more than echo or provide a counterpart to a concept already present in the film. Music can also direct attention to an object on the screen and establish emotionally

---

[42] K. Kalinack, *Settling the Score* (Madison, WI: University of Wisconsin Press, 1992).

[43] C. Palmer, *The Composer in Hollywood* (New York: Marion Boyars, 1990).

[44] C. Bullerjahn and M. Guldenring, "An Empirical Investigation of Effects of Film Music Using Qualitative Content Analysis," *Psychomusicology* 13 (1994): 99-118.

laden inferences about that object... Music heightens the sense of reality of or absorption in film, perhaps by augmenting arousal, and increasing attention to the entire film context and inattention to everything else.... Münsterberg suggested that the psychological processes underlying film were more similar to those of music than to visual art or drama, which on the surface might seem more similar. Experimental evidence since then has shown that music influences the interpretation of film narrative and that the music becomes integrated in the memory with the visual information.[45]

Importance of Music in the Advertising Industry

Music is a common element in commercials. It has been shown through various studies that music is involved in mood inducement and that it affects behaviour and preferences in a variety of contexts. Studies on consumers indicate that music does influence what products they will select. Because of the profound importance of music in influencing the moods of people, the advertising industry also relies heavily upon music. They use the best musical lyrics to seduce people into buying their products, sometimes incorporating catchy jingles from the works of famous musicians into their commercials.

E. M. Brand argues that music in supermarkets is:

designed to make shopping more enjoyable and perhaps to help distract attention from the total cost of the shopping cart full of merchandise.... Carefully selected music proves highly

---

[45] Cohen, "Music as a Source of Emotion in Film."

successful in creating a pleasant, relaxed atmosphere in which to shop.[46]

Studies also provide evidence that features such as humor, sex, colour and music in a commercial can directly influence our attitudes. For instance, Gerald J. Gorn of the University of British Columbia (Canada) has shown through his experiments on human subjects that when people hear music while being exposed to a product, this music can directly affect their product preferences. In addition, stimuli such as music and colours are so important that many North American commercials contain very little product information; instead they are comprised mainly of stimuli that can arouse emotions, such as music and colours (and other visual imagery such as female models).[47]

Interestingly, in one of Gorn's experiments, among all the subjects in the study who made the choice of the product based on the preferred music, 91% were not even aware that the preferred music was involved in influencing their decision. This could be partly due to the fact that people have their ego (which is termed 'cognitive bias' in the language of psychology), which is a result of their attempt to think well of themselves. Due to the cognitive bias, people try to convince themselves and the researchers that their minds cannot be manipulated by anything and that they always make rational decisions.[48]

---

[46] E.A. Brand, *Modern Supermarket Operation* (New York: Fairchild Publications, 1963).

[47] Gerald J. Gorn, "The Effects of Music in Advertising on Choice Behavior: A Classical Conditioning Approach," *Journal of Marketing* 46 (Winter 1982): 94-101.

[48] A.G. Greenwald, "The Totalitarian Ego: Fabrication and Revision of Personal History," *American Psychologist* 35, no. 7 (1980): 603-618.

Another reason for this lack of awareness on the part of the subjects about their minds being manipulated by music could be that music sometimes acts on the subconscious, as a subliminal message. There is scientific evidence for this, which will be discussed in detail later in the section on 'Role of Music in the Suicide among Youth.' In the end, Gerald Gorn suggests to advertisers (capitalists and industrialists) that they reach their viewers 'through emotionally arousing features' such as music, so as to manipulate and influence their choice of products.[49]

In a study by Ronald Millman and his colleagues at Loyola University, it was demonstrated that when slow music was played in the aisles of supermarkets, sales were 38.2% higher (as reflected in the sales receipts) as compared to sales when similar but fast music was played. When the customers who were exiting the supermarket were questioned, one-third of the shoppers were not aware that there was any kind of music being played, and 29% of the shoppers completely denied that fact that there was any music played in the market.[50]

Again, as pointed out in the previous study by Gorn, this study affirms that the majority of the customers were unaware that their minds were being manipulated by music. It can also be deduced that advertisers use music to sell products while lying about their actual worth and quality.

---

[49] Gorn, "The Effects of Music in Advertising on Choice Behavior: A Classical Conditioning Approach."

[50] Rosenfeld, "Music, The Beautiful Disturber."

Chapter 4

Music Made Me Do It

"$\mathcal{M}$usic can move us to tears or to dance, to fight or to make love.... It is created by people to affect and communicate with other people. In one sense, it's no surprise that music grabs us — it's supposed to. But once you look at the process, it seems quite miraculous that people can bowl one another over just by jiggling sound waves."[1]

(Anne H. Rosenfeld, psychologist and musician)

According to the ancient Greeks, the root word for music is 'muse,' which referred to the spirit beings responsible for the inspiration of all arts. It seems that those 'spirit beings' are the satanic forces at work in music because, according to the Qur'an, Satan misleads human beings by his seductive voice. Interestingly, one of the Webster's dictionary definitions for the word 'muse', the root of 'music', is 'a source of inspiration.' Humans have two main sources of inspiration outside of themselves: Allah (﷾) and Satan. While both communicate ideas to willing listeners, Allah (﷾) communicates through inspiration and through His sacred scriptures, whereas Satan is an aggressive liar who desires to stir rebellion against Allah (﷾). In the realm of

---

[1] Rosenfeld, "Music, The Beautiful Disturber."

social psychology, there is plenty of evidence demonstrating that music has a direct influence on the behaviour of people.

Comparison between Soft, Slow Music and Fast, Loud Music

In general, there are two major types of music, although the classification is somewhat arbitrary and there is some overlap:

1. Slow and soft music (such as ballads, folk music, classical music and religious hymns)

2. Fast and loud music (such as hard rock, heavy metal and punk)

The following is a comparison between the two types of music with respect to their effects on the society:

Slow, soft music swings the head of its listener, while fast, loud music swings the pelvis of its listener — although all types of music make the listener oblivious and forgetful of Allah (ﷻ). Slower music may depress its listeners due to its soft tone, especially when it has a sad theme, whereas faster music may make them aggressive due to its loud beat and hyper stimulation.

A cursory look at the lives of some of the traditional music composers tells us about the depression in their lives. The musical genius Ludwig van Beethoven contemplated committing suicide during his life. Classical composer Mozart had a premature death at the age of thirty-five.

The German philosopher and poet Friedrich Nietzsche considered music an attempt to give form and beauty to the dark, chaotic forces in the soul — to make them serve a higher purpose.[2] Yet Nietzsche was always cynical of God and even declared that "God is dead." He became permanently insane during the last ten years of his life.

Most songs of all types have the same theme of sex as their pivotal point, as was shown in the scientific studies in the previous chapter. In general, slow, soft songs inspire listeners to engage in illicit sex by presenting premarital love as a norm in the society, while fast, loud songs do so by stimulating sexual desires and even instigating violence in their listeners. The slower, softer songs often elevate women to the level of sex goddesses, whereas many others degrade women to the level of sex objects, as will be shown later in this chapter. To draw an analogy, slow and soft music resembles alcohol in that it kills slowly, whereas fast and loud music acts like drugs that are more stimulating than alcohol, such as cocaine, heroin, MDMA (Ecstasy), MDEA (Eve), LSD or PCP (angel dust).

The above discussion makes it clear that while different categories of music may have different methods of actions, they are not really different from each other in terms of their results and their evil influence upon the society. This is because all of them emanate from the same fountain of corruption. Loud music with a fast pace destroys its listeners more quickly, whereas softer, slower music is a slow killer. This may not be obvious at times, but that should not mislead anyone to think that soft, slow music is angelic and humble; it is just that its dangers are more subtle.

All forms of music are prohibited in the teachings of the Qur'an and Sunnah. Various types of music are related to one

---

[2] Friedrich Nietzsche, *The Birth of Tragedy and The Case of Wagner* (New York: Vintage Books, 1967).

another just as cigars are related to cigarettes, and research on one form of music applies to the other types as well. In fact, with the advent of modern acoustic technology, the traditional types of songs evolved into pop and rock songs. The filth and corruption that was lying hidden in traditional music became very obvious with the advent of modern technology such as radios, tape-recorders, amplifying speakers, music television stations, cables, dish networks, CD players, DVDs, the Internet, and portable devices such as Walkmans, iPods, and mp3s.

Although most music has a message of sexuality and rebellion against authority, the reason that the contemporary pop music culture is gaining more fame and momentum, as compared to more traditional types of music, is due to the fact that people become desensitized with the passage of time. Hence, singers and musicians must continually take the explicitness of the message of promiscuity and 'freedom' to higher levels. Only by increasing the intensity of their filthy message can those singers and musicians keep on amusing and gratifying the lowest desires of their listeners and viewers.

Role of music in the rebellion of youth against parents

Music, whether from radio or recordings, is a popular form of entertainment for young people. It has been shown that youth between the ages of 11 and 14 spend 16.6 hours per week, and teenagers from 15 to 18 years old spend about 21.4 hours per week, listening to music on radios, CDs or various other media.[3]

---

[3] Donald F. Roberts, U.G. Foehr and V.J. Rideout, *Generation M2: Media in=*

Parents may perceive it to be innocent and normal when children and teenagers listen to music, but in reality, sometimes unbeknownst to the parents, music has deep psychological implications for children and teenagers. Music makes the children rebellious towards their parents.

In the 1989 issue (Sept 22/29) of the *Journal of American Medical Association,* physicians Elizabeth Brown, MD and William Hendee, MD noted that most teenagers listen to music in the privacy of their homes and interpret on their own the ideas presented in the music, without any guidance from their elders. In addition, adolescence is the time when teenagers begin to develop standards of behaviour and morality in light of the moral standards of adults. Brown and Hendee argue:

> In this context, music, a powerful medium in the lives of adolescents, offers conflicting values. The explicit sexual and violent lyrics of some forms of music often clash with the themes of abstinence and rational behaviour promoted by adult society.[4]

Professor Allan Bloom writes: "Though students do not have books, they most emphatically do have music. Nothing is more singular about this generation than its addiction to music."[5]

American poet and author Robert Bly writes that the rock music of the 1950s and 1960s played an important role in the teenage liberation movement, the time when "Elvis Presley let his

---

=*the Lives of 8- to 18-Year-Olds* (Palo Alto, CA: Kaiser Family Foundation, 2010).

[4] Brown and Hendee, "Adolescents and their Music: Insights into the Health of Adolescents."

[5] Bloom, *The Closing of the American Mind.*

pelvis move to the music." He continues:

> The popular heroes of the late 1950s, James Dean, Elvis
> Presley, Marilyn Monroe, and Jack Kerouac, all took part in
> that struggle to loosen everyone up, and were loved for it...[6]

Robert Bly is arguing here that rock music was one of the
major factors that contributed towards the teenage liberation
mentality.

It is a fact that young people are the target audience for the
music industry, although people in other age groups also listen to
music. Young people spend an average of 2-1/2 hours a day
listening to music, out of 7-1/2 hours a day of total media
exposure.[7] According to key statistics from the Recording
Industry Association of America website, in 2008, sales of
recorded music (including full-length CDs and cassettes, singles,
music videos, DVDs, digital downloads, optical discs and LPs) in
the U.S. exceeded eight billion dollars, and young people between
the ages of 10 and 19 accounted for about 18% of the total sales.
The purchase of music in other countries is following the same
trend as seen in the U.S., although at a slower pace.

Many young people report feeling that the music they listen to,
and the artists who create that music, act as role models for them.
They feel a connection because they think that the singer knows
what mental conflicts they are going through and how they feel.
This idea of the artist becoming the role model can be described in
the language of psychology in terms of 'social learning theory.'

---

[6] Robert Bly, *The Sibling Society* (New York: Addison-Wesley Publishing
Company, 1996).

[7] Roberts, Foehr and Rideout, *Generation M2: Media in the Lives of 8- to 18-
Year-Olds.*

According to this theory, an individual's antisocial, aggressive responses are normally shaped by early experiences with parents and other significant adults. When these role models are unavailable, children seek out others to replace them, in their desire to imitate their superiors. In such situations, music and song — and those who play or sing it — may fill these gaps, providing the listener with a sense of identity and peer acceptance. The likelihood of imitation increases when the model is perceived as attractive or similar to the self.

In today's society, children and youth are spending much more time by themselves in front of electronic media devices, in part because more and more mothers are working instead of spending time with the children. Being left alone has forced many children and youth to seek out new role models and people to help them with the tough decisions they face. Popular music and songs tell the teenagers what they want to hear the most.

As pointed out earlier, adolescence is a time of great stress, when the limbic system is already activated due to the high levels of sex hormones. At this time, music and drugs, both of which also act on the limbic system, may cause overstimulation. Moreover, at this stage of adolescence, teenagers are at a turning point in determining the future directions of their lives. When music offers values that are in conflict with the values taught to them by their parents, teachers and the society, they become confused.

According to Dr. Paul King, a foremost expert in the area of child and adolescent psychiatry, young people who do not identify with the traditional values of their society have to identify themselves with something. All youngsters seek a higher power or authority that approves of what they are feeling and doing. In such a situation, music provides them with a justification and approval for their actions.[8]

One school specialist, with vast experience in dealing with difficult children, confirmed that the influence of music continued to surface in his counseling sessions with students. In the November/December 1989 issue of *Media Update*, he said:

> Time after time I saw them pattern their actions after the immoral behaviour of their rock stars. The kids showed their allegiances by the vocabulary they picked up, the song titles printed on their book jackets, by the posters they hung on the walls of their rooms at home, by the music they listened to in their cars, and by the clothes they wore.

Sometimes the rebellion of youth against their parents does not remain limited to forsaking their parents in nursing homes. Occasionally some rebellious youth go so far as to kill their parents. Again, music is a contributing factor.

On January 9, 1988, in the Jefferson township of New Jersey, a youth named Thomas Sullivan murdered his mother, Betty-Ann, in the basement of their house; then he set fire to the house in order to kill his father and younger brother. Finally, he ran outside and committed suicide by cutting his wrists. His father woke up in time, due to the sound of the fire alarm, but found his wife dead in a pool of blood in the basement of the house. The dead body of Thomas Sullivan was found in the backyard the next morning. Police later mentioned that Thomas had been a talented student, an outstanding sportsman and a Boy Scout. Then he became immersed in rock music and was a fan of Ozzy Osbourne.

---

[8] King, "Heavy Metal Music and Drug Abuse in Adolescents."

Thomas' father told the police that all week before murdering his mother, his son Thomas had been singing a song 'about blood and killing your mother.'[9]

Similarly, according to an article in *US News & World Report* on October 28, 1985, a 14-year-old girl, who was fascinated with pop music, stabbed her mother to death. Although these are extreme cases, they do show that music has the power to make a person mentally deranged and violent. There may not always be a simple one-to-one correlation between listening to music and committing violence, just as there is no simple one-to-one correlation between smoking and developing cancer, but the fact of the matter is that there is a direct connection in both cases.

Smoking is not the only cause of lung cancer, although it is one of the most prominent reasons. Neither is listening to music the only cause of youth violence, but it does play a significant role, as will become obvious in the next section.

Role of music in suicide among young people

In the modern age, music has played a major role in the increasing trend of suicide among young people. Allah (ﷻ) tells us:

﴿ ... وَلَا تَاْيَْسُواْ مِن رَّوْحِ ٱللَّهِ ... ﴿٨٧﴾﴾   (سورة يُوسُف : ٨٧)

﴿...And never despair of the mercy of Allah...﴾ *(Qur'an 12: 87)*

Similarly, in soorat az-Zumar (the Groups), Allah (ﷻ) says:

---

[9] Ankenberg and Weldon, *The Facts on Rock Music.*

﴿ ... لَا تَقْنَطُوا مِن رَّحْمَةِ ٱللَّهِ إِنَّ ٱللَّهَ يَغْفِرُ ٱلذُّنُوبَ جَمِيعًا ... ﴿٥٣﴾ ﴾

(سورة الزُّمَر : ٥٣)

﴾...Despair not of the mercy of Allah, verily Allah forgives all sins...﴿
(Qur'an 39: 53)

The Arabic name for Satan is *Iblees,* which means 'the one who despairs,' and one of the greatest tricks of Iblees is to cause people to despair of the mercy of Allah (ﷻ). Part of the modern condition is creating despair. For example, one of the ways to manifest despair is by watching television. The news on television portrays a 'doom and gloom' image of the world where everything is hell-bound. This is a Satanic ideology, an extreme state of despair that Satan loves to foster, where people kill themselves due to extreme despair and loss of faith. One should never despair. It is an evil state to enter upon, but this same despondent message is given to the youth in music, with a much more powerful tone. Just like drugs can depress people so much that some of them commit suicide, music can have similar consequences.

Music can be a powerful depressant, and it can nurture a suicidal mood in its listeners. Anyone listening to songs about heartbreak, rejection, pain, misery and loss definitely feels the depressing effects upon them. As pointed out by psychologist Aaron Beck and associates, hopelessness is considered the most important contributing factor, and a key psychological state, among people who commit suicide.[10]

---

[10] A.T. Beck, R.A. Steer, M. Kovacs and B. Garrison, "Hopelessness and Eventual Suicide," *American Journal of Psychiatry* 142 (1985): 559-563.

Those people who consider music to be a harmless form of entertainment do not actually understand the power of music. They do not realize what is being massaged into their psyches along with music. When a person listens to music, old memories are triggered, whether the music is sad or joyous. People can remember the words of songs more easily than prose. Hence, music can evoke feelings of melancholy, which may cause unbearable depression to the point that the listener commits suicide.

For example, a large proportion of country and western music, along with the blues, has always been associated with depressing lyrics and tales of woe, which in turn make the listener feel miserable. In a study published in 1992, researchers Steven Stack and Jim Gundlach assessed the link between country music and metropolitan suicide rates. The results of their multiple regression analysis of forty-nine major U.S. cities showed that the greater the amount of airtime devoted to country music, the greater the rate of suicide among white Americans. Based on the findings of their study, Stack and Gundlach hypothesized that country music nurtures in its listeners:

> a suicidal mood through its concerns with problems common in the suicidal population, such as marital discord, alcohol abuse, and alienation from work.[11]

Country music and songs often convey the idea of fatalism or hopelessness. They reflect despair and the futility and hypocrisy of the illusion of modern life. For example, a feeling of pessimism and bitterness permeates many country songs about farmers. The

---

[11] Steven Stack and Jim Gundlach, "The Effect of Country Music on Suicide," *Social Forces* 71, no. 1 (1992): 211-218.

Nitty Gritty Dirt Band, when singing about a man whose farm had been auctioned off, chanted the following lines:

Worked this place all my life,
Broke my heart, took my wife.
Now I got nothing to show.[12]

Similarly, many country songs repeatedly depict the lonesome and often abusive features of life among the lower socioeconomic classes.[13] They describe the banality or dullness of life. For example, Alfred Reed's song "How Can a Man Stand Such Things and Live?" suggests a connection between suicide and impoverishment, and Billy Hill's 1989 hit song "There's Too Much Month at the End of the Money" echoes the feelings of despair associated with problems of financial strain.[14]

Another common theme in the country music genre that can foster suicidal feelings is the issue of marital strife and dissolution. In one study published in the *Journal of Marriage and Family* in 1990, researcher Steven Stack reported the results of a content analysis of 1,400 hit country songs. It was found that about 75% of those songs had the bitter experiences of love as at least one of their themes.[15] In all these cases, the depressing themes conveyed in country music might be nurturing the suicidal mood in the listeners.

---

[12] Stack and Gundlach, "The Effect of Country Music on Suicide."

[13] Schaefer, "Slow Country Music and Drinking."

[14] Stack and Gundlach, "The Effect of Country Music on Suicide."

[15] Steven Stack, "New Micro Level Data on the Impact of Divorce on Suicide, 1959-1980: A Test of Two Theories," *Journal of Marriage and the Family* 52 (1990): 119-127.

When it comes to rock music, it in fact not only depresses listeners but also encourages them to commit suicide by giving them the message that "suicide is the only solution" and that it is the only way out of the depths of hopelessness. According to the Centers for Disease Control and Prevention, suicide is currently the third leading cause of death among Americans aged 10 to 24. Each year, about 4,400 youths kill themselves, and many more attempt to do so.[16] The following are just a few examples of nationally publicized cases of suicides under the influence of music:

On December 23, 1985, 18-year-old Raymond Belknap and 20-year-old James Vance climbed out of a bedroom window and went to a nearby playground after listening to pop singer Judas Priest's song entitled "Beyond the Realms of Death." Once there, Belknap placed a shotgun under his chin, pulled the trigger and died immediately. Vance then took his turn in the same manner, but the gun slipped forward and disfigured his face; he died three years later as a result of his wounds. On the day of the shootings, the two had played music all day long. While listening to Judas Priest's album, they started chanting "Just do it, just do it," became violent and ended up committing (or attempting to commit) suicide.[17]

The families of the victims brought legal action against Judas Priest. The bereaved parents claimed that a subliminal message, "Do it," was present in the song, which portrayed a hopeless view on life, and that it drove the two boys to commit suicide. The

---

[16] "Suicide Prevention", Centers for Disease Control and Prevention, last modified October 15, 2009,
http://www.cdc.gov/violenceprevention/pub/youth_suicide.html.

[17] Pamela Marsden Capps, "Rock on Trial: Subliminal Message Liability," *Columbia Business Law Review* 27 (1991).

music and its suggestive lyrics, combined with the continuous beat and rhythms, encouraged and mesmerized the victims into believing that the answer to life was death. (Belknap v. Judas Priest, Nev. Dist. Ct., August 24, 1990)[18]

In October 1984, 19-year-old John McCollum committed suicide by shooting himself in the head after listening to Ozzy Osbourne's song "Suicide Solutions." This song includes the lyrics:

The reaper's traveling at full throttle
It's catching you but you don't see
The reaper is you and the reaper is me...
Suicide is the only way out...
Get the gun and try it
Shoot, shoot, shoot.

McCollum was still wearing the headphones when his body was found. As reported by Chuck Philips in his *Los Angeles Times* article on October 04, 1990, entitled "Just Weeks After Judas Priest Case, Ozzy Osbourne Faces Similar Suits Over Subliminal Messages," the boy's guardian sued Osbourne and his record company. The subliminal messages allegedly present in Ozzy Osbourne's song were blamed for the suicide shooting of McCollum.

There is additional anecdotal evidence to support the connection between rock music and suicide. In February 1986, 18-year-old Philip Morton, of the city of Delafield, Wisconsin, hanged himself from a closet door. At the time of his suicide, he was listening to rock band Pink Floyd's album *The Wall*, which

---

[18] Ibid.

includes such songs as "Goodbye Cruel World" and "Waiting for the Worms." Those songs were playing continuously in the background.[19]

Steve Boucher, 16 years old, killed himself by putting a gun to his head and pulling the trigger. His parents protested that the cause of their son's suicide was his obsession with AC/DC's song "Shoot to Thrill." In fact, Steve was sitting under his favourite AC/DC poster when he pulled the trigger and killed himself.[20]

Michael Waller was another teenager who committed suicide in 1991. His parents filed a lawsuit against Ozzy Osbourne's "Suicide Solution" song.

In all of the cases described above involving lawsuits by parents, the legal actions against the singers, musicians and record producers were dismissed by the courts because, unfortunately, music is constitutionally protected speech under the First Amendment of the United States constitution.[21] Just because the artists and producers in question were not held legally responsible, however, does not mean that they bear no blame for the incidents. Social scientific evidence presented in this book clearly suggests that adolescents often give more credence to the opinions of musical performers about life than to what their parents say. They often try to emulate the clothing and attitudes of their favourite singers.

---

[19] Terry Watkins, "It's Only Rock 'n' Roll... But It Kills," accessed on November 1, 2010, http://www.av1611.org/rockm.html.

[20] Ibid.

[21] Mike Quinlan, J.D. and Jim Persels, J.D., "It's Not My Fault, the Devil Made Me Do It: Attempting to Impose Tort Liability on Publishers, Producers, and Artists for Injuries Allegedly 'Inspired' by Media Speech," *Southern Illinois Law Journal* 18, no. 417 (Winter 1994).

In each of the cases described above, would the youths have even thought of committing these crimes if it were not for the songs suggesting it to them? Their families knew about their fascination with certain kinds of songs and were aware that they were listening to them dozens of times, over and over again. The lyrics of those songs very likely influenced them to make their fatal decisions. These are just a few examples out of the countless incidents of violence perpetrated under the influence of music.

Role of music in subliminal seduction

Subliminal messages refer to communications directed to the subconscious mind; they are hidden suggestions that are perceived only by the subconscious. This is achieved by projecting the messages so quickly or faintly that they are received by the listener at a level below that of conscious awareness.[22] They can be audio subliminal messages (hidden behind music) or visual subliminal messages (airbrushed into a picture and flashed on a screen so quickly that we do not consciously see them).

Owing to its seductive power, music plays a superb role in disseminating both audio and visual subliminal messages to the minds of people. For example, words are uttered so quickly in a song that we do not consciously remember them, or words in a song are masked by musical tones or rhythms so that we do not consciously hear them.

To understand subliminal seduction, we have to understand how our minds work. Our conscious mind has the capacity to

---

[22] Capps, "Rock on Trial: Subliminal Message Liability."

distinguish between right and wrong. The moral sense of right and wrong has been revealed to us as mentioned in the Qur'an:

(سورة الشَّمس: ٨) ﴿فَأَلْهَمَهَا فُجُورَهَا وَتَقْوَىٰهَا ۝﴾

﴾And inspired it [with discernment of] its wickedness and its righteousness.﴿ *(Qur'an 91: 8)*

On the other hand, our subconscious mind does nothing with the information presented to it except to store it. When wrong values are passed to the brain in the form of subliminal messages, they bypass our conscious mind, which is capable of judging right from wrong. They are stored directly into our subconscious memory, and, hence, destroy the sense of morality.

The use of subliminal messages was first brought to the attention of the public in 1957, when James Vicary asserted that his company, Subliminal Projection Co., had developed a device that would flash a message on a movie screen every five seconds for just the smallest fraction of a second. A movie theatre in New Jersey used the device for six weeks, flashing the messages 'Drink Coca-Cola' and 'Hungry? Eat Popcorn.' On the days when the subliminal messages were shown, popcorn sales increased by 58%, and sales of Coke increased by 18%. In general, there was public outrage at the invention because people considered it an attempt to manipulate the mind.[23]

There have been various incidents where the use of subliminal messages has been found in the media. For example, in the Christmas shopping season of 1973, several parents complained to the Federal Trade Commission (FTC) and the Federal

---

[23] Ibid.

Communications Commission (FCC) that the subliminal message 'Get it' was used in a national TV commercial for a children's game. As a result, Premium Corporation of America, the maker of the game, voluntarily stopped running the commercial, "claiming the subliminal's presence was due to a misguided employee."[24]

Subliminal messages are used in music just as they are used in television, movies and other modes of communication. In fact, in music, they have an added advantage in that the mesmerizing influence of music very efficiently masks and transmits the subliminal messages contained in it.

One of the problems with subliminal messages is that sometimes they are so quick, so vague and so subtle that it is difficult to monitor them.[25] By their nature, subliminal messages are extremely similar to the whispers of Satan, which he instills into the hearts of human beings in a very subtle way, and which are very effective on humans. The Qur'an says, regarding the whispers of Satan:

(سورة النَّاس : ٥) ﴿ٱلَّذِى يُوَسْوِسُ فِى صُدُورِ ٱلنَّاسِ ۝﴾

﴿[Satan] who whispers [evil] into the breasts of mankind.﴾

(Qur'an 114: 5)

﴿فَوَسْوَسَ إِلَيْهِ ٱلشَّيْطَنُ قَالَ يَٰٓـَٔادَمُ هَلْ أَدُلُّكَ عَلَىٰ شَجَرَةِ ٱلْخُلْدِ وَمُلْكٍ لَّا يَبْلَىٰ ۝﴾ (سورة طه : ١٢٠)

﴿Then Satan whispered to him; he said: O Adam, shall I direct you to the tree of eternity and possession that will not deteriorate?﴾

(Qur'an 20: 120)

---

[24] Ibid.
[25] Ibid.

The effectiveness of subliminal messages has been shown experimentally in various studies published in different scientific journals. As cited above, in James Vicary's movie theatre experiment, there was a significant increase in the sales of popcorn and Coke when subliminal messages were shown.

Likewise, in January 1958, Seattle radio station KOL broadcast subconscious messages along with other recordings; the messages included "How about a cup of coffee?" and "Someone is at the door." The results of that experiment revealed that several listeners either made or thought about coffee, and some went to the door or checked around for people at the door. Similarly, KYA in San Francisco used subliminal messages during their program to tell their listeners to write to the station. In six days, the station received about eighty-seven response letters.[26]

One method employed by the music industry to create subliminals involves the placing of a short word or phrase under a drumbeat; this involves a conscious decision and action when recording the songs. For example, in the first suicide case mentioned in the previous section (Belknap v. Judas Priest), it was found that the words "Do it" were deliberately placed in the song as a subliminal message. Pamela Marsden Capps notes that:

> The court found that the words, "Do It," were a combination of the singer's exhalation on one track and a Leslie guitar on another track. There was, however, testimony indicating that the message was intentional including: the regularity of the words, "Do It," in relationship to the drum beats where the words are located, the presence of a 'punch-in sound' where the record button was pressed previous to a number of

---

[26] Ibid.

appearances of the words, "Do It," and computer analysis showing that the singer's breath occurred milliseconds after each "Do It" on the record.[27]

In the case in which McCollum committed suicide after listening to Osbourne's "Suicide Solution," subliminal lyrics were also involved:

> The Institute for Bio-Acoustics Research, Inc. (IBAR) was hired to evaluate "Suicide Solution." Not surprisingly, they found subliminal lyrics that weren't included in the copyright 'lead sheet.' The subliminal lyrics are sung at one and one-half times the normal rate of speech and are not grasped by the first time listener. However, they claim the subliminal lyrics *are audible enough that their meaning and true intent becomes clear after being listened to over and over again.*" What are some of the hidden subliminal lyrics? *"Why try, why try? GET THE GUN AND TRY IT! SHOOT...SHOOT...SHOOT,"* — followed by a hideous laughter![28]

The purpose of this discussion is to inform the readers that music and singing are not simply harmless forms of entertainment. Whether in the East or West, musicians and singers who are the apostles of Satan — intentionally or unintentionally — introduce subliminal lyrics into songs. Those subliminal messages embedded in music — about promiscuity, drugs and revolting against elders and religious traditions — ultimately affect the behaviour of their listeners and can destroy the moral fabric of the society within a few decades.

---

[27] Ibid.
[28] Watkins, "It's Only Rock 'n' Roll... But It Kills."

Role of music in the depiction
of women as sex objects

It has been shown in the previous sections of this book that sex is the most common theme of music. One feature that is common in youth-oriented music relating to courtship and sexual relationships is the depiction of women as sex objects. Such songs feature sex-driven males competing with one another for females who are viewed merely as sexual objects or conquests, and whose only value lies in their physical appearance.[29] This depiction of men as sexually insatiable and women as sexual objects is especially widespread in music videos.[30] In emerging adults, the frequent viewing of such content is strongly linked to the endorsement of women as sexual objects. This was shown by media researcher L. Monique Ward (a psychologist at the University of Michigan) in a study published in the 2002 issue of the *Journal of Youth and Adolescence*.[31]

Repeated exposure to such depictions may also result in internalization of these gender roles that show sexually degrading behaviour as central to both males and females. This suggests that portrayal of women as sex objects could affect the sexual behaviour of emerging adolescent girls and boys, and a detailed

---

[29] L. Monique Ward, "Talking About Sex: Common Themes about Sexuality in Prime-time Television Programs Children and Adolescents View Most," *Journal of Youth and Adolescence* 24 (1995): 595-615. Also see J. Gow, "Reconsidering Gender Roles on MTV: Depictions in the Most Popular Music Videos of the Early 1990s," *Communication Reports* 9 (1995): 151-161.

[30] S.A. Seidman, "An Investigation of Sex-role Stereotyping in Music Videos," *Journal Broadcast Electron* 36 (1992): 209-216.

[31] Ward, "Talking About Sex: Common Themes about Sexuality in Prime-time Television Programs Children and Adolescents View Most."

scientific study published in the August 2006 issue of the medical journal *Pediatrics* confirms this contention.[32]

Steven Martino, PhD, a researcher at Rand Corporation in Pittsburgh, Pennsylvania, and his associate scientists conducted a national longitudinal telephone survey of 1,461 adolescents aged between 12 and 17 years. Participants were first interviewed at baseline in 2001, when they were 12 to 17 years old, and most were virgins at that time. The subjects of the study were asked how frequently they listened to any of more than a dozen musical artists who were the most popular among the youth then. Follow-up interviews were conducted one and three years later, in 2002 and 2004, to see whether their choice of music had influenced their subsequent behaviour.

The study found that teenagers who listened to a lot of music with degrading sexual messages (depicting women as sex objects) were almost twice as likely to become involved in sexual activities within the following two years, as compared to the teens who listened to little or no sexually degrading music. In its August 7, 2006 article "Study: Sexy Lyrics Lead to Sex Sooner," the Associated Press quoted Dr. Martino as saying:

> Exposure to lots of sexually degrading music 'gives them a specific message about sex.' Boys learn they should be relentless in pursuit of women and girls learn to view themselves as sex objects.

Commenting on the influence of music content on adolescent sexual behaviour, Dr. Martino writes:

---

[32] Steven C. Martino et al., "Exposure to Degrading Versus Nondegrading Music Lyrics and Sexual Behavior Among Youth," *Pediatrics* 118, no. 2 (August 2006): 430-441.

Musicians who incorporate this type of sexual imagery in their songs are not simply modeling an interest in healthy sexual behaviour for their listeners; they are communicating something specific about what are appropriate sexual roles for men and women. These lyrics are likely to promote acceptance of women as sexual objects and men as pursuers of sexual conquest.[33]

Another interesting finding reported by Dr. Martino was the observation that the time spent listening to music in general and changes in sexual behaviour were directly proportional. In other words, the more time teenagers spent listening to any kind of music, the earlier they started their sexual activities. This was true regardless of the sexual content of music. One likely explanation for this phenomenon, according to Dr. Martino, is that when teens listen to popular music, no matter what its content is, it results in heightened physiologic arousal and sexual behaviour among such teens 'through a process of excitation transfer.'[34]

Dr. David Walsh, a psychologist who heads the National Institute of Media and the Family, told the Associated Press on August 7, 2006 that the results of Dr. Martino's study on the teenagers make sense because "the brain's impulse-control center undergoes 'major construction' during the teen years at the same time that an interest in sex starts to blossom." With the addition of sexually arousing lyrics, Dr. Walsh continued, "it's not that surprising that a kid with a heavier diet of that... would be at greater risk of sexual behaviour."

---

[33] Martino et al., "Exposure to Degrading Versus Nondegrading Music Lyrics and Sexual Behavior among Youth."

[34] Ibid.

Natasha Ramsey is a teen-editor for Sexetc.org, a web site produced at Rutgers University that provides sex education for teens. In an interview reported by the Associated Press, Natasha mentioned that the reason she and other teens listen to sexually explicit songs is because they like the beat. She further added:

> I won't really realize that the person is talking about having sex or raping a girl. Even so, the message is being beaten into the teens' heads. We don't even really realize how much.... Teens will try to deny it, they'll say 'No, it's not the music,' but it IS the music. That has one of the biggest impacts on our lives.[35]

If we look at any song that has sex and romance as its theme, we will notice that the emphasis is always on the physical appearance of a woman, thus portraying her as a sexual commodity. Never do we find such songs praising the intelligence of woman or her spiritual status. Based on the above-mentioned research, women lose sight of the value of chastity and modesty under the influence of music and songs, because they are brainwashed to believe that they are sex objects and that men compete with each other to win them.

While such behaviour may be appropriate for animals, human beings must act like human beings. Women must remember that they are not sex objects in the way that they are portrayed in the music. Modesty (*hayâ'*) is the most valuable asset for both women and men. It is so important that the Prophet Muhammad (ﷺ) regarded it as a salient feature of Islamic faith:

> Abu Hurayrah (﵁) narrated that the Prophet (ﷺ) said: «Faith has seventy-something or sixty-something branches. The highest of them is testifying that there is none worthy of worship other

---

[35] Ibid.

than Allah, while the lowest of them is removing something harmful from the road, and ḥayâ' is a branch of faith. » (recorded by Ibn Abi Shaybah; al-Albani graded it sound with a good chain of narration)

'Imrân bin Ḥusayn said that the Prophet (ﷺ) said: «Ḥayâ' does not bring anything except good.» (Muslim)

Narrated Abdullah ibn 'Umar (ﷺ): «The Prophet (ﷺ) passed by a man who was admonishing his brother regarding ḥayâ' and was saying: You are very shy, and I am afraid that might harm you. Hearing that, Allah's Apostle (ﷺ) said: Leave him, for ḥayâ' is (a part) of faith.» (Bukhari)

The meaning of ḥayâ' encompasses modesty, bashfulness, shyness, moral conscience and self-respect. Its root word in the Arabic language is *ḥayât,* which means 'life' or 'existence.' It means that the life of any nation lies in its moral conscience and modesty. When shamelessness and immodesty prevail in a nation, it will result in the death of the nation. Ḥayâ' is part of the natural inclination instilled by Allah (ﷻ) in human beings.

Muslim women and men also must not forget their lofty status as the children of Prophet Adam (ﷺ). Both women and men are recipients of a soul created by Allah. He has invested both genders with inherent dignity and has made men and women the trustees of Allah on earth, as mentioned in the Qur'an in various places:

﴿۞ وَلَقَدْ كَرَّمْنَا بَنِىٓ ءَادَمَ ... ۝﴾   (سورة الإسراء: ٧٠)

❨And We [Allah] have certainly honoured the children of Adam...❩
                                                        (Qur'an 17: 70)

﴿ثُمَّ سَوَّىٰهُ وَنَفَخَ فِيهِ مِن رُّوحِهِۦ وَجَعَلَ لَكُمُ ٱلسَّمْعَ وَٱلْأَبْصَٰرَ وَٱلْأَفْـِٔدَةَ﴾

قَلِيلًا مَّا تَشْكُرُونَ ۝   (سورة السَّجدَة : ٩)

❨Then He proportioned him and breathed into him from His [created] soul and made for you hearing and vision and hearts; little are you grateful.❩   *(Qur'an 32: 9)*

وَإِذْ قَالَ رَبُّكَ لِلْمَلَـٰئِكَةِ إِنِّي جَاعِلٌ فِي ٱلْأَرْضِ خَلِيفَةً ... ۝   (سورة البَقَرَة : ٣٠)

❨Your Lord said to the angels: Indeed, I will make upon the earth a successive authority...❩   *(Qur'an 2: 30)*

Islam elevated the status of both women and men to the highest status that any civilization can imagine, as is also evident in some of the following hadiths of Prophet Muhammad (ﷺ): «A man came to the Prophet Muhammad (ﷺ) asking: O Messenger of Allah, who among people is the most worthy of my good companionship? The Prophet said: Your mother. The man said: Then who is next? The Prophet said: Your mother. The man further asked: Then who is next? Only then did the Prophet say: Your father.» (Muslim)

«Whoever supports two daughters until they mature, he and I will come on the Day of Judgment like this (and he pointed with his two fingers held together).» (Muslim)

«Seeking knowledge is mandatory for every Muslim [male and female].» (recorded by Ibn Mâjah and graded as sound by al-Albâni)

Marriage of music and television — darkness upon darkness

Among the senses given to human beings by Allah (ﷻ), the senses of hearing and seeing are the strongest. In the Qur'an, Allah (ﷻ) reminds us:

قُلْ هُوَ ٱلَّذِىٓ أَنشَأَكُمْ وَجَعَلَ لَكُمُ ٱلسَّمْعَ وَٱلْأَبْصَـٰرَ وَٱلْأَفْـِٔدَةَ قَلِيلًا مَّا تَشْكُرُونَ ﴿٢٣﴾

(سورة المُلك: ٢٣)

❨Say: It is He [Allah] Who has produced you, and made for you hearing and vision and heart; little are you grateful.❩ *(Qur'an 67: 23)*

Music and singing affect the emotions of human beings in two different ways. Music-induced emotions can be conveyed by the tone of voice of the singer (plus the sounds of the musical instruments), and they can also be conveyed by nonverbal expressions such as laughing, crying, attractive gestures (of the female singer especially), or dancing. The effects of music-induced emotions are much greater when the visual dimension is combined with the audio dimension. In music videos, there are dramatic visual effects that mesmerize their viewers owing to their combined audio-visual power. Listen, for example, to Dr. Brown and Dr. Hendee, who are considered authorities in the area of clinical medicine:

> There is a concern that the marriage between television and music is powerful and synergistic. Multisensory input reinforces any message, specifically by enhancing learning and recall.[36]

---

[36] Brown and Hendee, "Adolescents and their Music: Insights into the Health of Adolescents."

Many researchers have emphasized the detrimental effects of the combination of music and television. In a laboratory study published in the journal *Youth Society* in 1986, regarding the effects of music television (MTV), researchers Greeson and Williams found that when selected music videos were watched by seventh and tenth graders for just one hour, their concepts about premarital sex changed. These students were then more likely to approve of premarital sex as compared with a control group of adolescents.[37] Music videos were clearly able to transform the viewpoint and moral sense of their viewers.

In the same vein, a behavioural study reported by Rehman and Reilly found that when participants were shown violent music videos, they became desensitized to any kind of violence committed in the real world immediately after viewing the videos.[38] It is clear that many of the messages, both in the lyrics and in the visualization of those lyrics, are sexual in nature. For example, in Paul McCartney's song entitled "We Got Married," the lyrics go: "Going fast, coming soon, we made love in the afternoon." Aerosmith's song "Love in an Elevator" includes the lyrics: "Lovin' it up as I'm going down."

As the new medium of music videos has been introduced into the society, social scientists have started to study their effects, and they have found that music videos can have a profound impact upon their viewers. Recently, there has been growing concern about the pernicious effects of rock music and music

---

[37] L.E. Greeson and R.A. Williams, "Social Implications of Music Videos for Youth: an Analysis of the Contents and Effects of MTV," *Youth and Society* 18 (1986): 177-189.

[38] S. Rehman and S. Reilly, "Music Videos: a New Dimension of Televised Violence," *Pennsylvania Speech Communication Annual* 41 (1985): 61-64.

videos on adolescents, because both contribute to a breakdown of morality and to the high teenage pregnancy rate in the United States.[39]

In one study, researcher Thomas N. Robinson, of the Stanford University Center for Research in Disease Prevention (in Palo Alto, California), and his associates examined the associations among media, music exposure and self-reported alcohol use. They collected baseline and eighteen-month follow-up data on media usage (which included watching television, videos and music videos, among others) and lifetime and thirty-day alcohol use from a sample of 1,533 students who were ninth-graders in six public schools in San Jose, California. They found that for each one-hour increase in watching music videos, there was a 31% increased risk of the young person beginning to drink alcohol within the next eighteen months. The authors of the study noted: "Increased television and music video viewing are risk factors for the onset of alcohol use in adolescents."[40]

In a similar study performed by Rubin and his colleagues, it was revealed that the meanings of a song from the music video version were more potent and had a greater effect upon the viewers than the audio version alone of the same song.[41] Hence, the visual counterpart to the music could be even more damaging when the audio and video dimensions were combined. The effect

---

[39] Tipper Gore, *Raising PG Kids in an X-rated Society* (Nashville: Abingdon Press, 1987).

[40] Thomas N. Robinson, Helen L. Chen and Joel D. Killen, "Television and Music Video Exposure and Risk of Adolescent Alcohol Use," *Pediatrics* 102, no. 5 (1998): e54-e59.

[41] R.B. Rubin, A.M. Rubin and E.M. Perse, "Media Use and Meaning of Music Video," *Journalism Quarterly* 63 (1986): 353-359.

of audio-visual versions of music on the viewers is more powerful and synergistic.

People carrying music on their heads — a prophecy in hadith

The Prophet Muhammad (ﷺ) said: «Soon there will be people from my Ummah who will drink wine, calling it by other than its real name. **There will be instruments of music and singing on their heads**, and they will listen to female singers. Allah (ﷻ) will cleave the earth under them and turn others into apes and swine.» (recorded by Ibn Mâjah and graded as sound by al-Albâni)

Hence, one of the signs of the end of times is that people will carry musical instruments 'on their heads.' Today when we watch people walking with headphones on their heads playing the music, we see this nearly 1400-year-old prophecy come true. Commenting on the recent invention of musical instruments for the head, medical researchers Elizabeth F. Brown, MD and William R. Hendee, PhD observed that during the early era of rock music, radios were large and hard to carry around, but for today's youth, "music is particularly ubiquitous" because:

> Music became portable with the advent of transistor radios. Recent innovations in miniaturization and the development of light high-quality headphones have made it possible for teenagers to envelop themselves constantly in rock music.[42]

---

[42] Brown, "Adolescents and their Music: Insights into the Health of Adolescents."

It is not surprising, although it is regrettable, that our modern industrialized society has generated an entertainment industry so ubiquitous that people today can amuse themselves anywhere on the planet. While walking, running, working, or even sleeping, they can listen to or watch videos of their favourite tunes, with the help of miniature music players such as iPods, cell phones or PDAs.[43] In fact, some of the garment companies sell their customers a 'personal stereo,' which consists of a jacket with a built-in radio and speakers conveniently attached right inside the hood.[44]

Allan Bloom contends that a huge number of the youths in their teens and early twenties are addicted to music today. When these young people are at school or in family gatherings, their minds are still daydreaming and yearning to go back to their world of music. In fact, in this age when music is everywhere — in the home and outside the home, on the road and in the library, in the car and in the shopping malls — nothing prevents them from being connected with their music.[45]

Lamenting the condition of the new generation, which is so preoccupied with the music on its head, Professor Bloom continues:

> But as long as they have the Walkman on, they cannot hear what the great tradition has to say. And, after its prolonged use, when they take it off, they find they are deaf.[46]

---

[43] Personal Digital Assistants, also known as 'handheld computers' or 'palmtops.' [Editor]

[44] Ron Chepesiuk, "Decibel Hell: The Effects of Living in a Noisy World," *Environmental Health Perspectives* 113, no. 1 (January 2005): A35-A41.

[45] Bloom, *The Closing of the American Mind.*

[46] Ibid.

Before the advent of Islam, the method of worship of pagan Arabs of Makkah involved clapping and singing while they were circumambulating the *Kaaba* (the House of Allah), as mentioned in the Qur'an:

﴿وَمَا كَانَ صَلَاتُهُمْ عِندَ ٱلْبَيْتِ إِلَّا مُكَآءً وَتَصْدِيَةً ... ۝﴾

(سورة الأنفال : ٣٥)

◆And their prayer at the House was not except whistling and handclapping...◆
(Qur'an 8: 35)

Today, with the prevalence of music, the wheel of jâhiliyah has come full circle, bringing us face to face with the same ancient paganism. Music is present even in the House of Allah, indicating the pathetic and somnambulant (sleepwalking) state of some of the Muslims. These days, some Muslims are so obsessed with modern technology that they are talking on their cell phones while performing *ṭawâf* (the circumambulation of the Kaaba that is one of the rites of the pilgrimage to Makkah). As Adnan Mâlik noted in his January 17, 2005 Associated Press report, their cell phones are ringing, and some have ringtones set to the musical lyrics of famous pop music singers such as Michael Jackson.

Similarly, some people set their cell phone ringers to music and do not feel any shame when their cell phones ring with the music while they are in congregational prayers in the mosques, hence disturbing the concentration of Muslims standing next to them in prayer. This is the result of the obsession of some Muslims with music. May Allah (ﷻ) protect us from such an obsession with music. Âmeen.

Chapter 5

Positions of the Companions, the Four Imams and other Islamic Scholars

$\mathcal{J}$t is important to mention here the opinions of the various Companions of the Prophet Muhammad (ﷺ), as well as the tâbi'oon, regarding the position of music in Islam. Imam Qurtubi, in his tafseer *Al-Jâm'il-Ahkâm ul-Qur'an*, and Imam Aloosi, in his tafseer *Rooh al-Ma'âni,* mention that the Companions (may Allah be pleased with them) unanimously agreed that music and singing are prohibited, but they allowed particular exceptions specified by the authentic Sunnah. This includes the four Rightly-guided Caliphs (may Allah be pleased with them); the jurists among the Companions, such as Ibn 'Abbâs, Ibn 'Umar, Ibn Mas'ood and Jâbir ibn Abdullah; and the general body of the Companions (may Allah be pleased with them all).

Position of the Companions of the Prophet (ﷺ)

Abdullah ibn Mas'ood (ﵞ)

Ibn Mas'ood (ﵞ), the distinguished Companion of Prophet Muhammad (ﷺ), said: "Singing fosters hypocrisy in the heart."[1]

Abdullah ibn 'Abbâs (ﵞ)

"The duff is prohibited, and the musical instruments are prohibited."[2]

'Uthmân ibn 'Affân (ﵞ)

"Ever since I took the pledge on the hand of the Prophet Muhammad (ﷺ), I have not played music, told a lie, or touched my private parts with my right hand."[3]

'Umar ibn al-Khaṭṭâb (ﵞ)

Once 'Umar ibn al-Khaṭṭâb (ﵞ) passed by a group of pilgrims. He saw a man singing, and the rest of them were listening to his song. 'Umar (ﵞ) said to them: "May Allah make you deaf, may Allah make you deaf." (*Ithâf as-Sâdatul Muttaqeen*)[4]

'Â'ishah aṣ-Ṣiddeeqah, the Mother of the Believers (ﵞ)

Once 'Â'ishah (ﵞ), the wife of the Prophet Muhammad (ﷺ), went to the house of her brother, whose daughters were sick. When she got there, she saw a singer with long hair who was

---

[1] Ibn al-Qayyim, *Ighâthat ul-Lahfân min Maṣâ'id ash-Shayṭân.*

[2] Ibn al-Qayyim, *Ighâthat ul-Lahfân min Maṣâ'id ash-Shayṭân.*

[3] Suhrawardi, *'Awârif al-Ma'ârif.*

[4] Mufti-Mohammad Shafee, *Islam and Music,* ed. Mohammad 'Abdul-Mu'izz (Karachi: Maktaba Darul Uloom, 2002), 14.

trying to amuse the sick girls by shaking his head as he sang. Upon seeing him, 'Â'ishah (ﷺ) immediately ordered: "Oh! This is Satan! Get him out. Get him out."[5]

Qâsim ibn Muhammad

Qâsim ibn Muhammad was a nephew and student of 'Â'ishah (ﷺ), the Mother of the Believers. He also was one of the well-known 'seven jurists of Madinah.' Once when a man asked him about music and singing, Qâsim replied: "I dislike it and forbid people from singing." The man further asked: "Is it ḥarâm?" Imam Qâsim said to him: "Listen, my nephew! When Allah is going to separate right from wrong on the Day of Judgment, where is He going to put music and singing?"[6]

When the commandments of the Qur'an, the hadiths of the beloved Messenger (ﷺ), and the understanding of his Companions (may Allah be pleased with all of them) are all taken together, it is quite clear that Islam has called for a prohibition on using and listening to musical instruments. To clarify the point further, the position of the four great Imams and other Islamic scholars will be presented in the following pages.

---

[5] Bayhaqi, *Sunan al-Kubrâ,* ed. Muhammad 'Abdul-Qâdir Ata (Beirut: Dar al-Kutub al-'Ilmiyah, 1423 AH/ 2003 CE). See the chapter on: Testimony, Section 64: The person who sings and makes it his/her profession. Hadith # 21010, 10:378.

[6] Ḥârith ibn Asad al-Muḥâsibi, *Risâlah al-Mustarshideen* (Halb, Maktab al-Matboo'at al-Islamia, 1383 AH).

Position of the four Imams
and other Islamic scholars

Among the Islamic scholars, all four imams including Imam Abu Ḥanifah, Imam Shâfiʻi, Imam Mâlik and Imam Aḥmad ibn Ḥanbal (may Allah have mercy on them) agree that listening to music is ḥarâm in Islam.

<u>Imam Abu Ḥaneefah</u>

Imam Abu Ḥaneefah (80-148 AH) forbids 'listening to all musical instruments, all types of tambourines, hand drums, and even the striking of sticks.'[7]

<u>Imam Shâfiʻi</u>

Imam Shâfiʻi (150-204 AH) said about music and singing: "Verily, song is loathsome; it resembles the false and vain thing. The one who partakes of it frequently is an incompetent fool whose testimony is to be rejected."[8]

In addition, it has been clarified by many of his closest students that Imam Shâfiʻi's position on the issue of music is that of prohibition.

<u>Imam Mâlik</u>

As for Imam Mâlik (93-179 AH), it is generally understood that he found it to be ḥarâm, except for certain forms of innocent singing (without instruments and without mixed gatherings), which he allowed. Imam Ibn Taymiyah mentioned that when

---

[7] Aloosi, *Rooḥ al-Maʻâni.*

[8] Imam Muhammad ibn Idrees Shâfiʻi, *Kitâb al-Umm* (Egypt: Maktaba al-Kulliyât al-Azhar, 1381 AH), 8:311.

Is-hâq ibn Moosâ asked Imam Mâlik about the view of people of Madinah regarding singing, Imam Mâlik replied: "Here, in fact, that is done only by the sinful ones."[9]

Imam Ahmad ibn Hanbal

Imam Ahmad ibn Hanbal (164-241 AH) forbade all but those forms of music that have been mentioned as exceptions in the Sunnah. Imam Ibn al-Jawzi writes in his book *Talbees Iblees* that when Imam Ahmad was asked by Abdullah, his own son and student, about his position on music, the Imam replied: "Singing sprouts hypocrisy in the heart; it does not please me."[10]

Dahhâk

"Music and singing results in the loss of wealth, anger of Allah and destruction of the heart."[11]

Imam Ibn Taymiyah

The great revivalist and Islamic scholar Imam Ibn Taymiyah states in his *Majmoo' al-Fatâwa*:

The *madh-hab* (school of juristic thought) of the four imams is that all instruments of musical entertainment are harâm. It is authentically related in *Saheeh al-Bukhâri* and other compilations that Prophet Muhammad (ﷺ) foretold that some of his Ummah would seek to make lawful: fornication, the wearing of silk, the drinking of wine, and musical instruments (*ma'âzif*); and that such people would be turned into apes and swine. The term *ma'âzif* means musical

---

[9] Shaykh ul-Islam Ibn Taymiyah, *Risâlah Waj'd wa Samâ'* (Lahore: Al-Hilal Book Agency, 1365 AH).

[10] Ibn al-Jawzi, *Talbees Iblees.*

[11] Ibid.

entertainment, as has been mentioned by the scholars of the Arabic language. It is the plural of *mi'zafah*, the instrument upon which one makes musical sounds. None of the disciples of these imams has mentioned the existence of any dissension from the consensus on the prohibition of all instruments of musical entertainment.[12]

Ibn 'Abdul-Barr

Ibn 'Abdul-Barr said:

Among the types of earnings which are ḥarâm (forbidden) by scholarly consensus are ribâ (interest), the fee of a prostitute, bribes, payments for wailing over the dead and singing, payments to fortune-tellers and astrologers, payments for playing flutes (musical instruments), and all kinds of gambling.[13]

Ḥasan al-Baṣri

Abu Bakr al-Khallâl mentioned that it is reported that Ḥasan al-Baṣri, the great teacher of the purification of hearts, said:

Duffs have absolutely no relation to the affairs of Muslims, and the students of Abdullah (ibn Mas'ood) used to tear them apart.[14]

It must be noted, however, that according to the works of the Muslim jurists, it is permissible to play the duff on certain occasions of joy such as weddings, since that is not designed

---

[12] Shaykh ul-Islam Ibn Taymiyah, *Majmoo' al-Fatâwa* (Riyadh: Mat'ba ar-Riyadh, 1381 AH), 11:576.

[13] Ibn 'Abdul-Barr, *al-Kâfi*, quoted in Shafee, *Islam and Music*.

[14] Muhammad Nâṣir ad-Deen Al-Albâni, *Taḥreem Alât at-Tarab* (The Prohibition of Musical Instruments) (Egypt: Maktaba Ad-Daleel, 1996).

solely for entertainment and pleasure but instead for announcements and such.

Ḥârith ibn Asad al-Muḥâsibi

One of the imams of Islamic spirituality, Ḥârith ibn Asad al-Muḥâsibi, explicitly stated his position on singing: "Music and singing are prohibited for us just like the meat of a dead animal is prohibited."[15]

Junaid al-Baghdâdi

Another great authority on *tasawwuf* (Islamic spirituality), Shaykh Junaid al-Baghdâdi, said: "If you notice that a student of spirituality is asking for permission to listening to *samâ'* (religious songs), then this means that he still has spiritual defects in him."[16]

Al-Fudayl ibn Iyâd

This statement of the great Islamic scholar of the science of purification of hearts, al-Fudayl ibn Iyâd, can be considered no less than an axiom and a golden rule of thumb: "Ghinâ' is a prelude to zinâ."[17]

Imam Abu Ḥamid al-Ghazâli

Imam al-Ghazâli, after a long discussion about the permissibility of religious singing in his book *Iḥyâ' 'Uloom-ud-Deen* (Revival of the Islamic Sciences), clarifies that listening to music and singing that are accompanied by women, the use of musical instruments, or lustful poetry is completely prohibited in

---

[15] Al-Muḥâsibi, *Risâlah al-Mustarshideen.*

[16] Suhrawardi, *'Awârif al-Ma'ârif.*

[17] Ibid.

Islamic teachings.[18]

Imam an-Nawawi

Imam an-Nawawi, the great hadith scholar whose two collections of hadith, *Riyâḍ aṣ-Ṣâliḥeen* and *Forty Hadiths,* have gained widespread acceptance in the Muslim Ummah, said the following about music:

> It is unlawful to use musical instruments — such as those which drinkers are known for, like the mandolin, lute, cymbals, and flute — or to listen to them. It is permissible to play the tambourine [*duff*] at weddings, circumcisions, and other times, even if it has bells on its sides. Beating the kuba, a long drum with a narrow middle, is unlawful.[19]

Ibn Qudâmah

Ibn Qudâmah gave the following verdict about listening to music:

> Musical instruments are of three types, which are ḥarâm. These are the strings and all kinds of flutes, and the lute, drum and stringed instruments and so on. Whoever persists in listening to them, his testimony should be rejected.[20]

---

[18] Imam Abu Ḥamid Al-Ghazâli, *Iḥyâ' 'Uloom ud-Deen* (Karachi: Darul Isha'at Publishers, 1978).

[19] Muhammad ash-Shirbini al-Khatib and Yaḥya ibn Sharaf an-Nawawi, *Mughni al-Muhtaj,* quoted in Shaykh Nuh Ha Mim Keller, *Reliance of the Traveller* (Maryland: Amana Publications, 1994), 775.

[20] Muwaffaq ad-Deen Ibn Qudâmah, *Al-Mughni.* (Egypt: Dar al-Minar, 1367 AH), 9:173.

Shaykh Shahâb ud-Deen Suhrawardi

Renowned Islamic scholar Shaykh Shahâb ud-Deen Suhrawardi is the founder of the Suhrawardi school of spirituality. He authored a book entitled *'Awârif al-Ma'ârif*, which can be regarded as the *magnum opus,* or masterpiece, on the subject of the science of purification of the hearts. He devoted two chapters of the book to singing; in the first chapter, he discussed the permissibility of religious singing, and in the second chapter, the prohibition of other types of singing. Throughout the entire discussion, he did not deviate in the slightest from the stand of the Prophet's Companions (may Allah be pleased with them) and the mainstream Islamic scholars: that religious singing is permissible only under limited conditions. He writes in the second chapter:

> When people indulge in samâ' (listening to religious singing), they waste a lot of time. The taste in their prayers is reduced. Those people become addicted to going to the gatherings of samâ'. In order to seek pleasure from the singers, they arrange for these get-togethers more and more frequently, even though it is not a hidden matter that Sufi scholars consider such kind of gatherings as impermissible and rejected.[21]

Abu Ali ar-Rudhbâri

Another scholar of the science of purification of the heart, Shaykh Abu Ali ar-Rudhbâri, was once asked about a man who sought pleasure with musical instruments and claimed that "such an act is *halal* (permissible) for me because I have reached such a (spiritual) station that different conditions do not affect me."

---

[21] Suhrawardi, *'Awârif al-Ma'ârif.*

Shaykh Abu Ali retorted: "Yes, that person has reached a station. But where? In the hellfire!"[22]

Shaykh Aḥmad Sirhindi Farooqi

Shaykh Aḥmad Sirhindi Farooqi (also known as *Mujaddid Alf Thâni,* or 'reviver of the second millenimum') was largely responsible for the reassertion and revival of Islam in India in the second millennium AH against the Moghul emperor Akbar and his anti-Islamic government. He wrote:

Religious music, singing and dancing in reality belong to amusement and vain play.... There are so many Qur'anic verses, hadiths and narrations of scholars of Islamic jurisprudence about prohibition of music and singing that it is hard to count them. In spite of that, if someone tries to bring an abrogated hadith or unreliable narration to prove the permissibility of music, then his claim will be rejected because no Islamic jurist in any period in Islamic history has given a fatwa in favour of music and singing or dancing.... Some immature Sufis of our times, by using the actions of their teachers as a pretext, have made religious music and singing as their religion and consider it as a form of worship. The Qur'an tells us about such people:

❨Who took their religion as distraction and amusement.❩ *(Qur'an 7: 51)*

...All praise is due to Allah, and it is of His blessings that our spiritual teachers did not suffer from this disease and kept followers like us away from such matters.[23]

---

[22] Ibn Ḥajar Al-Haythami Al-Makki, Kaff ar-Ra'â', quoted in *Shafee, Islam and Music.*

[23] Shaykh Aḥmad Farooqi Sirhindi, *Maktubât Mujaddid Alf Thâni* (Collected=

Shaykh 'Abdul-Aziz ibn Bâz

Shaykh 'Abdul-Aziz ibn Bâz, who was the Grand Mufti of Saudi Arabia and an authority on Islamic sciences, issued the following verdict about music and singing:

> Listening to music and singing is ḥarâm, and it is an evil practice. It hardens the hearts and prevents people from remembrance of Allah and establishing the prayers.[24]

Shaykh Nuh Ha Mim Keller

Nuh Ha Mim Keller is a contemporary scholar. Formerly a Catholic, he became Muslim in 1977 at al-Azhar in Cairo and later studied the traditional Islamic sciences of Hadith, Shâfi'i and Ḥanafi *fiqh* (Islamic jurisprudence), legal methodology and tenets of faith in Syria and in Jordan, where he has lived since 1980. He has the following to say about music:

> Some people claim that recorded music is not actually music because it comes from recording, and it does not come from a musician. This is an unreliable position, because the amount of revenue generated by the recorded music in the U.S. in the year 2002 was around 12 billion U.S. dollars, and the amount for live musicians was 1.7 billion U.S. dollars. So obviously they are not buying it because it is not music. There are six *Ṣaḥeeh* (authentic) hadiths that expressly forbid musical instruments. Hence, if there is fear of Allah (*taqwâ*) and faith (*eemân*) in the heart, the ruling is clear, i.e., the primary basis for musical

---

=Letters), trans. Syed Zawwar Hussain Shâh (Karachi: Idara Mujaddadia, n.d.), *Book 1, Letter 266.*

[24] Abu Sâd, *Playing and Listening to Music and Singing: In Light of Qur'an and Sunnah* (in Urdu) (Karachi: Dar-ut-Taqwa, 2003).

instruments is that they are forbidden (*harâm*). It is clear from the hadiths, and the hadiths are authentic in their chains of transmitters. There is no doubt that the Prophet (ﷺ) said it, and he said it for our benefit.... What is music? If you look at the nature of music, it is pure, unadulterated expression of the musician's self (*nafs*). So why let it into your *nafs*...?

People who think it is permissible to listen to records and jazz concerts are blind, and the jurists (*fuqaha*) who give out legal verdicts (*fatâwa*) making music permissible are blind, because part of fatwa consists in 'purification of the self' (*tazkiyatun-nafs*). Allah tells us in the Qur'an what the Islamic Law (*Sharia*) is doing in our lives:

❴He has succeeded who purifies it [his own self]❵ (*Qur'an 91: 9*)

This is the fatwa interest. It is not to let people do anything they want. The interest of fatwa is often lost sight of in our times by the jurists (*muftis*) who often do not have any clue about it and do not know about *tazkiyatun-nafs* — what will be the effect of music on the soul of the person that you are giving the fatwa to, what will happen to his religion (*deen*) when you give him this fatwa. This is an interest that the person giving the fatwa must be conscious of it and he must be observing. And how many people giving legal verdicts (fatwas) are not jurists (*muftis*) in our times, even if they memorized all the books of all the schools of thought (madh-habs) and they are Imam of al-Azhar or whoever else. If they gave the fatwa that music is OK, then they do not understand the effect of music on human psyche (*nafs*).[25]

---

[25] Shaykh Nuh Ha Mim Keller, "Is Listening to the Recorded Music Permissible?",

http://www.sunnipath.com/Resources/Questions/QA00004456.aspx. Permission=

Muhammad Taqi Usmani (former Justice)

Renowned Islamic scholar and former Judge of the Islamic Sharia Court of Pakistan, Muhammad Taqi Usmani, writes:

At the time of the Prophet Muhammad (ﷺ) and during the time of his Companions, non-Muslim people of the world were fond of musical and other entertainments. It was quite possible to create such entertainments in order to convey the message of Islam to them, but the Companions of Prophet Muhammad (ﷺ) did not try to amuse people by dramas, music and plays; instead, they conquered the hearts of people by presenting their exemplary character to them... Today, if we are not willing to change our non-Islamic habits and customs for the sake of Islamic preaching, and we want to propagate the message of Islam by merely making dramas, musical shows and films, then only Shaytân could be the inventor of such ideas.[26]

Conditions under which Singing is Permissible

Since it was mentioned in the above discussion that certain exceptions do exist, they will be elucidated here. The exception concerns singing and playing the duff on the occasions of celebrations. As far as the rest of the musical instruments (other than the duff) are concerned, they are not permissible under any circumstances. It must also be noted that most of the music employed these days in weddings goes beyond the Islamic zone of

---

=to use this quote was confirmed in a personal communication from Shaykh Nuh Ha Mim Keller; for further information, consult http://www.sunnipath.com.

[26] Justice Muhammad Taqi Usmani, *Islâh-e-Muashara* (in Urdu) (Reform of Society) (Karachi: Maktaba Darul Uloom, 1998).

permissibility. The duff is a round hand drum that resembles a tambourine without the metal disc attachments. We know that it was allowed on special occasions, like weddings and *Eids* (the two Islamic celebrations, one at the end of the fasting month of *Ramadan* and the other at the culmination of the *hajj*). We find this in the following hadiths: «It has been narrated by 'Â'ishah (ﷺ), the wife of the Prophet, that once the Prophet Muhammad (ﷺ) came home, and at that time, two little girls were singing songs about the battle of Buath. The Prophet (ﷺ) lay down on the bed and turned his face away. Then Abu Bakr came and scolded her, saying: These musical instruments of Satan in the house of the Prophet of Allah (ﷺ)! Prophet Muhammad turned to him and said: Leave them. In the words of 'Â'ishah (ﷺ): When Abu Bakr got busy in other matters, I told the two girls to leave, and they left. That was the day of Eid. The Abyssinians were playing in the mosque with shields and lances. Then either I asked the Messenger (ﷺ), or he himself said: Do you want to have a look? I said yes, so he let me stand behind him, with my cheeks against his cheeks, and said: Carry on, Banu Arfidah. When I became bored, he asked: Is that enough for you? I said yes. He said: Then you may leave.» (Bukhari)

Muhammad ibn Hâtib al-Jumahi relates that the Messenger of Allah (ﷺ) said: «The difference between the unlawful and the lawful (in marriage celebrations) is the duff and the voice.» (recorded by Ibn Mâjah and Tirmidhi, who considered its chain of narration reliable)

«It was narrated by 'Â'ishah (ﷺ) that when she prepared a lady as a bride for a man from the *Anṣâr* [the Muslim citizens of Madinah who gave refuge to the Prophet (ﷺ) and the other Muslim emigrants from Makkah], the Prophet (ﷺ) said: O

'Â'ishah! Haven't you got any amusement (for the wedding), as the Anṣâr like amusement?» (Bukhari)

Hence, on the occasions of marriage and Eid, we have been allowed the singing and the duff as the previous hadiths clearly specify.

In Conclusion: the legal ruling on listening to music and singing

As stated in the beginning of the book, in Islamic Sharia, the correct approach to an issue is an essential element in deriving a ruling. This requires that we understand the Islamic commandments through the text of the Qur'an and the Sunnah. Then we take that understanding and apply it to the issue as it exists in reality. By combining our understanding from the Qur'an and the Sunnah and applying it to the issue, we derive the fatwa on the permissibility or impermissibility of the issue at hand. In doing so, we also look at the harms and the benefits related to the issue. The approach of the Islamic Sharia is to weigh the benefits and harms of everything, because the ultimate aim of Sharia is to benefit the society.

We can dissect the problem into three parts:

1. Musical instruments such as duffs, pianos, guitars and flutes
2. Lyrics
3. Singers or composers

We have looked at the evidence from the Qur'an and the Sunnah regarding music and singing. We have also looked at the positions taken by the Companions of the Prophet (may Allah be pleased with them) as well as our great Imams and other Islamic scholars. Furthermore, we have scientifically looked at the harms caused by music to individuals and the society. Hence, when we apply our understanding from all of these sources to the issue of listening to music and singing, we give the following decisive ruling with regards to music:

Musical instruments that are designed solely for entertainment are ḥarâm, with or without singing. Moreover, the use of the sounds of musical instruments generated by any means whatsoever (digitally produced or computer-generated or even produced by the mouth of the singer) is also ḥarâm. However, the majority of Islamic scholars permit the use of the duff when played on special occasions by men or women in separate-gender gatherings. Note that the natural sounds (such as the waterfall sound or chirping of the birds) used in songs do not constitute musical sounds.

As far as the songs are concerned, if their lyrics consist of anything that is unlawful, if the environment in which singing is carried out is unlawful (such as singing in mixed gender gatherings, vain amusement and entertainment, and singing by professional singers), or if they prevent one from his or her obligatory duties, then they are ḥarâm. If the songs are free from the above-mentioned things, and they are NOT accompanied by any musical instruments (except the duff) or the sound of musical instruments generated by any means whatsoever (such as digitally produced or computer-generated), then it is permissible to sing them.

Chapter 6

Critical Analysis of Arguments Used in Favour of 'Islamic' Music

$\mathcal{I}$s there such a thing as 'Islamic' music? Can we listen to 'Islamic' music? Can music be used to further the noble cause of the spread of Islam? Is the subject of music a highly controversial issue in Islam? The purpose of this chapter is to provide answers to all these questions by logically analyzing some of the arguments that some Muslims use in favour of music.

If we simply look at the Islamic history, we will notice that there is not a single Islamic scholar who took music as his profession. Since human nature needs novelty, Islam is acutely aware of the fact that even religious music eventually leads to ḥarâm music. In fact, there is nothing Islamic about 'Islamic music,' just like the terms 'Islamic bingo' or 'Islamic beer' or 'Islamic socialism' do not exist in the vocabulary of Islam. If we put the 'halal' label on a beer bottle, it will not make it pure; that is only a deception to the eyes. Alcohol can still not be used to inspire us for any noble cause or simply as a mild entertainment. Similarly, if we recite the name of Allah (﷾) while slaughtering a pig, this will not make the pork halal. By the same token, if we call the interest (earned on our money deposited in the banks) a profit, it will still be usury, which is absolutely forbidden in Islam.

So it is manifestly erroneous for Muslims — particularly some scholars who follow the so-called 'modernist' trend set by modernist scholars and intellectuals — to use terms such as 'Islamic music.' They confuse Islam and music and are thus responsible for the confusion of Muslims and for leading them astray. Some of them even suggest that the Companions and tâbi'oon listened to music and singing, and that they saw nothing wrong with it. However, they cannot produce hadiths with authentic chains of narration going back to these Companions and tâbi'oon, which would prove what they falsely attribute to them with respect to music. Imam Muslim mentioned in his introduction to his *Saheeh Muslim* that Abdullah ibn Mubarak said: "The chain of narration is part of religion. Were it not for the chain of narration, whoever wanted to could say whatever he wanted to."

Listening to music is a non-Islamic practice that has been clearly prohibited by Allah (ﷻ) and His messenger (ﷺ), so there can never be such a reality as 'Islamic music.' Music and Islam are as far apart from each other as East and West. Based on the evidence from the Qur'an, the Sunnah and the verdicts of the Islamic scholars, we can say:

Oh! Music is music, and Islam is Islam,
And never the twain shall meet.

In the following pages, we will address some of the most common arguments put forward by people in favour of music. The response to each argument contains a critical and logical analysis of that argument.

Prohibition of music — Is it a controversial issue or a matter of consensus in Islam?

Argument:

Music is a highly controversial issue in Islamic fiqh. Many eminent scholars have considered it forbidden, but there are other eminent scholars — classical and contemporary — who permit singing and the use of musical instruments.

Response:

The best question to ask such people is: "Are you able to name one scholar who claimed that music was a highly controversial issue in Islamic fiqh?"

No doubt it is true that some contemporary scholars hold the usage of musical instruments permissible, with certain conditions attached. Nevertheless, it does not render the issue a controversial one in Islamic law.

Here we must understand a fundamental maxim that rules the Islamic spirit and law. The fact that a handful of scholars hold a view that opposes the overwhelming majority neither makes the issue controversial nor makes the difference a tolerable one. This axiom is agreed upon among the jurists, and this becomes apparent when they discuss the principle that states: "There is NO censure in issues of disagreement, while the censure is only in issues of consensus."[1]

The scholars explained the meaning of 'issues of disagreement' by stating that odd or weak opinions are

---

[1] Haytham bin Jawwad Al-Haddad, "Music: A Simple Matter of Disagreement?", accessed June 1, 2007, http://www.islamicawakening.com.

excluded from this principal altogether, rendering them open for censure. For this reason, Ibn al-Qayyim, in his work *I'lâm al-Muwaqqi'een,* explains at length the difference between issues subject to *ijtihâd* (using one's knowledge of the Qur'an and the Sunnah to derive rulings on matters not specifically mentioned in either source of Islamic law) with conditions attached, and issues not subject to ijtihâd, even if there may be scholars who held a contrary opinion.

Failing to differentiate between the two issues, or not implementing this rule, leads to major legal problems.[2] In fact, this may lead to the destruction of the Ummah. Although this might come as a surprise to us, it is important that we open our hearts and minds to certain truths. If we were to read through the works on comparative Islamic fiqh, especially the voluminous manuals such as *al-Mughni, al-Majmoo', Fath al-Bâri, 'Umdat al-Qâri* or *at-Tamheed,* we would rarely find a legal issue that is free from any dispute; and if we were to accommodate differences at every legal dispute, we would end up with no Islam at all. It is precisely for this reason that the scholars would often say: "One who deliberately seeks out religious allowances becomes a heretic."

It must be noted that just because there happens to be any level of difference of opinion over an issue, this does not necessarily render the difference as a tolerable one. The tolerable difference is where there is room for ijtihâd, which occurs only when the difference of opinions is a major one. Moreover, it must be performed objectively and sincerely.[3]

---

[2] Ibid.

[3] Ibid.

Having said that, let us focus our attention on the tiny minority of scholars in the past who have been reported as considering music to be permissible; they include Ibn Ḥazm, Shawkani, an-Nabulsi and al-Ghazâli. It must be noted that none of those scholars lived in the first two centuries after the death of the Prophet (ﷺ). In the period closer to Prophet Muhammad (ﷺ), his Companions and the pious predecessors, pioneers of Islamic tasawwuf and all four great Imams, music and singing accompanied with music were considered prohibited in Islam.

Ibn Ḥazm did not accept the hadith of *Ṣaḥeeḥ al-Bukhari* regarding the prohibition of music. Ibn Ḥazm was no doubt a virtuous and astute scholar, but his personality was full of contradictory qualities. He belonged to the school of Dhâhiri fiqh (those who apply only literal wordings of Qur'an and Sunnah in assessment of judicial issues), which is obsolete and outdated now. In the area of Hadith assessment and verification, Ibn Ḥazm held some very abnormal and unfounded views. Al-Ḥâfidh ibn 'Abdul-Hâdi, the accomplished Hadith scholar and student of Ibn Taymiyah, says of Ibn Ḥazm that "he often errs in his critical assessment of the degrees of traditions and on the conditions of their narrators."[4] For example, he was not even aware of the name of Imam Tirmidhi, the famous compiler of the hadiths and student of Imam Bukhari.

Al-Ḥâfidh Dhahabi writes about Ibn Ḥazm:

Ibn Ḥazm's statement that Imam Tirmidhi is *majhool* (unknown) is a baseless claim. In fact, Ibn Ḥazm was

---

[4] Ḥâfidh Shams ud-Deen Abu Abdullah Al-Maqdisi Ibn 'Abdul-Hâdi Al-Ḥanbali, *Tabaqât Ulamâ al-Ḥadeeth* (Beirut: Al-Resalah Publishing House, 1996 CE/1417 AH).

completely unaware of Imam Tirmidhi and his book of hadiths *Jâmi' Tirmidhi*.[5]

Al-Ḥâfiḏẖ Ibn Ḥajar al-'Asqalâni, a well-known Hadith scholar, has the following to say about Ibn Ḥazm:

Ibn Ḥazm possessed great memory, but due to his excessive reliance on memory, he often made errors in his critical assessment of the degrees of hadiths and on the conditions of their narrators, and he would often suffer from the worst kind of whims.[6]

As far as Imam al-Ghazâli is concerned, he clarifies in his book *Iḥyâ' 'Uloom-ud-Deen* (after a long discussion about the permissibility of religious singing) that listening to music and singing accompanied by women, musical instruments, or lustful poetry is completely ḥarâm in Islamic teachings.[7] Hence, we can see that Imam al-Ghazâli placed strict conditions on listening to religious music. When we look at the most sophisticated musical instruments today, the environment in which music is played, and the lyrics of the songs, it is clear that all the prerequisite conditions for listening to religious music that were set forth by people like Imam al-Ghazâli are nullified. This makes the act of listening to music, and singing accompanied by it, an impermissible act based on the standards set forth by Imam al-Ghazâli.

Contemporary Islamic researcher Khalid Baig, in his path-breaking book *Slippery Stone*, discusses the position of al-Ghazâli in the following words:

---

[5] Ḥâfiḏẖ Shamsud-Deen Dhahabi, *Mizânul E'tidâl* (Cairo: Dar al- Iḥyâ' Kutub al-'Arabiyya, 1382 AH).

[6] Ibn Hajar al-'Asqalâni, *Lisânul Mizân*, ed. Shaykh 'Abdul-Fattah Abu Ghuddah (Beirut: 1423 AH/ 2002 CE).

[7] Al-Ghazâli, *Iḥyâ' 'Uloom ud-Deen*.

Interestingly, most people who refer to his arguments seem to forget his conditions. For example, few realize that al-Ghazâli declared samâ' to be impermissible for the youth, the target audience of most music business today. In other words, music fans have found in al-Ghazâli a convenient prop on which to hang the justification for their indulgence. But this is an exception of al-Ghazâli. Anyone who wants to seriously understand the issue must not separate al-Ghazâli's conditions from his arguments. When that is done, those invoking al-Ghazâli in support of their license may be in for a rude shock. Al-Ghazâli does use words like ḥarâm and *makrooh* [disliked] for activities and conditions that describe most of what is going on today even in the *nasheed* [Islamic songs] department, let alone the secular music.[8]

Let's take the case of scholars like 'Abdul-Ghâni an-Nabulsi, who was of the opinion that religious music is permissible. The verse of soorat al-Jumu'ah (Friday), which mildly rebukes amusement during the time of prayers, says:

$$\text{﴿وَإِذَا رَأَوْاْ تِجَـٰرَةً أَوْ لَهْوًا ٱنفَضُّوٓاْ إِلَيْهَا وَتَرَكُوكَ قَآئِمًا قُلْ مَا عِندَ ٱللَّهِ خَيْرٌ مِّنَ ٱللَّهْوِ وَمِنَ ٱلتِّجَـٰرَةِ وَٱللَّهُ خَيْرُ ٱلرَّٰزِقِينَ ١١﴾}$$

(سورة الجُمُعَة : ١١)

﴿And when they see some merchandise or amusement, they break away to it, and leave you [O Prophet] standing. Say: What is with Allah is better than amusement and merchandise, and Allah is the best of providers.﴾   *(Qur'an 62:11)*

An-Nabulsi claimed that the way amusement has been mentioned in this verse shows that there seems to be nothing

---

[8] Khalid Baig, *Slippery Stone: an Inquiry into Islam's Stance on Music* (Garden Grove, CA: Open Mind Press, 2008).

wrong with it.[9] He tried unsuccessfully to use this argument in defense of religious singing, and the widely circulated fatwa of al-Azhar also copied this argument in an attempt to prove that music and singing are legitimate.[10] This reasoning has been very strongly refuted by the famous commentator on the Qur'an Maḥmood Aloosi:

> Shaykh 'Abdul-Ghâni al-Nabulsi, may Allah forgive him, argued for the permissibility of lahwa from this verse of soorat al-Jumu'ah. You should know that that is based on a claim and a misconception. Even stranger is his argument from the conjunction between permissible trade and lahwa in the beginning of the verse. And that is also weird that he wrote epistles to show their permissibility that are used by a group attributed to Mawlânâ Jalâl ad-Deen ar-Roomi. These epistles revolve around arguments that are weaker than the waist of the baby gazelle... These are baseless lies that no sensible person can accept.[11]

Regarding Shawkani's position on music, it seems that he just followed Ibn Ḥazm due to his love for the Dhâhiri school of thought, which was initially strengthened by Ibn Ḥazm but is almost obsolete today. Otherwise, all the major Ḥanbali scholars — Imam Aḥmad ibn Ḥanbal, Imam Ibn Taymiyah, Ibn al-Jawzi,

---

[9] 'Abdul-Ghâni an-Nabulsi, *Iḍâḥ ad-Dalâlat fee Samâ' al-Âlât* (Explaining the Arguments for Listening to Instruments) (Damascus: 1302 AH).

[10] Dâr al-Iftâ al-Maṣriyah, http://www.dar-alifta.org, fatwa number 3280, dated 12 August 1980, quoted in Baig, *Slippery Stone: An Inquiry into Islam's Stance on Music*. This ruling was given by the Grand Mufti and Shaykh of Cairo's Al-Azhar, which has been a major centre of Islamic learning for over a thousand years. Michael Mumisa's English translation of this fatwa has been widely promoted by a Muslim music business in the UK.

[11] Aloosi, *Rooḥ al-Ma'âni*, soorat *al-Jumu'ah*, verse 11, 28: 417.

Ibn al-Qayyim, Ibn Qudâmah and others — regarded music as forbidden in Islam.[12]

The assumption about music being a controversial topic only underlines the lack of research on one's part. It has been clearly shown in this book that the vast majority of the scholars throughout Islamic history have agreed that music is forbidden. An obvious question that arises here is how can the vast majority of scholars from all legal schools throughout the past fourteen centuries agree on the prohibition of musical instruments, while the truth happens to be to the contrary? Would it not occur to us that by adopting the other view, we are implicitly imputing error on the part of a vast majority of the scholars throughout the past fourteen centuries? Why would Allah (ﷻ) order us on the one hand:

﴿ ... فَسْـَٔلُوٓاْ أَهْلَ ٱلذِّكْرِ إِن كُنتُمْ لَا تَعْلَمُونَ ۝ ﴾   (سورة النحل : ٤٣)

❰...So ask the people of the message if you do not know.❱

(Qur'an 16: 43)

while the Prophet (ﷺ) declared that the scholars are the inheritors of the prophets: «Certainly, the scholars are the inheritors of the prophets, for indeed the prophets did not leave behind *dinars* (gold) or *dirhams* (silver), but (they left their) knowledge. Whoever accepts it receives a great fortune.» (a sound hadith recorded by Abu Dâwood)

Yet, on the other hand, such a vast majority of the scholars would consent to an invalid legal opinion for over fourteen centuries? Would this not, in turn, cast doubt on the integrity of Islam, which was conveyed to us by none other than these scholars?

---

[12] See Chapter 5 for references to the Ḥanbali scholars mentioned here.

Hence, we should not wonder why and how a scholar would oppose such a vast majority of the scholars. The question more worthy of springing to mind is: How could such a vast majority of scholars be wrong in believing musical instruments to be forbidden?

To sum up, both Imam Qurtubi (in his tafseer *Aḥkâm ul-Qur'ân*) and Imam Aloosi (in his tafseer *Rooḥ al-Ma'âni*) mention that the Companions (may Allah be pleased with them) unanimously agreed upon the prohibition of music and singing but allowed particular exceptions specified by the authentic Sunnah. This includes the four Rightly-guided Caliphs and the jurists among the Companions such as Ibn 'Abbâs, Ibn 'Umar, Ibn Mas'ood and Jâbir ibn Abdullah, as well as the general body of Companions (may Allah be pleased with them). Imam Ibn Taymiyah wrote:

> The view of the four Imams is that all kinds of musical instruments are ḥarâm. It was reported in *Ṣaḥeeḥ al-Bukhâri* and elsewhere that the Prophet (ﷺ) said that there would be among his Ummah those who would allow zinâ, silk, alcohol and musical instruments, and he said that they would be transformed into monkeys and pigs... None of the followers of the Imams mentioned any dispute concerning the matter of music. (*Majmoo' al-Fatâwa*, 11/576)

Unintentional hearing of music

<u>Argument:</u>

How can we consider music to be forbidden in Islam when there is music everywhere? When we go to supermarkets, offices, restaurants, or stores, we are bombarded with music. There is no way to escape music in this technological age.

Response:

There is a difference between listening and hearing. If we happen to hear music against our free will, while we are in a certain public place, this does not justify listening to music. Imam Ibn Taymiyah commented on this matter:

Concerning (music) which a person does not intend to listen to, there is no prohibition or blame, according to scholarly consensus. Hence blame or praise is connected to listening, not to hearing. The one who listens to the Qur'an will be rewarded for it, whereas the one who hears it without intending or wanting to will not be rewarded for that, because actions are judged by intentions. The same applies to musical instruments that are forbidden: if a person hears them without intending to, that does not matter. (*Majmoo' al-Fatâwa*, 10/78)

Answers to some commonly raised objections

Argument:

We are listening to music and singing because everybody in the society is doing so.

Response:

The Qur'an tells us that the fact that something is done by the majority of people is not a justification to make it permissible. Music has been prohibited by Allah (﷾) and His Messenger (ﷺ). In fact, each of the prophets of Allah (peace be upon them all) came to this world at a time when the majority of people were not obeying Allah (﷾), to such an extent that the deviance appeared to be the norm in the society. The Qur'an tells us not to follow the majority:

$$﴿وَإِن تُطِعْ أَكْثَرَ مَن فِى ٱلْأَرْضِ يُضِلُّوكَ عَن سَبِيلِ ٱللَّهِ إِن يَتَّبِعُونَ إِلَّا ٱلظَّنَّ وَإِنْ هُمْ إِلَّا يَخْرُصُونَ ﴿١١٦﴾ ﴾$$

(سورة الأَنعَام: ١١٦)

❴If you follow most of those upon the earth, they will mislead you from the way of Allah. They follow nothing but assumption, and they are not but falsifying.❵   *(Qur'an 6: 116)*

The Qur'an also says:

$$﴿ ... وَإِنَّ كَثِيرًا مِّنَ ٱلنَّاسِ لَفَٰسِقُونَ ﴿٤٩﴾ ﴾$$

(سورة المَائدة: ٤٩)

❴...And indeed, many among the people are defiantly disobedient.❵   *(Qur'an 5: 49)*

The criterion between truth and falsehood is not the majority; it is the Qur'an and Sunnah. Any act or custom that passes the criteria set forth by the Qur'an and Sunnah is the truth. Dr. Muhammad Iqbal, the famous poet of Islam, said in one of his poetic verses:

Falsehood likes dual nature (hypocrisy)
  whereas truth is one.
Do not accept the compromise of truth and falsehood.
               (Kulliyât Iqbal)

Argument:

If this thing (music) is prohibited in Islam, why was this not clearly mentioned in the Qur'an? We only obey the commandments of the Qur'an.

Response:

This is another excuse propounded by people who indulge in the actions prohibited in Islam. This objection, which is not new, was raised by many hedonists (pleasure-seekers) and apologetics, as well as modernist Muslims, over the entire course of Islamic history. The Qur'an provides clear and conclusive proof of the prohibition of music in Islam, but we must go to the Sunnah of the Messenger of Allah (ﷺ) for further clarification of any commandment of Islam. The Qur'an is general and does not go into the fine details of the various commandments; it directs us to follow Prophet Muhammad (ﷺ) for guidance. The Qur'an tells us clearly:

﴿ ... وَمَا ءَاتَىٰكُمُ ٱلرَّسُولُ فَخُذُوهُ وَمَا نَهَىٰكُمْ عَنْهُ فَٱنتَهُوٓاْ ... ۝ ﴾

(سورة الحَشر : ٧)

﴿...And whatever the Messenger has given you — take. And whatever he has forbidden you — refrain from...﴾ *(Qur'an 59: 7)*

Mohammad Asad explains that the rejection of the Sunnah by some of the present day Muslims is the outcome of an inferiority complex from which those Muslims suffer when they are confronted with the dazzling Western civilization. He notes:

This 'Westernization' is the strongest reason why the Traditions of our Prophet and, along with them, the whole structure of the Sunnah have become so unpopular today. The Sunnah is so obviously opposed to the fundamental ideas underlying Western civilization that those who are fascinated by the latter see no way out of the tangle but to describe the Sunnah as an irrelevant and therefore not compulsory, aspect of Islam — because it is 'based on unreliable Traditions.' After that, it becomes easier to twist the teachings of the Qur'an in such a way that they appear to suit the spirit of Western civilization.[13]

---

[13] Muhammad Asad, *Islam at the Crossroads* (Lahore: Sh. Muhammad Ashraf Publishers, 1991).

Our beloved Prophet (ﷺ) prophesized in his hadiths about the kind of people among Muslims who would raise such objections to the commandments of Islam. One hadith narrated by Abu Rafi' goes as follows: «Let me not find one of you reclining on his couch when he hears something regarding me, which I have commanded or forbidden, saying: We do not know. What we found in Allah's Book, we have followed only that.» (recorded by Abu Dâwood and graded as sound by al-Albâni)

In another hadith narrated by al-Miqdam ibn Ma'dikarib, Prophet Muhammad (ﷺ) warned us: «Beware! I have been given the Qur'an and something like it, yet the time is coming when a man replete on his couch will say: Keep to the Qur'an; what you find in it to be permissible, treat as permissible, and what you find in it to be prohibited, treat as prohibited.» (recorded by Abu Dâwood and graded as sound by al-Albâni)

Argument:

I am listening to music just to kill time.

Response:

First of all, the person must realize that we do not kill time. Actually, it is time that kills us. With every breath, with every tick of the clock, as the time passes, we get closer to our final destination, to our grave, to our death:

(سورة النَّجْم: ٤٢)   ﴿وَأَنَّ إِلَىٰ رَبِّكَ ٱلْمُنتَهَىٰ ۝﴾

❨And that to your Lord [Allah] is the finality [return of everything].❩   *(Qur'an 53: 42)*

The Prophet (ﷺ) spoke to us about how much we lose when we waste our time, saying: «There are two blessings that many people squander: health and time.» (Bukhari)

One cannot dispute the fact that spending time in any entertainment consumes time that ought to be reserved for carrying out religious obligations and doing good deeds. We all know that we will be standing before Allah (ﷻ) to be questioned about how we spent our time. Did we spend our time wisely, or did we just kill it? Abi Barza Aslami narrated that Prophet Muhammad (ﷺ) said: «No one will be permitted to turn his two feet away on the Day of Resurrection until he is questioned about the following: about his life, how he spent it; his knowledge, how much he acted upon it; his wealth, how he earned it and spent it; and his body, how he employed it.» (a reliable hadith recorded by Tirmidhi)

Islam does not like people involving themselves in trivial pursuits. Furthermore, even if we accept that the persons who say, "I am just killing time by listening to music," are doing what they say, then they are also killing something else — their sense of morality, which is a major loss.

Hadith about two girls singing to 'Â'ishah, the Mother of the Believers

Argument:

Music is permissible in Islam because it is mentioned in a hadith that two girls were singing to 'Â'ishah (ؓ), the Mother of the Believers, and at that time, Prophet Muhammad (ﷺ) was there. In addition, there is another hadith about the Abyssinians playing in the mosque of the Prophet in which the Prophet (ﷺ) showed them to 'Â'ishah (ؓ). These hadiths can be used as evidence that music and singing is allowed in Islam.

Response:

People who try to make music permissible quote the hadith of 'Â'ishah (رضي الله عنها), which is as follows: «It has been narrated by 'Â'ishah, the wife of the Prophet (ﷺ), that once Abu Bakr (رضي الله عنه) came to her home, and at that time, two Anṣâri girls were singing songs about the battle of Buath. They were not professional singers. Abu Bakr scolded her, saying: These musical instruments of Satan in the house of the Prophet of Allah (ﷺ)! It was the day of Eid, so Allah's Messenger said to him: O Abu Bakr, there is an Eid for every people, and this is our Eid day.» (Bukhari)

Another version of this hadith provides additional details about this incident: «It has been narrated by 'Â'ishah (رضي الله عنها), the wife of the Prophet, that once the Prophet Muhammad (ﷺ) came home, and at that time, two little girls were singing songs about the battle of Buath. The Prophet (ﷺ) lay down on the bed and turned his face away. Then Abu Bakr came and scolded her, saying: These musical instruments of Satan in the house of the Prophet of Allah (ﷺ)! Prophet Muhammad turned to him and said: Leave them. In the words of 'Â'ishah (رضي الله عنها): When Abu Bakr got busy in other matters, I told the two girls to leave, and they left. That was the day of Eid. The Abyssinians were playing in the mosque with shields and lances. Then either I asked the Messenger (ﷺ), or he himself said: Do you want to have a look? I said yes, so he let me stand behind him, with my cheek against his cheek, and said: Carry on, Banu Arfidah. When I became bored, he asked: Is that enough for you? I said yes. He said: Then you may leave.» (Bukhari)

1. The first of these hadiths, which is widely quoted by people who try to justify the permissibility of music, has the Arabic sentence *'Endi jâriyatâni tughanniyâni,* which translates as

"There were two little girls who were singing." While explaining the word *jâriyah* in *'Umdatul Qâri*, his commentary of *Ṣaḥeeḥ al-Bukhâri*, Shaykh Ai'nee writes: "Among women, *jâriyah* refers to a little girl who has not reached the age of puberty, just like *ghulâm* refers to a little boy who has not reached the age of puberty."[14] This kind of singing is in no way similar to the kind of singing by sexually attractive female singers in the present day. In fact, in Islam there is no room for gatherings where men and women freely mix with each other and listen to each other's singing, even on the occasions of marriage or Eid.

2. In both versions of this hadith, it is stated that Abu Bakr objected to the singing by those girls. This in itself shows that Abu Bakr must have heard of the prohibition of music and singing from Prophet Muhammad (ﷺ), and that is why he thought that this prohibition included every instance. The Messenger of Allah (ﷺ) clarified to Abu Bakr that on the occasion of Eid, it is permissible (with limitations). In addition, the Prophet Muhammad (ﷺ) did not express his pleasure with this act. For this reason, he did not participate in the act, as he might have done if it were a commendable act; instead he turned his face away.[15] There is a difference between hearing something and listening to something.

3. Commenting on the above-mentioned hadiths of 'Â'ishah (ﷺ) in Bukhari, Imam Baghawi writes:

The poetic verses those girls were singing (in the hadith of *al-Bukhari*) were about battle and bravery, and in their mentioning there was a support to a religious matter (jihad).

---

14 Hasan 'Abdul-Ghaffar, "Islam and Music", *Meesâq*, January 2003.

15 Aloosi, *Rooḥ al-Ma'âni*, vol. 21.

Otherwise, those poetic verses, which discuss lewdness and evil deeds and express forbidden (harâm) matters, are not allowed to be recited in a song. That is why, if such verses were sung in front of the Prophet Muhammad (ﷺ), he would have spoken against it.[16]

4. 'Â'ishah (ﷺ), the Mother of the Believers, herself considered singing to be prohibited. That is why, in the first hadith of Bukhari mentioned above, she made a point of saying that these two girls were not professional singers. Al-Hâfidh Ibn Hajar al-'Asqalâni writes in explaining this hadith:

From this hadith, a group of Sufis has taken the proof of permissibility of singing and listening to singing. However, to refute their false claim, that portion of the hadith is enough in which 'Â'ishah (ﷺ) clarified that those two girls were not professional singers. Thus, if there was any doubt that might arise from the early wordings of the hadith, she eliminated that doubt. (*Fath al-Bâri*, vol. 2)

In fact, some of the scholars of Hadith have considered the narrations of 'Â'ishah (ﷺ), the Mother of the Believers, in *Saheeh al-Bukhâri* about the singing of girls as a proof and censure against music and singing. For example, Shaykh 'Abdul-Haqq Muhaddith Dehlavi states:

Some people have used the *hadeeth of Jâriyatain* (tradition about two girls) as a proof for the permissibility of singing but the truth of the matter is that this tradition is a proof against singing except at certain occasions such as Eid... The maximum that can be proved from this tradition is that on certain occasions such as Eid, etc. there is permission of

---

[16] Imam Baghawi, *Sharah as-Sunnah*, vol. 4 quoted in Shafee, *Islam and Music*.

singing. Otherwise, it is *ḥarâm* and it is still a musical instrument of Satan as it is obvious from the tradition.[17]

It must be noted here that the singing that Shaykh 'Abdul-Ḥaqq is referring to as ḥarâm is singing that is accompanied by musical instruments or singing consisting of anything unlawful in Islam.

Some people use the portion of this hadith about the Abyssinians playing in the mosque of the Prophet (ﷺ) as evidence that singing is allowed. However, they never mention that Bukhari included this hadith in his *Ṣaḥeeḥ* under the heading 'Chapter on Spears and Shields on the Day of Eid.' Those Abyssinian slaves were playing with weapons, not with musical instruments, and there is a huge difference between the two.

Pop culture in the name of Islam

Argument:

We can use 'Islamic' music to promote the noble cause of the spread of Islam. 'Islamic' pop music can do a good job in promoting the message of love and peace. After all, Muslim artists are using pious themes and purposes in their songs as a means to achieve a positive end.

Response:

These days, we have many nasheed artists who make the rounds of Islamic conferences and conventions, singing in the name of Islam in order to entertain the attendees. They may have good intentions to remind the listeners of Islam and to make Islam

---

[17] 'Abdul-Ḥaqq Muhaddith Dehlavi, *Sharah Safr-us-Sa'adah* quoted in Shafee, *Islam and Music.*

attractive, especially to young people, by offering an alternative to pop music. Sad to say, in their desire to compete, some Muslim nasheed artists use musical instruments or digitally produced music in their 'Islamic' songs, and sometimes human voices are used to create the sounds of other musical instruments. Thus they make permissible what has been forbidden in Islam. A new type of pop culture is growing around some of these performers, who in reality have become Muslim pop stars. These Muslim singers do not realize that they only deceive themselves, as Allah tells us:

﴿ يُخَٰدِعُونَ ٱللَّهَ وَٱلَّذِينَ ءَامَنُوا۟ وَمَا يَخْدَعُونَ إِلَّآ أَنفُسَهُمْ وَمَا يَشْعُرُونَ ۝ ﴾

(سُورَة البَقَرَة: ٩)

﴿They [think to] deceive Allah and those who believe, but they deceive not except themselves, and perceive [it] not.﴾ *(Qur'an 2: 9)*

Yvonne Ridley is a British journalist and activist who came to prominence in September 2001 after she was captured by the Taliban in Afghanistan while working for London's *Daily Express*. She was held hostage for eleven days and said that she was treated with respect during her captivity. She promised her captors that she would read the Qur'an after her release, and she later did. She accepted Islam in 2003. In her recent thought-provoking article, Ms. Ridley has the following to say about the newly emerging pop culture in the name of Islam:

> Eminent scholars throughout history have often opined that music is ḥarâm, and I don't recall reading anything about the Ṣaḥâbah whooping it up to the sound of music. Don't get me wrong. I'm all for people letting off steam, but in a dignified manner and one which is appropriate to their surroundings.[18]

---

[18] Yvonne Ridley, "Pop Culture in the Name of Islam," last modified April=

Commenting on one such Islamic singing event held in London, Ms. Ridley continues:

> The reason I am expressing concern is that just a few days ago at a venue in Central London, sisters went wild in the aisles as some form of pop-mania swept through the concert venue. And I'm not just talking about silly, little girls who don't know any better; I am talking about sisters in their 20's, 30's and 40's, who squealed, shouted, swayed and danced. Even the security guys who looked more like pipe cleaners than bulldozers were left looking dazed and confused as they tried to stop hijabi sisters from standing on their chairs. Of course the stage groupies did not help at all as they waved and encouraged the largely female Muslim crowd to "get up and sing along." (They're called 'Fluffers' in lap-dancing circles!)

> ...Apparently the sort of hysteria... is also in America, and if it is happening on both sides of the Atlantic, then it must be creeping around the globe and poisoning the masses. Islamic boy bands like 786 and Mecca 2 Medina are also the subject of the sort of female adulation you expect to see on American Pop Idol or the X-Factor. Surely Islamic events should be promoting restrained and more sedate behaviour.[19]

Sadly enough, many of those Muslim 'artists' claim that they are furthering the 'noble cause' of the spread of Islam by using music. However, Islam does not permit its followers to use negative means to achieve a positive end. Music cannot be used as a means to promote virtue. Such Muslim 'artists' claim that they are promoting the message of peace and love through their music.

=24, 2006 http://www.islamicawakening.com/viewarticle.php?articleID=1261.
[19] Ibid.

The fact of the matter is that our attempt to promote idealistic concepts is very similar to the Christians using emotional language and idealism to promote what they cannot defend using convincing, rational arguments. The result of Christian attempts to sugarcoat their inconsistencies ended up in people turning away from them. We must not expect any different results.

The Muslim public has lost faith in the so-called 'music for peace and love,' since they have realized that it does not deal with real life problems. It only numbs their sense of pain regarding the global suffering. In the current atmosphere, how can music contribute to stopping the Western troops from attacking innocent people in Muslim countries? How will the music stop the Israelis from shedding the blood of innocent women and children in Lebanon and Palestine? In fact, have we ever noticed violence magically turning to peace because of music? Let us be sincere and truthful to ourselves and not deceive ourselves by using fancy slogans such as 'music for peace and love.'

Let us ask a simple question: Is there any proof suggesting that music has achieved any such noble goals? The answer to this question is a simple 'NO.' In fact, in the history of Islam, music has done nothing to promote peace and love. It has only corrupted the Muslim youth throughout Islamic history.

Imam Shâfi'i's famous statement about music clarifies that music cannot be used for pious themes and purposes:

I visited Baghdad and I saw something which has been invented by heretics, and it is known as *taghbeer*. They divert people from paying attention to the Qur'an through the use of taghbeer.[20]

---

[20] Ibn al-Qayyim, *Ighâthat ul-Lahfân min Maṣâ'id ash-Shayṭân*.

Taghbeer was a practice invented in Baghdad. People would gather, and a singer would sing poems stressing the importance of the hereafter and disliking this world. The singing was accompanied by musical instruments and sometimes dancing. Imam Shâfi'i regarded such a thing as an act of heresy, even though those people were using music for pious themes and purposes.

Discussing the non-compromising attitude of Islam, Muhammad Taqi Usmani writes in his book *Reform of Society*:

The question is: if a people of a certain period or region could be attracted to Islam through the use of music, then would it be permitted to sing Qur'an to them, accompanied by the use of a guitar and piano, for the sake of the 'preaching of Islam'? If it were possible that people of a certain area would accept Islam when they saw the photograph of Prophet Muhammad (peace be upon him), then would Muslims (God forbid) agree to print an imaginary photograph of the Prophet? If some people may accept Islam if they are impressed by the dance and singing of Muslim women, then should we send groups of women dancers to those people for the purpose of 'preaching' Islam? What kind of thought process is this, that whenever acts of evil become predominant and rampant in the world, people not only make them permissible (halal) but also start considering them inevitable for the preaching and progress of Islam.... At the time of the Prophet Muhammad (ﷺ) and during the time of his Companions, non-Muslim people of the world were fond of musical and other entertainments. It was quite possible to create such entertainments in order to convey the message of Islam to them, but the Companions of Prophet Muhammad (ﷺ) did not try to amuse people by dramas and plays; instead, they conquered the hearts of people by presenting their exemplary character to them. As a result of that, the Prophet's Companions waved the flag of *tawḥeed* (Oneness of Allah) to all corners of the world. Today, if we are not willing to change our non-Islamic habits and customs for the sake of Islamic preaching, and we want to propagate the message of Islam by merely making dramas, musical shows and films, then only Shayṭân could be the inventor of such ideas.[21]

Sufism and music

Argument:

Most of the Sufi scholars regarded listening to religious music and singing as permissible; therefore, we can listen to music.

Response:

This is not true. In fact, the founding fathers of Islamic spirituality and tasawwuf took an uncompromising stand against music. Being the experts on the science of purification of the hearts, the early Sufi scholars were quite aware of the corrupting influence of music on the human soul. Only a tiny minority of some of the later Sufis regarded Islamic singing — **without** the use of musical instruments — as permissible, but with stringent conditions attached to it. However, those are only a tiny minority of the total body of actual Sufis. We may find plenty of contemporary pseudo-Sufis who regard music and singing as permissible, but as far as the pioneers and the greatest of the Sufi scholars are concerned, they regarded music as ḥarâm.

---

[21] Usmani, *Islâh-e-Muashara.*

In chapter 5 of this book, the verdicts of Islamic scholars such as Ḥasan al-Baṣri, Ḥârith ibn Asad al-Muḥâsibi, Shaykh Junayd al-Baghdâdi, Shaykh Shahâb ud-Deen Suhrawardi and Shaykh Aḥmad Sirhindi Farooqi have already been given; it should be clear to the reader that those scholars took an unequivocal stand against music. It is hoped that after reading those definitive verdicts from Islamic scholars, it will be clear to the reader that the real Sufi scholars, who were also experts in the knowledge of Hadith, have always considered music to be ḥarâm. What we see with the present day Sufis — such as *qawwâlis*,[22] nasheeds with musical instruments and dancing in ecstasy — is completely against Islam. It has no basis in our religion.

Music and Islamic worship

Argument:

Music and singing can be used to express our love for God, and listening to religious music can elevate us to higher spiritual stations. This is why some of the Sufis regarded music as permissible.

Response:

In Hinduism, Christianity, Sikhism and other religions, music entered into the acts of worship, but Islamic worship has no place for music in it whatsoever. In response to this argument, it would be most appropriate to quote one of the greatest of the Islamic spirituality scholars to explain the position of music in Islamic

---

[22] Qawwâli is a traditional form of devotional music, found in Pakistan and India and associated with Chisti Sufism. One well-known contemporary singer (qawwâl) was Nusrat Fateh Ali Khan. [Editor]

worship. In a letter to one of his students, Shaykh Aḥmad Sirhindi criticized some of the pseudo-Sufis who were addicted to religious music and singing:

Alas! In this group of Sufis, there are many who try to find the solution to their restlessness in listening to religious music and singing, and they try to find their beloved [Allah] in the songs of the singer. For this purpose, they have made music and dancing as their way even though they must have listened to the hadith of Prophet Muhammad (ﷺ): «Allah has not put a cure in anything ḥarâm.» [Narrated by Umm Salamah in Ṭabarâni with an authentic chain]... If they had the slightest knowledge of the reality of ṣalâh (prayers), they would have never been attracted towards religious music and singing. When they did not find the path of truth, they took the path of falsehood. O my dear brother! Just like a difference that exists between prayers and singing, a difference of similar amount exists between the excellence and perfection achieved by prayers as compared to the states caused by listening to singing. A hint is enough for a wise person.[23]

Some people say that they want to play music to express their love of God. Is this the only way to express our love? The question to ask is whether the Companions of Prophet Muhammad (ﷺ) expressed their love through playing music. The answer is no. The Companions (may Allah be pleased with them) used to recite the Qur'an, utter remembrances of Allah (ﷺ), give charity, perform voluntary fasting, feed the poor and needy, and pray voluntary late night prayers to express their love of Allah (ﷺ). If there was any better way to please Allah (ﷺ), the Companions would have done it. Actually, the Companions of

---

[23] Sirhindi, *Maktubât Mujaddid Alf Thâni* (Collected Letters), Letter 261.

Prophet Muhammad (ﷺ) knew the corrupting influence of music on worship and therefore they stayed away from it. Dr. Muhammad Iqbal, the great Islamic poet and Islamic scholar, clarified in his famous lectures that the real Islamic spirituality does not permit music, in order to prevent the corruption of the mystical experience with music. He said:

> Indeed with a view to secure a wholly non-emotional experience the techniques of Islamic Sufism at least take good care to forbid the use of music in worship, and to emphasize the necessity of daily congregational prayers in order to counteract the possible anti-social effects of solitary contemplation.[24]

Fundraising in Islamic Gatherings through Musical Entertainment

Argument:

'Islamic' music can be used to promote the noble cause of Islam. Entertainment sessions containing music and singing can be used to attract Muslim teenagers and adults to Islamic conferences and conventions in order to raise funds for Islamic projects.

Response:

Nowadays, Islamic conventions and conferences are held frequently, and they are sometimes accompanied by musical entertainment. A lot of people are attracted to these gatherings due

---

[24] Sir Muhammad Iqbal, *The Reconstruction of Religious Thought in Islam* (New Delhi: Kitâb Bhavan, 1994).

to the entertainment factor, although some Muslims who fear Allah (ﷻ) go there to seek Islamic knowledge, and prominent Islamic scholars are invited to disseminate the sacred knowledge of Islam. According to a hadith mentioned previously: «Certainly, the scholars are the inheritors of the prophets, for indeed the prophets did not leave behind dinars or dirhams, but (they left their) knowledge. Whoever accepts it receives a great fortune.» (a sound hadith recorded by Abu Dâwood)

We must remember that the heirs of the prophets should be respected, and Islamic conventions should not be polluted with the presence of singers and comedians on the stage. In the Qur'an, Allah (ﷻ) told the Prophet (ﷺ) and his followers in clear terms to stay away from those people who introduce entertainment in religion, and to remind people with the Qur'an (for example, in Islamic gatherings and conventions):

$$﴿وَذَرِ ٱلَّذِينَ ٱتَّخَذُواْ دِينَهُمْ لَعِبًا وَلَهْوًا وَغَرَّتْهُمُ ٱلْحَيَوٰةُ ٱلدُّنْيَا وَذَكِّرْ بِهِۦٓ ... ٧٠ ﴾$$

(سورة الأنعَام: ٧٠)

❮And leave those who take their religion as amusement and diversion and whom the worldly life has deluded. But remind [them] with the Qur'an...❯   *(Qur'an 6: 70)*

The Qur'an and Sunnah tell us that Prophets Abraham and Ishmael (peace be upon them) taught people in the Arabian Peninsula how to pray and how to perform the rituals of hajj. However, over the next few centuries, the people of that region completely disfigured the religion brought forth by Prophet Abraham. They introduced entertainments into it, and a few thousand years later, when Prophet Muhammad (ﷺ) was sent as a prophet in that area, the ritual of hajj was reduced to a business festival. Ṭawâf was replaced by naked men and women clapping, shouting and dancing while circumambulating the House of Allah (ﷻ), as described in the Qur'an:

$$﴿وَمَا كَانَ صَلَاتُهُمْ عِندَ ٱلْبَيْتِ إِلَّا مُكَاءً وَتَصْدِيَةً ... ٣٥﴾$$

(سورة الأنفال : ٣٥)

❲And their prayer at the House [the Kaaba] was not except whistling and handclapping...❳   *(Qur'an 8: 35)*

Hence, the acts of worship were replaced with acts of entertainment.

If we read about the life of Prophet Muhammad (ﷺ), we will notice that he enjoyed time with his family. In following the Sunnah, Muslims are encouraged to take part in entertainment along with their families. They are encouraged to have their meals with family, play with their children and have picnics with relatives. These are considered Islamic entertainments. One of the issues of this era is that Muslims do not spend much time with their families. When at home, they give their time to cable or satellite television; if there is time is remaining, they spend it on the Internet. The world of virtual reality is much more exciting to them than spending time with their spouses and children. They think that entertainment lies outside their homes, but in reality, the true entertainment lies with their very families.

We must remember that Islamic conventions are not entertainment centers where we have 'Islamic' singers on the stage, entertaining and amusing their audiences and outside in the hallways, with young Muslim boys and girls in mixed gatherings laughing and chatting, completely unaware of the Islamic concept of ḥayâ'. Muslims are to be eloquently solemn and exemplary for others and not show any frivolousness.

Islam holds a unique position among all the other religions of the world in that Islam does not permit compromise with the ways and customs of secularists and modernists. Allah (ﷻ) warned the Prophet Muhammad (ﷺ), as well as all the true believers:

﴿وَدُّوا۟ لَوْ تُدْهِنُ فَيُدْهِنُونَ ۝﴾   (سورة القَلَم: ٩)

﴿They wish that you would soften [in religious commandments], so they would soften [toward you].﴾   *(Qur'an 68: 9)*

Islam clearly prohibited the use of non-Islamic methods in the preaching of Islam:

﴿لَآ إِكْرَاهَ فِى ٱلدِّينِ قَد تَّبَيَّنَ ٱلرُّشْدُ مِنَ ٱلْغَىِّ ... ۝﴾   (سورة البَقَرة: ٢٥٦)

﴿There shall be no compulsion in [acceptance of] the religion. The right course has become clear from the wrong...﴾
(Qur'an 2: 256)

Permissible entertainment in Islam

Argument:

We need some entertainment in our lives, so we listen to music because it is the most common entertainment.

Response:

The last refuge taken by Muslims while defending the enjoyment of music is to claim: "Listening to music is just entertainment, and we need entertainment in our lives." It is true that all of us need entertainment in our lives, but the truth of the matter is that listening to music is not merely entertainment. As has been shown in the previous chapters, there is a lot of corruption and filth that comes along with this entertainment. It is similar to the case of alcohol or gambling (such as the lottery); they are also forms of entertainment, but there are a multitude of harms that come along with them. Since their harm is greater than their benefit (as stated in the Qur'an), alcohol and gambling are prohibited in Islam. We must also bear in mind that music is not the only form of entertainment that is prohibited in Islam. Gambling, intoxication, reading vulgar literature, using animals (cattle or chickens, for example) as targets in archery, and cruel sports like cockfighting or dog fighting are all forms of entertainment. Yet all these 'entertainments' are prohibited according to Islamic teachings.

Islam is a complete and comprehensive religion that addresses all aspects and needs of our lives, and this includes our need for diversions and recreation. It provides lawful means for us to fulfil our needs. Imam Bukhari narrates in *Al-Adab al-Mufrad* that the Companions of the Prophet (may Allah be pleased with them) used to throw watermelons to each other, but in times of seriousness, they proved themselves to be true men of action.

In the Sunnah, we see that the Companions (may Allah be pleased with them) participated in many different forms of lawful entertainment and play. They engaged in sports like footraces, horseracing, wrestling, and archery. They spent time in lighthearted conversation. Pastimes are permissible as long as they provide the participant with relaxation or exercise, and at the same time do not compromise the laws of Islam in terms of dress, intermingling of men and women, music, gambling, betting or anything else.

Hence, Islam is not against lawful forms of entertainment. However, according to Islam, listening to music, and singing accompanied by music, is NOT an acceptable entertainment.

Examples of Permissible and Impermissible Entertainments

Permissible	Impermissible
Participating in sports like footraces, horseracing,[25] wrestling, swimming and archery	Gambling
Spending time in lighthearted conversation with family members and friends	Drinking alcohol
Listening to Islamic poetry without any musical instruments in gender-segregated settings	Listening to music or to singing accompanied by music
Playing with your spouse and children	Playing chess
Listening to beautiful-sounding Qur'anic recitation by various reciters	Reading, watching or listening to vulgar materials
Going on picnics with family or friends and enjoying the beauty of nature	Cruel animal sports such as bullfights, cockfights and the like
Hiking and sailing	

---

[25] The permissible type of horseracing involves no gambling, no intermingling of the sexes, and no alcohol or other ḥarâm activities.

Examples of Islamic Gatherings
without any musical entertainment

Argument:

It is very hard to have Islamic gatherings without the use of any musical entertainment. How can we attract Muslim youth to Islamic conventions without having any musical entertainment? The fact is that music is a strong force, and we are afraid that Islamic gatherings may not be very effective if we do not use 'Islamic' music.

Response:

It is entirely possible to have Islamic meetings without the use of music. In fact, the Islamic gatherings that are free of such entertainment prove to be highly effective and influential upon the lives of their attendees. Here are a few examples of Islamic gatherings without any musical entertainment:

1. Hajj and *'umrah* (the minor pilgrimage). Every year, millions of Muslims travel to Makkah to perform the holy rites of the hajj and 'umrah, and to Madinah to visit the Prophet's Mosque. All the pilgrims visit the holy Kaaba and carry out specific rituals. During hajj, they also congregate in the vast valley of 'Arafah from noon until sunset to engage in prayer, glorifying Allah (ﷻ) and begging His forgiveness. In spite of all the hardships of travel, overcrowding and high temperatures, the experiences of hajj and 'umrah are so moving and spiritually invigorating that most Muslims return to their countries having undergone a complete spiritual transformation. Many Muslims make sincere repentance of their sins, intend never to commit those sins again and pledge to uphold their daily prayers and other religious obligations. The number of Muslims who attend the annual 'Islamic convention' of hajj is more than two million.

2. 'Umrah during Ramadan. More than one million Muslims perform 'umrah during the month of Ramadan and gather in Makkah to attend the blessed night prayers during the last ten days, especially on the twenty-seventh of Ramadan. Yet in those blessed Muslim gatherings, there are no 'entertainment sessions.' Muslims do not come to these gatherings to amuse themselves; they attend these conferences with seriousness and humility. It is interesting to note that a few decades ago, most Muslims performing hajj or 'umrah were elderly people who desired to carry out these obligations before their death. However, the situation is completely different now. Presently, a large proportion of the pilgrims to hajj and those performing 'umrah are young men and women in their thirties, even though youth is the time when people are said to need the most entertainment. These Muslim men and women attend such Muslim gatherings with elegance and sincerity; consequently, they reap the fruits of these congregations in the form of new spiritual strength and vigor.

3. Friday congregational prayer. A third example of an Islamic gathering is the weekly meeting of Muslims for the Friday congregational prayer, which is preceded by a sermon from the Imam, similar to a speech given in any Islamic convention or conference. This event, which takes place every week at every major mosque on the face of this earth, is no less than an Islamic conference or convention. Yet there is one thing completely absent from it, and that is any entertainment session. In spite of the absence of any entertainment in these weekly assemblies, Muslims — young and old, practicing and non-practicing —

attend the prayer submissively. The Friday congregational prayers do not have musical entertainment like that found in many weekly church gatherings, yet Muslims (including many who do not perform the five daily prayers regularly) try not to miss this weekly faith-enhancing experience.

The approach of Islam — nip the evil in the bud

Islam is a religion that is in complete accordance with human nature. The Islamic approach to dealing with vice and corruption in the society is to nip the evil in the bud. For example, *'âb'* (Father) was one of the names of Allah (ﷻ) in almost all the primitive religions, as well as in Christianity and Judaism. However, Prophet Muhammad (ﷺ) abrogated that name of Allah (ﷻ) for us to call upon in our prayers. The reason is quite obvious: *Shirk* (polytheism, or associating partners with Allah) and anthropomorphism crept into the creed of Christianity through this door. The Christian theologians made Prophet Jesus the son of God.

It was the same case with gambling. Other religions were lenient regarding gambling, and today gambling takes place even inside churches, under the name of 'bingo.'

Music was no different. With the exception of Islam, music entered almost all other religions of the world at their inception. In the beginning, the hymns seemed very innocent because they were wearing the 'sacred' garments of religion. Today, when traditional religious music has taken off its coat, the monster of rock music has emerged out of it. In early Christianity, music was strictly forbidden, as stated in the Bible:

Take thou away from me the noise of thy songs; for I will not hear the melody of thy viols.[26] (Amos 5:23, King James Version)

Woe unto them that rise up early in the morning, that they may follow strong drink; that continue until night, till wine inflame them! And the harp, and the viol, the tabret,[27] and pipe, and wine, are in their feasts: but they regard not the work of the LORD, neither consider the operation of his hands. (Isaiah 5:11-12, King James Version)

In early Christianity, singing with the accompaniment of instruments was strictly forbidden. The only thing permitted was to sing with voices only, without any musical instruments. However, with the passage of time and growing secularization of the Christian societies, music crept into the churches. Puritan intellectual John L. Girardeau wrote about the introduction of music into Christianity:

It deserves serious consideration, moreover, that notwith-standing the ever-accelerated drift towards corruption in worship as well as in doctrine and government, the Roman Catholic Church did not adopt this corrupt practice until about the middle of the thirteenth century.[28]

That was the time when Luther, like other Christian reformers, declared instrumental music to be permissible and urged his followers to use it in the service of God: "I would like to see all the

---

[26] Viols were bowed, stringed musical instruments used during the sixteenth to eighteenth centuries; they are different from violins. [Editor]

[27] A tabret is a percussion instrument similar to a tambourine. [Editor]

[28] John L. Girardeau, *Instrumental Music in the Public Worship of the Church* (Richmond, VA: Whittet and Shepp, 1888), 158-159, quoted in Baig, *Slippery Stone: an Inquiry into Islam's Stance on Music*.

arts, especially music, used in the service of Him who gave and made them."[29] Today, music has become an important part of worship in many churches.

If there are minute benefits in music, its harms are much more than its benefits. The ruling of the Qur'an in such issues is clear:

$$﴿۞ يَسْـَٔلُونَكَ عَنِ ٱلْخَمْرِ وَٱلْمَيْسِرِ قُلْ فِيهِمَآ إِثْمٌ كَبِيرٌ وَمَنَـٰفِعُ لِلنَّاسِ وَإِثْمُهُمَآ أَكْبَرُ مِن نَّفْعِهِمَآ ... ﴾ (سورة البَقَرَة: ٢١٩)$$

❨They ask you [O Muhammad] about alcoholic drink and gambling. Say: In them is great sin, and [some] benefit for people, but their sin is greater than their benefit.❩   *(Qur'an 2: 219)*

The same principle can be applied to all addictions including drugs, alcohol, gambling, music, TV, wasting time in web surfing and Internet chatting, and idle talk. The Islamic approach of nipping evil in the bud can also be seen in commandments of the Qur'an not to go close to zinâ or even to the means and routes to zina:

$$﴿وَلَا تَقْرَبُوا۟ ٱلزِّنَىٰٓ إِنَّهُۥ كَانَ فَـٰحِشَةً وَسَآءَ سَبِيلًا ٣٢﴾ (سورة الإسرَاء: ٣٢)$$

❨And do not approach unlawful sexual intercourse. Indeed, it is ever an immorality and is evil as a way.❩   *(Qur'an 17: 32)*

Allah, the Exalted, the Almighty commands us not to go close to any form of shameful deed, whether committed openly or secretly:

---

[29] Martin Luther, *Luther's Works*, preface to the Wittenberg Hymnal (1524), 53:316, (1965) quoted in Baig, *Slippery Stone: an Inquiry into Islam's Stance on Music.*

$$\{\ ...\ \text{وَلَا تَقْرَبُوا الْفَوَاحِشَ مَا ظَهَرَ مِنْهَا وَمَا بَطَنَ}\ ...\ ﴿١٥١﴾\}$$

(سورة الأنعام: ١٥١)

❨...And do not approach immoralities — what is apparent of them and what is concealed...❩   *(Qur'an 6: 151)*

The modernist writers on Islam do not realize what the end result would be if we began the practice of making forbidden things permissible in Islam. The bitter fruits of such additions or deletions in divine injunctions can be seen in other religions. Christianity made music and gambling permissible in order to show their enlightenment; today music, singing and dancing are done inside the churches in the name of religion. The same kind of dancing is done in the name of religion in Hindu temples.

It may be of interest to readers to note that some of the greatest musicians entered into the music business through the route of religious music. The late Egyptian musical singer Umm Kalthum used to sing religious songs with her father when she was a child; later on, she became the queen of Arabic music. Similarly, Elvis Presley's early introduction to music came from gospel singing in church and in school; later on, he emerged as the king of rock and roll and pop music.

Islam knows that the more people are exposed to the evils in society, the more they become desensitized to them. Thus, if children are exposed to lascivious songs, suggestive music and sexy dances in their childhood, their whole worldview of sexual morality will be tarnished. Their moral uprightness will be destroyed from their very childhood. The natural inclination with which they were born, which was instilled by Allah (ﷻ), will be disfigured. They will lose the ability to distinguish between modesty and immodesty, morality and immorality, and chastity and promiscuity.

Ibn al-Qayyim writes in *I'lâm ul-Muwaqqi'een* (vol. 2) about this approach of Islam:

Among Islamic scholars, some consider the use of the duff to be disliked, even on the occasion of marriages. The reason for this approach is based on the rule of Islamic Sharia known as *sadd bâb zaree'ah*, which means that some of the permissible acts are forbidden because they may result in a back door for the introduction of prohibited acts in the society. It is similar to the idea that exchanging gifts among people is an act of Sunnah, but it is prohibited to present gifts to a government official or to someone who has given us a loan, because this paves a way for bribery and usury (interest) and creates corruption in the society. Similarly, to stare at the face of a woman (who is not a person's wife) intentionally is prohibited because in this way the germs of fornication are nourished in the society, even though someone could argue that by looking at the beautiful female faces, we are only enjoying the artistry of Allah.[30]

Similarly, Imam Ibn Taymiyah, weighing the harms and benefits of music and religious music and singing (like qawwâlis), stated:

But their harms are much more than their benefits. It is similar to the case of alcohol and gambling, in which there are some benefits for people but the harms of alcohol and gambling are much more. It is for this reason that Islamic law has not made them permissible.[31]

---

[30] Ibn al-Qayyim al-Jawziyah, *I'lâm ul-Muwaqqi'een* (Lahore: Ahl Hadeeth Academy, 1976).

[31] Ibn Taymiyah, *Risâlah Waj'd wa Samâ'.*

In conclusion, Islam prohibits music and singing because they lead a person to commit sins. Hence, Islam takes preventive measures rather than suffering the consequences. As explained by Ibn al-Qayyim, this is based on the Islamic juristic idea of preventing an evil before it actually materializes. Based on this Islamic principle, preventing harm is given precedence even over achieving possible benefits.

Music creates heedlessness and a hole in one's soul

Music, by its very nature, creates heedlessness of remembrance of Allah (ﷻ). This is why musical instruments are known in the Arabic language as *malâhi*, meaning instruments that prevent one from the remembrance of Allah (ﷻ). Music is not food for the soul; on the contrary, it creates a hole in one's soul. It clouds the minds of the listener and takes him or her into a delusional state, far from the remembrance of Allah (ﷻ) — making the listener oblivious to the purpose of his creation on this earth. Allah (ﷻ) says:

﴿وَٱلشُّعَرَآءُ يَتَّبِعُهُمُ ٱلْغَاوُۥنَ ۝ أَلَمْ تَرَ أَنَّهُمْ فِى كُلِّ وَادٍ يَهِيمُونَ ۝ وَأَنَّهُمْ يَقُولُونَ مَا لَا يَفْعَلُونَ ۝ إِلَّا ٱلَّذِينَ ءَامَنُوا۟ وَعَمِلُوا۟ ٱلصَّٰلِحَٰتِ وَذَكَرُوا۟ ٱللَّهَ كَثِيرًا ... ۝﴾ (سورة الشُّعَرَاء: ٢٢٤-٢٢٧)

﴿And the poets — [only] the deviators follow them; do you not see that in every valley they roam and that they say what they do not do? Except those [poets] who believe and do righteous deeds and remember Allah often...﴾
(Qur'an 26: 224-227)

It is clear that singing and music are closely related to poetry; in fact, they are inseparable. Allah (ﷻ) has made it clear that the ones who follow the poets are people who have strayed from the right path. The only exception made by Allah (ﷻ) in the Qur'an are the poets who remember Allah (ﷻ) frequently, and we know that very few poets in the history of Islam fall under this category. Of course, there are no legal objections to Muslims practicing the art of poetry in defense of Islam and its values. In fact, Sultan Bahoo, the famous poet from the subcontinent, said in one of his poetic verses:

Whatever moments are spent in heedlessness (not remembering Allah) are spent in a state of disbelief in Allah.
This is the lesson taught to me by my spiritual teacher.

Poetry accompanied by musical instruments takes its listeners into a delusional state of heedlessness and invites them to a culture of permissiveness and liberalism. There is a clear link between music and behaviour, and then crime by extension, as shown in this book using scientific evidence.

In addition, most soft, romantic songs have lyrics that border on shirk, where the person who is the object of one's desire or love is put on a pedestal equal to or above Allah (ﷻ), and the person who is in love is constantly thinking of that person, thus turning away from Allah (ﷻ) and remembrance of Him. This takes a person's heart into a state of hypocrisy. Ibn al-Qayyim writes that one of the characteristics of such singing is that it:

distracts the heart and prevents it from contemplation and understanding of the Qur'an, and from applying it. Among the signs of hypocrisy is one's rarely remembering Allah (ﷻ) and one's laziness in rising to prayer, along with its poor performance.... A person's addiction to song peculiarly makes listening to the Qur'an a heavy weight upon his heart, hateful to his ears. If this is not hypocrisy, then hypocrisy has no reality.[32]

There are two types of memory: short term and long-term. As the name implies, short-term memory lasts for a shorter period of time than long-term memory. Converting short-term memory to long-term memory (a process known as coordination) requires rehearsal. This involves, among other things, repetition, rhyming, and emotional attachment to the incident or the message.

If we look at songs, we find that all these factors are available to make them a part of the long-term memory of a person. There is repetition in the lyrics of the songs, and there is rhyming as well. In addition, music arouses emotions in its listeners. Hence, music and songs become part of the long-term memory of a person who indulges in music. When the memory of a person is flooded with music and the lyrics of songs, it becomes hard for that person to contemplate the Qur'an and its message. It becomes hard for such a person to engage in remembrance of Allah (ﷻ) as mentioned in the Qur'an:

﴿يَـٰٓأَيُّهَا ٱلَّذِينَ ءَامَنُوا۟ ٱذْكُرُوا۟ ٱللَّهَ ذِكْرًا كَثِيرًا ۝﴾   (سورة الأحزاب : ٤١)

❨O you who have believed! Remember Allah with much remembrance.❩   *(Qur'an 33: 41)*

Dr. Bilal Philips is a Western convert to Islam and a contemporary Islamic scholar.[33] In one of his public speeches, Dr. Philips pointed out that when he accepted Islam in 1971, he learned about the prohibition of music, so he stopped listening to

---

[32] Ibn al-Qayyim, *Ighâthat ul-Lahfân min Maṣâ'id ash-Shayṭân.*

[33] See the next chapter for his detailed biography.

his record collection. When he used to invite non-Muslim friends to his house to tell them about Islam, he would sense that they felt uncomfortable having discussions with no music in the background. They found something amiss.

Actually, that is the trick of the Western society. Whether you are at work, shopping in a department store, or using a restroom, there is background music. It ensures that you are immersed in worldly pleasures and materialistic desires so that you neglect to remember Allah (ﷻ). It ensures that you do not have time to think about the purpose of your creation.[34] On the other hand, Allah (ﷻ) makes us think by addressing us:

(سورة التكوير : ٢٥-٢٦)   ﴾وَمَا هُوَ بِقَوْلِ شَيْطَانٍ رَجِيمٍ ۝ فَأَيْنَ تَذْهَبُونَ ۝﴿

❨And the Qur'an is not the word of a devil, expelled [from the heavens]. So where are you going?❩   *(Qur'an 81: 25-26)*

This question put forth by the Qur'an makes us remember that the purpose of our creation, our death and our life after death is different from the purpose depicted in the words of Satan, that is, music. The Qur'an is the word of Allah (ﷻ), whereas music is the word of Satan. Music is a delusion of this world, which paralyzes one's mind and does not let him or her think about the fundamental question, "So, where are you going?"

Music affects the bestial souls of human beings, not their angelic souls

Now let us have a philosophical examination of the idea that music is food for the human soul. First of all, we know that human

---

[34] Dr. Bilal Philips, *Silence*, audio recording of lecture in Saudi Arabia, n.d.

beings are made of two things: dust and soul. It is mentioned in various places in the Qur'an that our body is made from the soil of this earth. For example:

﴿وَمِنْ ءَايَـٰتِهِۦ أَنْ خَلَقَكُم مِّن تُرَابٍ ...﴾ (سورة الرُّوم: ٢٠)

﴿And among His signs is that He created you from dust...﴾

(Qur'an 30: 20)

Then Allah (ﷻ) sends an angel to blow the spirit into this material being, as He (ﷻ) mentions:

﴿فَإِذَا سَوَّيْتُهُۥ وَنَفَخْتُ فِيهِ مِن رُّوحِى فَقَعُوا۟ لَهُۥ سَـٰجِدِينَ﴾ (سورة صّ: ٧٢)

﴿So when I have proportioned him and breathed into him of My [created] soul, then fall down to him in prostration.﴾ *(Qur'an 38: 72)*

This soul blown into human beings is unique to humans; they do not share it with other living creatures on this planet. Allah (ﷻ) refers to the dual nature of human beings when He describes the creation of Adam (عليه السلام):

﴿قَالَ يَـٰٓإِبْلِيسُ مَا مَنَعَكَ أَن تَسْجُدَ لِمَا خَلَقْتُ بِيَدَىَّ أَسْتَكْبَرْتَ أَمْ كُنتَ مِنَ ٱلْعَالِينَ﴾ (سورة صّ: ٧٥)

﴿[Allah] said: O Iblees [Satan], what prevented you from prostrating to that which I have created with My Hands...?﴾

(Qur'an 38: 75)

The human body is made from the ingredients of this world, but the soul is blown into the body by an angel. A human being consists of both a body and a soul; he or she is at once a physical being and a spirit. The human body possesses desires similar to those of animals (such as hunger, thirst, and sexual urges), whereas the human soul strives for heavenly desires. It is due to the presence of the soul that a human being is regarded as the best of the creations of Allah (ﷻ). Thus, human beings are a combination of a celestial element (the spirit) and a terrestrial element (the body or flesh).

Islamic scholars make a second classification according to which the human being possesses not only the *rooḥ* (soul), but also a *nafs,* which is the type of soul present in animals as well as in human beings. Hence, humans have two souls, or spiritual powers, analogous to this dual nature. Shâh Waliullah Dehlavi, in his famous book *Hujjatullah al-Bâlighah*, writes that Allah (ﷻ) has given human beings two kinds of powers. One power is due to the higher, angelic soul, which exists only in humans; it urges humans to grow close to Allah, the Exalted, the Almighty, and to perform good deeds. The other power is due to the lower, animal or bestial soul, which urges them to perform acts that are unworthy of being a human. These two powers are always in conflict in the human being.[35]

It is mentioned in the Qur'an that Allah (ﷻ) has created everything in pairs:

﴿سُبْحَٰنَ ٱلَّذِى خَلَقَ ٱلْأَزْوَٰجَ كُلَّهَا مِمَّا تُنۢبِتُ ٱلْأَرْضُ وَمِنْ أَنفُسِهِمْ وَمِمَّا لَا يَعْلَمُونَ ۝﴾ (سورة يّس: ٣٦)

﴿Exalted is He who created all pairs — from what the earth grows and from themselves and from that which they do not know.﴾
(Qur'an 36: 36)

Allah (ﷻ) has endowed human beings with a dualistic nature, not only with respect to the body and soul but also with respect to

---

[35] Shâh Waliullah Muhaddith Dehlavi, *Hujjatullah al-Bâlighah* (Karachi: Darul Isha'at, n.d.).

a pair of souls (angelic and carnal). In describing the dualistic nature of human beings, Syed Muhammad Al-Naquib Al-Attas, a contemporary Islamic thinker, writes:

> Man also has two souls (*nafsân*) analogous to his dual nature: the higher, rational soul (*al-nafs al-nâtiqah*); and the lower, animal soul (*al-nafs al-hayawâniyyah*). When God proclaimed the reality of His Lordship to man, it is the rational soul that knows God. In order for man to fulfil his Covenant with God, to constantly confirm and affirm the Covenant within his total self so that it is enacted as action, as work (*'amal, i.e., with reference to 'ibâdah*) performed in obedience to God's Law (*i.e., the Sharia*), the rational soul must assert its supremacy and exert its power and rule over the animal soul, which is subject to it and which must be rendered submissive to it.[36]

Music affects this bestial or carnal soul of humans. The angelic soul of a human being is not affected by music (or, if anything, it is negatively influenced). If music were influencing only the angelic soul in humans, then animals would remain unaffected by music, but we know from everyday experience and observation that this is not the case. When songs are sung to camels, they are so powerfully affected that they start to run rapidly, bearing heavy burdens, until they fall down in a state of exhaustion. A cow produces more milk if music is played while it is being milked. Some owners of pig farms play music at their farms because in their experience, the pigs eat more food and become fatter when they listen to music. When a flute is played in front of a snake, it becomes mesmerized by the sound. Ibn al-Qayyim wrote:

---

[36] Muhammad Al-Naquib Al-Attas, *Islam and Secularism* (Delhi: New Crescent Publishing Company Company, 2002).

The thing which is activated and excited by listening to songs and music is the animal (carnal) soul, not the human soul or 'angelic soul.' What is presented as a proof of this (by Islamic scholars) is the influence on animals and birds when singing and music are played to them.[37]

Cure for the disease: listening to recitation of the Qur'an

People might ask, "If we quit listening to music, what would we replace it with?" In fact, listening to the recitation of the noble Qur'an is the best substitute and solution to this problem. As has been shown in the previous sections, music acts like a drug. In today's age of electronics, music can be regarded as a 'plug-in drug.' Addiction is associated with the use of any narcotic drugs, and music is no exception. When we stop listening to music, we may suffer from withdrawal symptoms, but listening to the recitation of the noble Qur'an provides a cure for them.

We must remember that human beings have a dualist nature: a terrestrial element as well as a celestial element. The angelic soul, which is centered in the heart, is on a continuous search for peace and tranquility. When people listen to music, which is not meant to be the food for the soul, it only keeps their souls engaged temporarily. As soon as the music or the song ends, they may be overcome with a feeling of emptiness.

The real tranquility for the angelic being (soul) comes from listening to the book of Allah (ﷻ), the Qur'an, which has a heavenly origin, similar to our soul. Recitation of the Qur'an is the

---

[37] Ibn al-Qayyim, *Ighâthat ul-Lahfân min Maṣâ'id ash-Shayṭân*, vol. 1.

true food for our soul. Listening to music deludes a person and shuts off his or her contemplating faculties, while listening to the Qur'an makes the person reflect upon the purpose of his or her creation. Allah (ﷻ) has made our hearts only for His remembrance. Recitation of the Qur'an has the power to cure the hearts which are addicted to music because the Qur'an is a healing for the diseases of the heart, as Allah (ﷻ) mentions:

﴿وَنُنَزِّلُ مِنَ ٱلْقُرْءَانِ مَا هُوَ شِفَآءٌ وَرَحْمَةٌ لِّلْمُؤْمِنِينَ...﴾ ﴿٨٢﴾ (سورة الإسراء : ٨٢)

❮And We send down of the Qur'an that which is a healing and a mercy for the believers...❯   *(Qur'an 17: 82)*

﴿يَٰٓأَيُّهَا ٱلنَّاسُ قَدْ جَآءَتْكُم مَّوْعِظَةٌ مِّن رَّبِّكُمْ وَشِفَآءٌ لِّمَا فِى ٱلصُّدُورِ وَهُدًى وَرَحْمَةٌ لِّلْمُؤْمِنِينَ﴾ ﴿٥٧﴾ (سورة يُونس : ٥٧)

❮O mankind, there has come to you instruction from your Lord [the Qur'an], and healing for what [disease] is in the breasts and guidance and mercy for the believers.❯   *(Qur'an 10: 57)*

Shaykh Anwar Shâh Kashmiri, the renowned Indian Islamic scholar of Hadith, stated the following on this issue:

> The person who is overwhelmed and captivated by music and singing and it becomes hard for him or her to quit music, as you have observed the singers that they are always humming a song, then if such people desire to refrain from music, for them Prophet Muhammad (peace be upon him) prescribed that they should attach themselves to the Qur'an. They should do much recitation of the Qur'an and delve into it so much they attain tranquility only from the Qur'an.[38]

---

[38] Maulana Anwar Shâh Kashmiri, *Faidhul Bâri*, vol. 4 quoted in Shafee, *Islam and Music*.

The beauty of recitation of the Qur'an is that reciters and listeners never get bored by it. Continual recitation of it increases its sweetness, and repetition of it makes one love it more. Music and singing do not possess this quality. People quickly become bored after listening to a certain kind of song or music, and then they search for other artists and songs, which is how the music industry survives. On the other hand, no Muslim ever gets bored by the Qur'an; it does not lose its freshness. A well-known saying describes this miraculous quality of the Qur'an:

> Scholars are not satiated by it, repetition does not wear it out, and its wonders do not end. Whoever recites it speaks the truth.

The highest expression of 'melodization' in Islam is the recitation of the Qur'an, which has dramatic effects upon its listeners. Commenting on the recitation of the Qur'an, Louisa Young, a British journalist and author, writes:

> The simple pulse, the beating of the drum of the heart, is the repetitive rhythm which leads and propels meditation — the voyage into the heart — in all religions.... One Muslim ritual is the recitation of the Qur'an; the flowing, hypnotic rhythm of the Arabic words has often been compared to the heartbeat. Grief caused by the separation from God is assuaged by remembering God: "Verily in the remembrance of Allah do hearts find rest." This remembrance is *dhikr* — remembrance, the mental and verbal repetition of a verse of the Qur'an or one of the names of God.[39]

The eminent English intellectual and convert to Islam, Mohammad Marmaduke Pickthall, in his much celebrated and famous English translation of the noble Qur'an, described the

---

[39] Louisa Young, *The Book Of The Heart* (New York: Doubleday, 2003).

recitation of the Qur'an as "the inimitable symphony, the very sound of which moves men to tears and ecstasy."[40]

In praising the beautiful rhythm and rhetoric of the Qur'an, Professor A.J. Arberry, another British intellectual and historian, wrote in his translation of the Qur'an:

> In making the present attempt... to produce something which might be accepted as echoing however faintly the sublime rhetoric of the Arabic Koran, I have been at pains to study the intricate and richly varied rhythms which — apart from the message itself — constitute the Koran's undeniable claim to rank amongst the greatest literary masterpieces of mankind.[41]

Mâlik Bennabi, the renowned Algerian Muslim intellectual, has the following to say about the influence of the unmatched rhythm of the Qur'anic verses on people during the time of Prophet Muhammad (ﷺ):

> Some testimonies of this period, which have been recorded by tradition, provide us with ample information concerning the irresistible charm which Qur'anic verses exerted on the Bedouin soul. 'Umar [ibn al-Khaṭṭâb] himself was converted under the effect of this charm, while al-Walid ibn al-Mughirah, who personified the eloquence of the literary pride of his period, expressed his opinion concerning the "magic of the Qur'an". Answering Abu Jahl who asked him about his opinion of it, he said, "What do I think of it? By God, I think there is nothing of its like... it is too majestic to be matched!"[42]

---

[40] Mohammad Marmaduke Pickthall, *The Meaning of the Glorious Qur'an: Text and Explanatory Translation,* ed. Arafat K. El Ashi (Maryland: Amana Publications, 1996).

[41] Arthur John Arberry, *The Qur'an Interpreted: A Translation* (New York: Touchstone, 1996).

[42] Mâlik Bennabi, *The Qur'anic Phenomenon: An Essay of a Theory on the=*

Jubayr ibn Mut'im, a polytheist from Makkah who had not embraced Islam yet, came to visit Madinah and said: «I heard the Prophet (ﷺ) reciting soorat aṭ-Ṭoor (the Mount) in the sunset prayer. When he reached the verse: ﴿Or were they created out of nothing, or were they the creators? Or did they create the heavens and the earth? Rather, they are not certain. Or have they the depositories [containing the provision] of your Lord? Or are they the controllers [of them]?﴾ *(Qur'an 52: 35-37)*, my heart practically flew to Islam.» (Bukhari)

The Qur'anic recitation has profound effects upon its listeners. Charles le Gai Eaton, a former British diplomat who embraced Islam in 1959, describes this quality of the Qur'anic recitation:

> For the listener the sound [of Qur'anic recitation] — and for the reader the script — have a profound transforming effect.... it could be said that there is an effect upon the regions of the personality which are in practice concealed from conscious thought or control.... Because the Qur'an is the divine Word (in which we ourselves originated) it is able to fill every crevice of our being and, in a sense, to replace the debris which previously filled that space with something of heavenly origin.[43]

The human heart and body are pacified and responsive to the recitation of the Qur'an.[44] Listening to the poetic words of the Qur'an chanted by a beautiful voice can bring about profound

---

=*Qur'an*, trans. Mohamed El-Tahir El-Mesawi (Kuala Lumpur: Islamic Book Trust, 2001).

[43] Charles Le Gai Eaton, *Islam and the Destiny of Man* (New York: The Islamic Texts Society, 1985).

[44] Mushtaq, *The Intelligent Heart, The Pure Heart: An Insight into the Heart based on Qur'an, Sunnah and Modern Science.*

effects upon its listeners. Qadi 'Iyad (died 1149 CE), the great Mâliki Islamic scholar from Muslim Spain, notes this miraculous aspect of the Qur'an in his famous biography of the Prophet Muhammad (ﷺ) titled *Ash-Shifa*:

> The believer continues to be terrified and in awe of it when he recites it [the Qur'an], and it attracts him and it brings him joy by his heart's inclination to it and confirmation of it.[45]

The effects of Qur'anic recitation on the believers are described in the Qur'an when it is said:

$$\text{﴿ ... جُلُودُ ٱلَّذِينَ يَخْشَوْنَ رَبَّهُمْ ثُمَّ تَلِينُ جُلُودُهُمْ وَقُلُوبُهُمْ إِلَىٰ ذِكْرِ ٱللَّهِ}$$
$$\text{... ﴿٢٣﴾}\qquad\text{(سورة الزُّمَر : ٢٣)}$$

﴿...The skins shiver therefrom of those who fear their Lord; then their skins and their hearts relax at the remembrance of Allah...﴾

(Qur'an 39: 23)

Similarly, Allah (ﷻ) also mentions:

$$\text{﴿لَوْ أَنزَلْنَا هَٰذَا ٱلْقُرْءَانَ عَلَىٰ جَبَلٍ لَّرَأَيْتَهُ خَٰشِعًا مُّتَصَدِّعًا مِّنْ خَشْيَةِ ٱللَّهِ}$$
$$\text{... ﴿٢١﴾}\qquad\text{(سورة الحَشر : ٢١)}$$

﴿If We had sent down this Qur'an upon a mountain, you would have seen it humbled and coming apart from fear of Allah...﴾

(Qur'an 59: 21)

Commenting on this verse, Qadi 'Iyad wrote:

> This indicates that this is something unique to it. It can even seize someone who has no understanding of its meanings and does not know its explanation. This was related about a

---

[45] Qadi 'Iyad Ibn Moosâ al-Yahsubi, *Muhammad Messenger of Allah* (Ash-Shifa of Qadi 'Iyad), trans. Aisha Bewley (Scotland: Madinah Press, 1991).

Christian who passed by someone reciting and he stopped and wept. He was asked, "Why are you weeping?" He said, "Because it has broken my heart and because of the beauty of its arrangement." This awe has seized many before Islam and after it. Some of them became Muslim the first moment they heard it, believing in it, while some of them rejected it.[46]

Qadi 'Iyad mentioned those words about nine hundred years ago. Recently, the effects of Qur'anic recitation on our bodies have been shown via scientific experiments conducted separately by two Muslim scientists in two different parts of the world. One study was conducted in 1984, and experiments are still going on at the Akbar Clinics, Panama City, Florida in the United States by Dr. Ahmed Elkadi, who is using the most sophisticated, state-of-the-art instruments in his research.

In the series of experiments conducted and published by Dr. Elkadi, three groups of volunteers — Muslims who understood Arabic, Muslims who did not understand Arabic and non-Muslims who did not understand Arabic — listened to recitation of the Qur'an while physiological parameters, such as their heart rate, blood pressure and muscle tension, were monitored.

The results of his study showed very clearly that listening to the recitation of Qur'an resulted in relaxation of smooth muscles, reduction of the heart rate, and all the physiological changes that indicate a release from stress and anxiety. These effects were produced among Muslims and non-Muslims both, regardless of whether or not they understood the Arabic language. Another important observation was that when verses promising rewards (verses of persuasion) were recited, there was more stress

---

[46] Ibid.

reduction (for example, more tranquility in the heart rate) among the listeners, whereas listening to verses promising punishment (verses of dissuasion) caused comparatively fewer stress-reducing effects on the listeners.[47] This study demonstrates the beneficial effects of Qur'anic recitation on the human heart and body.

Dr. Muhammad Khair al-Irgisoosi carried out a similar scientific study as part of his PhD research at the University of Khartoum, Sudan, under the supervision of the world-renowned Islamic psychologist Dr. Mâlik Badri. The subjects of this study were patients who suffered from hypertension due to stressful lifestyles or other reasons. The results of this study also showed that listening to the recitation of the Qur'an contributed significantly to lowering the blood pressure among the patients. In some cases, their doctors even told them to stop taking their medication because their blood pressure readings had returned to normal levels.[48] These research findings support the results of the research going on at Akbar Clinics in the U.S.

In the same vein, Dr. Mohammad Usman Najati, one of the most famous contemporary Islamic psychologists, has the following to say about the significance of recitation of the Qur'an, based on his clinical experience with patients:

> The recitation of the Qur'an is not only the best cure for restlessness and mental agitation due to the feelings of guilty conscience, but also it is the best treatment for all the

---

[47] Ahmed Elkadi, "Health and Healing in the Qur'an," in *Islamic Perspectives in Medicine – A Survey of Islamic Medicine: Achievements and Contemporary Issues*, ed. Shahid Athar, M.D. (Indianapolis: American Trust Publications, 1993).

[48] Mâlik Badri, *Contemplation: An Islamic Psychospiritual Study* (London: The International Institute of Islamic Thought, 2000).

psychological and mental disturbances as well as mental depression. The Prophet (ﷺ) treated neurosis of people with the Qur'an.[49]

It is not thus surprising to note that the Companions of Prophet Muhammad (ﷺ) used to recite the Qur'an with beautiful voices. In various hadiths, Prophet Muhammad (ﷺ) emphasized that the recitation of the Qur'an should be done in the best natural voice possible. He said: «Beautify the Qur'an with your voices.» (recorded by Abu Dâwood and graded as sound by al-Albâni)

In another hadith, the Prophet (ﷺ) is reported to have said: «He who does not recite the Qur'an while beautifying it with his voice is not from among us.» (Bukhari)

In one hadith, al-Barâ' ibn 'Âzib reported: «A man was reciting soorat al-Kahf (the Cave), and there was a horse beside him, tied with two ropes. As he was reciting, a cloud overshadowed him, and as it began to come nearer and nearer, the horse began to trample violently. The man came to the Messenger of Allah (ﷺ) in the morning and mentioned the incident to him. The Prophet (ﷺ) said: That was tranquility, which descended as a result of the recitation of the Qur'an.» (Muslim)

We can easily understand from the above discussion that if we get these benefits from just listening to the Qur'an, then there will be even more benefits when we apply the Qur'an to our lives. We should not reduce the Qur'an to being merely a ceremonial book, to be used on special occasions for attaining blessings but not used as the code for our lives. The Companions of the Prophet Muhammad (ﷺ) used to apply every verse of the Qur'an to their

---

[49] Mohammad Usman Najati, *Hadeeth and Ilm un-Nafs* (Lahore: Al-Faisal Publishers and Traders, n.d.).

character. We too need to understand and apply the Qur'an to our lives. Lastly, we must remember that recitation of the Qur'an is not only aesthetically pleasing to our nature, but it also calms our hearts. As Allah (ﷻ) mentions:

﴿ ... أَلَا بِذِكْرِ ٱللَّهِ تَطْمَئِنُّ ٱلْقُلُوبُ ۝ ﴾   (سورة الرّعد : ٢٨)

❨...Unquestionably, by the remembrance of Allah hearts find rest.❩
(Qur'an 13: 28)

Chapter 7

Music and Society

"One quick way to destroy a society is through its music."
(Vladimir Lenin, 1870-1924 CE)

The older the disease, the deeper the roots of the disease in the body. Music is such a disease; it attacked the Muslim nation after the end of the rule of the Rightly-guided Caliphs. At that time, the immune system of the Muslim nation was strong, so the disease of music and singing affected only a small portion of the nation. Today, however, 1400 years later, when the defense system of the body of Muslims has weakened, this disease has spread into the whole body of Muslims, with the exception of a minority of pious Muslims. Today many Muslims have become so addicted to music that they cannot live without this 'entertainment.' They want to amuse themselves to death with music.

In the recent past, Muslims remained colonized by the European imperial powers for about two hundred years. Now, although Muslim countries are politically free, the effect of the post-colonial trauma has not faded from the minds of many Muslim inhabitants.

Today the moral decline of Muslims has reached such an extent that many think of listening to music as permissible, and they label as 'extremists,' 'fundamentalists' or 'mullahs' those Muslims who consider music to be forbidden. They do not realize that they themselves may actually hold views that could be called extreme, since the Muslims who consider music to be ḥarâm are actually on the middle path. Dr. Muhammad Iqbal wrote about such a situation in one of his poetic verses, which can be translated as follows:

What was inappropriate has slowly become appropriate,
The conscience of nations is changed in slavery.

(Kulliyat-e-Iqbal)

The only reason that some Muslims consider music to be permissible in Islam is due to the glare in their eyes from the prevalence and omnipresence of music in modern society. In these circumstances, deviant behaviour is practiced in the society to such an extent that people begin to consider it a norm. Their ability to distinguish between right and wrong becomes desensitized due to the powerful effect of their environment. We should remember that having a majority does not create truth. There is much reality in the oft-quoted saying, "One on God's side is a majority." Allah (ﷻ) tells us:

﴿قُل لَّا يَسْتَوِى ٱلْخَبِيثُ وَٱلطَّيِّبُ وَلَوْ أَعْجَبَكَ كَثْرَةُ ٱلْخَبِيثِ فَٱتَّقُوا۟ ٱللَّهَ يَـٰٓأُو۟لِى ٱلْأَلْبَـٰبِ لَعَلَّكُمْ تُفْلِحُونَ ۝﴾ (سورة المَائدة: ١٠٠)

﴿Say: Not equal are the evil and the good, although the abundance of evil might impress you. So fear Allah, O you of understanding, that you may be successful.﴾ *(Qur'an 5: 100)*

﴿وَإِن تُطِعْ أَكْثَرَ مَن فِي ٱلْأَرْضِ يُضِلُّوكَ عَن سَبِيلِ ٱللَّهِ إِن يَتَّبِعُونَ إِلَّا
ٱلظَّنَّ وَإِنْ هُمْ إِلَّا يَخْرُصُونَ ﴾ ١١٦ (سورة الأنعَام: ١١٦)

﴿And if you obey most of those upon the earth, they will mislead
you from the way of Allah. They follow nothing but assumption,
and they are not but falsifying.﴾   *(Qur'an 6: 116)*

Today some 'brave' Muslims have taken it one step further;
they are trying to prove that listening to music is in fact part of
Islam, and that it is an act of virtue. The Prophet Muhammad (ﷺ),
with the deep vision bestowed upon him as a prophet, described
this phenomenon of changing the criteria that differentiate evil
from good: «There were, before you, some of the children of
Israel who, if any one of them committed a sin, they would tell
him to stop doing the sin and make excuses for him. The [sinner
would persist, and the] next day they would sit with him, and eat
and drink with him as if they had not seen him sinning the day
before. When Allah (ﷻ) saw this, he sealed their hearts (and
cursed them) by the tongue of David and of Jesus, son of Mary.
﴿That was because they disobeyed and [habitually] transgressed.﴾
(Qur'an 5: 78) By the One Who has my soul in His hand, you will
enjoin what is good and right and forbid what is evil and wrong,
and you must take the sinner by the hand and lead him to the truth,
or Allah (ﷻ) will seal your hearts little by little and curse you like
he cursed them.» (recorded by al-Haythami with a sound chain)

There is a deep sociological understanding of human societies
presented in this hadith. The Prophet Muhammad (ﷺ) was quite
aware that in human societies which do not follow divine
revelation, the criterion of deviance and norm is relative. The
concept of 'deviation' does not have the same meaning in
Sociology as it does in the Qur'an. According to sociologists,

actions that offend 'conventional' norms (the normal ways of behaving in society) are deviant, but the criteria of deviance (wrong) and norm (right) are relative. In other words, when good is prevailing in a society, it is considered the norm, and evil is considered deviant; if evil becomes the predominant practice in a society, then evil is considered the norm in that society, and the good is regarded as deviant. In truth, though, the Qur'an and Sunnah present the absolute standards of right and wrong.

In this hadith, Prophet Muhammad (ﷺ) was telling his Companions that a time would come when the actual criterion of good and evil in society would be turned upside down. The hearts of Muslims would become accustomed to the evils of society, to the point that any acts of righteousness would be perceived as deviance. That is happening in the Muslim societies today because some Muslims have turned their backs on the absolute criterion of right and wrong given to them in the Qur'an. Due to the prevalence of music in society, many Muslims incorrectly believe that listening to and playing music and songs is not a sin. In accordance with the above-mentioned hadith, some Muslims even make desperate attempts to use the Qur'an to prove that music is permissible in Islam.

Sadly enough, some of the modernist Muslims do not even hesitate to cite the scriptures of other religions to serve their own purpose of proving that music is allowed in Islam. As the Prophet Muhammad (ﷺ) said in an authentic hadith narrated by Abu Sa'eed al-Khudri: «You will surely follow in the ways of those before you, inch by inch and step by step, so much so that if they were to enter the hole of a lizard, you would follow them. The Companions asked: O Messenger of Allah, (do you mean) the Jews and the Christians? He replied: Who else?» (Muslim)

Furthermore, we find that the whole world is obsessed with a satanic version of freedom — a concept of freedom in which all people should be free to do or say anything they wish, with no concern for the effect on other individuals, on their families, or on the society as a whole. In many schools and universities, we observe that an extreme concept of independence, free expression and secular thinking is encouraged. This idea of freedom unconstrained by social or moral conscience, of "It's my life, I'll do what I want," is a predominant, underlying theme of today's music. It is being used as a means for drilling ideologies that are totally contrary to Islamic Sharia and values into the minds of Muslims. We should try to avoid mimicking those Western values that are against our religion. Prophet Muhammad (ﷺ) warned us against the imitation of non-Muslims when he said: «Whoever imitates a people (nation) is one of them.» (recorded by Abu Dâwood and Aḥmad, and graded as sound by al-Albâni)

Commenting on this hadith, Mohammad Asad, a famous Austrian convert to Islam, writes in his book *Islam at the Crossroads*:

This well known hadith is not only a moral hint, but also an objective statement which lays down the inevitability of Muslims' being assimilated by any non-Muslim civilization they imitate in its external appearance.

Music and the life history of nations

If we look at the role of music in different societies over the course of history, we will notice that music and singing comprise one of the oldest and most classical weapons of Satan against human beings. When Satan was ordered by Allah (ﷻ) to bow down before Prophet Adam (ﷺ), he refused:

﴿وَإِذْ قُلْنَا لِلْمَلَٰئِكَةِ ٱسْجُدُوا۟ لِءَادَمَ فَسَجَدُوٓا۟ إِلَّآ إِبْلِيسَ قَالَ ءَأَسْجُدُ لِمَنْ خَلَقْتَ طِينًا ٦١﴾ (سورة الإسراء: ٦١)

﴿And [mention] when We said to the angels, "Prostrate to Adam," and they prostrated, except for Iblees. He said, "Should I prostrate to one You created from clay?"﴾   *(Qur'an 17: 61)*

Then Satan requested that Allah (ﷻ) give him respite and keep him alive until the Day of Judgment, so that he could misguide all the descendants of Adam (ﷺ) except a few.

﴿قَالَ ٱذْهَبْ فَمَن تَبِعَكَ مِنْهُمْ فَإِنَّ جَهَنَّمَ جَزَآؤُكُمْ جَزَآءً مَّوْفُورًا ٦٣ وَٱسْتَفْزِزْ مَنِ ٱسْتَطَعْتَ مِنْهُم بِصَوْتِكَ وَأَجْلِبْ عَلَيْهِم بِخَيْلِكَ وَرَجِلِكَ وَشَارِكْهُمْ فِى ٱلْأَمْوَٰلِ وَٱلْأَوْلَٰدِ وَعِدْهُمْ وَمَا يَعِدُهُمُ ٱلشَّيْطَٰنُ إِلَّا غُرُورًا ٦٤﴾ (سورة الإسراء: ٦٣-٦٤)

﴿[Allah] said, "Go, for whoever of them follows you, indeed Hell will be the recompense of you — an ample recompense. And incite [to senselessness] whomever you can among them with your voice, and assault them with your horses and foot soldiers, and become a partner in their wealth and their children and promise them." But Satan does not promise them anything except delusion.﴾   *(Qur'an 17: 63-64)*

This last verse is one of the verses cited by Imam Qurtubi in his tafseer as a proof of the prohibition of music. Moreover, as shown in Chapter 1, some of the commentators from the generation of the tâbi'oon, such as Mujâhid, Ḥasan al-Baṣri and Ḍaḥḥâk regarded Satan's 'inciting' humans to mean his use of music, song and amusement.

A student of history knows very well that there is a profound relationship between music and the life history of nations. History tells us that there is a direct proportionality between the decline of a nation and the prevalence of lewd art and music in the society. Vladimir Lenin, who was the co-founder of Communism, the first dictator of the Soviet Union and one of history's greatest experts on subversion and revolution, said: "One quick way to destroy a society is through its music."[1]

In describing the life history of nations and the factors resulting in their decline, Muslim poet Dr. Muhammad Iqbal writes:

> The life-history of nations shows that when the tide of life in a people begins to ebb, decadence itself becomes a source of inspiration, inspiring its poets, philosophers, saints, statesmen, and turning them into a class of apostles whose sole ministry is to glorify, by the force of a seductive art or logic, all that is ignoble and ugly in the life of their people.[2]

This reality is also summed up very succinctly in a couple of Iqbal's poetic verses:

Let me tell you about the fate of nations.
It starts with the swords and the spears.
And there are musical instruments in the hands of its people
when the nation is on its decline.[3]

---

[1] David A. Noebel, *The Marxist Minstrels: A Handbook on Communist Subversion of Music* (American Christian College Press, 1974).

[2] Dr. Sir Muhammad Iqbal, *Islam and Ahmadism* (Lahore: Sh. Muhammad Ashraf, 1980).

[3] Dr. Sir Muhammad Iqbal, *Bang-e-Dara* (Lahore: Shaykh Ghulam Ali and Sons, 1987).

One contemporary Muslim musician recently told his audience that the reason he was using a guitar in his musical shows was due to the fact that the guitar was invented by Muslims in Spain. Actually, it is not clear whether or not this is true, but even if we assume it to be historically correct, we have to see what happened to Muslims in Spain. After ruling Spain for 800 years, those Muslims suffered such a humiliating defeat, massacre and exodus from Spain that Islamic history can offer very few examples to match such a calamity. The Muslims of Spain forgot the purpose of their creation. They abandoned the lifestyle of the Companions of the Prophet (ﷺ) and indulged heavily in music and entertainment. As a consequence, those Muslims paid a heavy price for their heedlessness and indulgence in music when the Christians of Spain butchered them. Today, Muslims in Spain are mostly history, as well as a lesson for the later generations of Muslims.

When the fall of a nation begins, it resembles a huge sinking ship like the Titanic, on which the band keeps on playing songs while it is sinking, because the people playing the music are in a delusional state. The question to ask is: "Does it seem appropriate that a group of people are dancing on the deck of a sinking ship?" Anyone with a sound intellect would be surprised to see that.

Unfortunately, the study of history also tells us that people do not learn from the past; they tend to be deceived by Satan again and again, making the same mistakes. It was for this reason that Spanish-born American philosopher George Santayana said in his much-celebrated quote: "Those who do not remember the past are condemned to repeat it."

Debate in the royal court of Delhi:
Who is the best woman dancer?

In 1739 CE, Nadir Shâh Durrâni, king of Afghans, laid siege to Delhi, which was the capital of the Moghul Muslim Empire. While the capital was under siege, there was a debate going on about a 'very important' issue in the royal court of Muhammad Shâh Rangela, the Moghul king of that time. The question was whether a female singer named Jadan Baai was the best dancer, or whether it was another woman named Kamla Devii. The ruling elite and the society were so obsessed with music and singing that they did not even realize that death was hovering over their heads. When King Nadir Shâh conquered Delhi after a few days of siege, his soldiers killed thousands and thousands of Muslims in Delhi and raped hundreds of Muslim women.[4]

Emperor Wâjid 'Ali Shâh's fondness for music

Wâjid 'Ali Shâh (1827-1887 CE) was a Muslim ruler of Oudh, a state in India. He was deeply fond of music and dancing. He used to play the tambourine or hand-drum with his own hands; only when he got tired would he give it to his Prime Minister Naqi Ali to play.[5] It is clear what happens when a ruler puts away the sword and holds hand-drums instead. On the 31st of January 1856 CE, the British conquered the Islamic state of Oudh, and Wâjid 'Ali Shâh was sent to prison, where he may have had plenty of

---

[4] Dr. Shabbir Aḥmad, *Dastak* (in Urdu) (Florida).

[5] Maulana Abul-Kalâm Azad, *Ghubâr-e-Khatir (Emotions of the Heart)* (Lahore: Islamic Publishing House, 1982).

time to play musical instruments, sing and dance. An Arab poet has rightly said:

When a father plays the drum,
don't blame his children for dancing.[6]

Lessons from biographies of singers and musicians who died without repentance

When we look at the lives of singers, actors and artists, we notice that in many cases, their lives are filled with corruption that is far beyond our imagination. Their self-destructive lifestyles include abuse of narcotics, sexual permissiveness, alcoholism, nihilism, hedonism, insubordination and anarchism. Many of them die in unpleasant circumstances. In fact, many of them commit suicide or suffer premature deaths caused by accidents that occur while they are under the influence of drugs. They lead the worst lives, degraded to the levels of animals, because Allah ( ) and His Messenger ( ) have cursed those professions.

The Dutch painter Van Gogh committed suicide because the art to which he had devoted his life could not give him any true happiness or mental peace. Michelangelo, who was the creator of the statue of David, and who painted religious pictures on the walls of the Sistine Chapel, in the Pope's residence in the Vatican, was noted for his love for men. Michelangelo's homoeroticism is apparent in his poetry.

The German philosopher and poet, Friedrich Nietzsche (1844-1900 CE), considered music to be so essential to human life that it

---

[6] See the Appendix for the Arabic wording of the poetic verse.

could make life worth living. He regarded music as an attempt to give form and beauty to the dark, chaotic forces in the soul — to make them serve a higher purpose.[7] Nietzsche loved music so much that he made it equivalent to religion. On the other hand, Nietzsche hated God so much that he declared that "God is dead."[8] The fact of the matter is that God is still alive, and He (﷾) will always be alive. Nietzsche, however, died in 1900 CE after remaining permanently insane for the last ten years of his life.

The musical genius Ludwig von Beethoven was so arrogant that people could not stand his rude behaviour. He had several romantic attachments with women, but none was successful, and he never married. Problems in his life led him to contemplate committing suicide. The classical composer Mozart had an early death at the age of thirty-five.

The despair and emotional disturbance in the life of musical genius Elvis Presley can be seen from the fact that he died as a result of an overdose of a combination of drugs. Many other music stars died because of drug abuse, including Brian Jones of the Rolling Stones, Dennis Wilson of the Beach Boys, Sid Vicious of the Sex Pistols, Jimi Hendrix, Jim Morrison of The Doors, folk musician Tim Hardin and pop and R&B singer Frankie Lymon. Similarly, many traditional music singers in Muslim countries died due to excessive intake of alcohol.

Why is this so? The reason for the corrupt lives and the tragic, premature deaths of many singers and artists is that Allah (﷾) and His Messenger (ﷺ) have prohibited all such professions which

---

[7] Nietzsche, *The Birth of Tragedy and The Case of Wagner*.

[8] Friedrich Nietzsche, *Thus Spoke Zarathustra: A Book for All and None* (New York: Modern Library, 1995).

spread vice and corruption in the society. The Qur'an tells us about the fate of such people in no unclear terms:

$$﴿إِنَّ ٱلَّذِينَ يُحِبُّونَ أَن تَشِيعَ ٱلْفَٰحِشَةُ فِي ٱلَّذِينَ ءَامَنُوا۟ لَهُمْ عَذَابٌ أَلِيمٌ فِي ٱلدُّنْيَا وَٱلْءَاخِرَةِ وَٱللَّهُ يَعْلَمُ وَأَنتُمْ لَا تَعْلَمُونَ ۝﴾$$

(سورة النُّور: ١٩)

❨Indeed, those who like that immorality should be spread [or publicized] among those who have believed will have a painful punishment in this world and the Hereafter. And Allah knows and you do not know.❩   *(Qur'an 24: 19)*

People who engage themselves in sowing the seeds of corruption through seductive art and music ultimately harm only themselves. They choose to forget their Creator and Lord, so Allah (ﷻ) makes them forget their own selves by immersing them in sex, drugs and rock and roll. In the words of the Qur'an:

$$﴿وَلَا تَكُونُوا۟ كَٱلَّذِينَ نَسُوا۟ ٱللَّهَ فَأَنسَىٰهُمْ أَنفُسَهُمْ أُو۟لَٰٓئِكَ هُمُ ٱلْفَٰسِقُونَ ۝﴾$$

(سورة الحَشر: ١٩)

❨And be not like those who forgot Allah, so He made them forget themselves. Those are the defiantly disobedient.❩ *(Qur'an 59: 19)*

Chapter 8

It is Never Too Late —
Inspiring Stories from History

" $\mathcal{T}$ he only difference between the saint and the sinner is that every saint has a past, and every sinner has a future."

(Oscar Wilde)

If we look at the style of the Qur'ân, we notice that one of the ways it presents its message is through narration of real stories. The Qur'an itself is a narrative. One of the reasons for this is that a story can convey a message in a simple form, whereas it may be hard to convey the same message in the form of dry exposition. Human beings need stories from which they can draw meanings for their life. Another reason is that a story is a part of history, and the Qur'ân tells us to learn from history. Allah (ﷻ) says:

(سورة الأعرَاف: ١٧٦) ﴿فَٱقۡصُصِ ٱلۡقَصَصَ لَعَلَّهُمۡ يَتَفَكَّرُونَ ١٧٦﴾

﴿...So relate the stories, that perhaps they will give thought.﴾

(Qur'an 7: 176)

In this chapter, we relate some inspiring true stories having to do with music. These stories of conversion and moral revival are mentioned in order to clarify that according to Islamic teachings, it is never too late to mend our ways. The door of repentance is wide open until we are in the throes of death, as the Prophet (ﷺ) said: «Allah (ﷻ) accepts the repentance of His servant as long as death has not reached his collarbone.» (a reliable hadith recorded by Tirmidhi)

If someone has committed evil deeds but has repented sincerely and changed his or her life around for the better, then Allah (ﷻ) has certainly promised to grant them mercy and forgiveness. Our history is filled with glittering examples of those who made sincere repentance to Allah (ﷻ), their Creator, as will be shown in this chapter. Repentance is the most noble and beloved form of obedience in the eyes of Allah (ﷻ). He loves those who repent. It is because of His love for His creation that He tests them with sins, so that He may shower His blessings and favours upon them after they repent. In several places in the Qur'an, Allah (ﷻ) tells human beings to repent:

$$﴿ ۞ قُلْ يَـٰعِبَادِىَ ٱلَّذِينَ أَسْرَفُوا۟ عَلَىٰٓ أَنفُسِهِمْ لَا تَقْنَطُوا۟ مِن رَّحْمَةِ ٱللَّهِ ۚ إِنَّ ٱللَّهَ يَغْفِرُ ٱلذُّنُوبَ جَمِيعًا ۚ إِنَّهُۥ هُوَ ٱلْغَفُورُ ٱلرَّحِيمُ ۝ ﴾ (سورة الزُّمَر: ٥٣)$$

❨Say: O My servants who have transgressed against themselves [by sinning], do not despair of the mercy of Allah. Indeed, Allah forgives all sins. Indeed, it is He who is the Forgiving, the Merciful.❩   *(Qur'an 39: 53)*

$$﴿ يَـٰٓأَيُّهَا ٱلَّذِينَ ءَامَنُوا۟ تُوبُوٓا۟ إِلَى ٱللَّهِ تَوْبَةً نَّصُوحًا عَسَىٰ رَبُّكُمْ أَن يُكَفِّرَ عَنكُمْ سَيِّـَٔاتِكُمْ وَيُدْخِلَكُمْ جَنَّـٰتٍ تَجْرِى مِن تَحْتِهَا ٱلْأَنْهَـٰرُ ... ۝ ﴾$$

(سورة التَّحْريم: ٨)

{O you who have believed, repent to Allah with sincere repentance. Perhaps your Lord will remove from you your misdeeds, and admit you into gardens beneath which rivers flow [paradise]...}

(Qur'an 66: 8)

True repentance turned a sinner into a scholar — the story of Zazân the Tâbi'i

Shaykh 'Abdul-Qâdir Jilâni narrates an interesting incident that occurred during the time of Abdullah ibn Mas'ood ( ), the noble Companion of Prophet Muhammad ( ):

One day Abdullah ibn Mas'ood was passing by a town near the city of Kufa [in Iraq]. In one house, there was a gathering of corrupt people who were busy drinking alcohol in a party. A musician named Zazân was playing the flute and singing in his beautiful voice. When Abdullah ibn Mas'ood heard his voice, he said: "What a sweet-sounding voice it is. I wish this voice would have been used in the recitation of the Qur'an."

After saying those words of advice, Abdullah ibn Mas'ood put a cloak on his head and went on. Zazân overheard Ibn Mas'ood's words and asked his friends in the party, "Who was that person?" They told him, "That person is a famous Companion of the Prophet Muhammad ( ), and he said it because he heard your voice." Upon hearing that, Zazân went into a strange spiritual state. He broke all his musical instruments, went straight to Abdullah ibn Mas'ood and started crying. Ibn Mas'ood hugged him and started to cry himself and then said: "Why should I not love that person who has repented from playing his musical instruments and whom Allah loves?"

After repenting, Zazân became a disciple of Abdullah ibn Mas'ood and learned the Qur'an and Islamic knowledge from him. Later, he became an Islamic scholar and an authority of his age in the Islamic sciences.[1]

Turning point in the life of a genius — Imam Mâlik ibn Anas

Imam Mâlik belonged to a family of scholars. His father Anas was an Islamic scholar, as were three of his paternal uncles. As a child, Imam Mâlik used to play with pigeons, which he kept as pets. He had a beautiful voice and was inspired to become a singer when he grew up. However, there was a turning point in his life. His older brother Nadhar ibn Anas was a great Islamic scholar who was quite famous in the city of Madinah. At that time, nobody knew Imam Mâlik. One day, Anas (Imam Mâlik's father) addressed a question about Islamic jurisprudence to both of his sons, Nadhar and Mâlik. Imam Mâlik could not answer the question, but Nadhar answered it correctly. His father said to Mâlik: "Playing with pigeons has destroyed you." Imam Mâlik later narrated this incident and said that when he heard that reply, he became angry and jealous of his brother. His sense of competition was ignited. He went to Ibn Hurmuz and studied Islamic sciences with him for seven years.

There was another incident that contributed equally as a turning point in Imam Mâlik's life. When he was young, Imam

[1] 'Abdul-Qâdir Jilâni, *Ghaniyat uṭ-Ṭalibeen* (Karachi: Nafees Academy, 1989). Also Muwaffaq ad-Deen Ibn Qudâmah, *Kitâb ut-Tawwâbeen* (Karachi: Darul Isha'at, 1999).

Mâlik told his mother about his ambition to become a singer in the future. His mother did not scold him, but in a very gentle and loving manner, she told him: "My son, you do not have the looks of a singer; therefore, you cannot become a singer." Upon hearing that, Imam Mâlik decided to study Islamic sciences to become an Islamic scholar.[2]

Advice of 'Umar ibn 'Abdul-'Aziz to the teacher of his sons

Muslim Caliph 'Umar ibn 'Abdul-'Aziz (died 101 AH) is regarded as the fifth Rightly-guided Caliph, due to his sense of justice and fear of Allah (عزّ وجلّ). He was not very religious in his early life because he was born into a royal family. The environment in which he was raised was filled with music and singing, and he had access to all the pleasures of life that a person could imagine. No one in the royal family could compete with 'Umar in wearing fashionable clothes, and when he was appointed governor of Madinah in 87 AH, there were thirty camels needed just to carry his personal belongings.

When he was appointed Caliph of the Muslim nation in 99 AH, that event proved to be a major turning point in his life. He abandoned the luxurious life in which he had indulged, and he became the epitome of a humble, pious, God-fearing and just ruler. The extent of his piety can be recognized by the fact that when he died, the Christian king of Rome paid him a tribute by calling him a person who is a reincarnation of Jesus Christ (عليه السلام).

---

[2] Dr. Hesham Al-Awadi, *The Four Great Imams* audio CD (California: Awakening, 2004).

While saying those words, tears were coming from the king's eyes.[3]

Due to his upbringing in a royal family, Caliph 'Umar ibn 'Abdul-'Aziz was quite aware of the harms and pernicious effects of music and singing. When he sent his sons to their teacher Sahal, 'Umar wrote him a letter of advice, in which he emphasized:

> The first concept you would want to instill into these children through your teaching is to hate the instruments of music. The beginning of musical instruments is from Shayṭân and their end is with the wrath of Allah. I have heard from authentic scholars that going to the places with musical instruments, listening to songs and to be fond of them fosters hypocrisy in the heart, very much like water promotes the growth of grass. I swear that it is easier for a wise person not to go to such places and be safe from their pollution as compared to having hypocrisy strengthened in his heart (and then trying to find cure for it).[4]

'Umar ibn 'Abdul-'Aziz did not restrict his commands to his sons; he made no concession to his Muslim subjects either. He sent an order to all his governors:

> Those non-Arab people entertain themselves with those things which Satan has made attractive in their eyes. You should stop your Muslim subjects from those objects. By Allah, now time has come that people must stop those things after getting the knowledge of the commandments from the Book of Allah.

---

[3] Abâd Shah Puree, *Bright Stars of Preaching and Forbearance* (in Urdu) (Lahore: Al-Badar Publications, 1991).

[4] Jalâl ud-Deen as-Suyooṭi, *Tafseer Dur Al-Manthoor*, quoted in Shafee, *Islam and Music*.

Therefore, you must forbid them from indulging in frivolous activities and music and singing. If they do not stop, you may give them punishment.[5]

Dr. Bilal Philips — Journey from nightclub guitarist in Toronto to PhD in Islamic fiqh

Allah (ﷻ) says in the Qur'an:

﴿يَٰٓأَيُّهَا ٱلَّذِينَ ءَامَنُوا۟ تُوبُوٓا۟ إِلَى ٱللَّهِ تَوْبَةً نَّصُوحًا عَسَىٰ رَبُّكُمْ أَن يُكَفِّرَ عَنكُمْ سَيِّـَٔاتِكُمْ وَيُدْخِلَكُمْ جَنَّٰتٍ تَجْرِى مِن تَحْتِهَا ٱلْأَنْهَٰرُ ... ﴿٨﴾﴾

(سورة التَّحْريم: ٨)

《O you who have believed, repent to Allah with sincere repentance. Perhaps your Lord will remove from you your misdeeds, and admit you into gardens under which rivers flow [paradise]...》 *(Qur'an 66: 8)*

The door of repentance is open for anyone. There are some individuals who carry out exemplary repentance, and Dr. Bilal Philips from Canada is one such example. After embracing Islam in 1971, he went to Saudi Arabia and received his Bachelor of Arts in *Uṣool ad-Deen* (the principles of the religion) from the Islamic University of Madinah in 1979, then his Master of Arts in Islamic Theology from the University of Riyadh. After teaching Islamic studies to high school students in Riyadh from 1979 to 1987, he went to the University of Wales and completed his PhD in Islamic Studies there.

---

[5] Abu Abdullah Muhammad Ibn Sa'd, *Kitâb at-Tabaqât al-Kabeer* (New Delhi: Kitab Bhavan, n.d.).

At one of his lectures, a group of youths asked Dr. Philips to comment on the position of music in Islam and to give a personal example of how he was involved in music in the past and how he stopped. Dr. Philips told them that he not only used to listen to music but also played music — different types of rock music. During the 1970s, he played the guitar and sang with a group in a nightclub in Toronto. After he became Muslim, no one told him right away about the prohibition of music in Islam, so he continued to play in the nightclubs of Toronto and Vancouver. Dr. Philips told the Muslim youth:

> After becoming Muslim, I found while in the nightclub as if I were in a different world. The other members of my music group were all taking drugs, and in the nightclub everybody was 'high' on something, and I was the only one who was sane there. There was no way I could be part of it, so by myself I decided to stop it. I sold all my equipment and my records. I got rid of it, and later on I found out by studies that according to Islamic teachings, music is ḥarâm.[6]

Dr. Bilal Philips reminded the Muslim youth that music has a very strong effect on its listeners. It can be overwhelming and addictive. The effect is so strong that people can recall in an instant a song that they heard several years ago. The whole song is still there, with all its words, because it has taken a spot in the heart of its listener. Eventually, music and singing fill up the heart, and it becomes extremely difficult for its listener to reflect on the Qur'an, because the Qur'an and music cannot coexist and occupy the same space.

---

[6] Dr. Bilal Philips, *Discussion with the Youth,* audio recording of lecture in Riyadh, Saudi Arabia, n.d.

Dr. Philips also emphasized that the effects of music on its listeners can be very subtle and slow. People think that music is not affecting them because they are only listening to music during study or as a pastime, but if we keep on feeding data into any system, the effects start to show up, albeit slowly. Dr. Philips advised the young Muslims to keep the company of pious people, because we can easily get sucked back into the corrupt life if we hang around people who listen to music all the time. He also said:

> So for a Muslim to get away from it means getting rid of all the records and CDs, because you cannot keep these things around you and say, "I am going to stop," because any time you feel the desire, you can listen to it. Try to remove the obvious products, which can trap you.[7]

Egyptian female singers turn to religion in repentance

The world of music and media looks extremely dazzling and alluring from the outside. The fame and glamour associated with this world, and the competition to attain them, can make a person lose his or her sanity. The music and film industries are portrayed as eye-catching and attractive through the seductive power of media, but they are awfully dark when seen from the inside. The bleak and depressing side of this field often goes unrecognized because many who enter this black hole get lost and never return. However, there are some blessed souls who have managed to escape from the darkness of the music industry and who have decided to lead the lives of true Muslims. Recently an interesting

---

[7] Philips, *Discussion with the Youth.*

phenomenon has occurred in Egypt, where an increasing number of celebrities have appeared on television and radio shows to announce their decision to leave fame behind and devote themselves to God.

One of those celebrities is the former Egyptian dancer Sahar Hamdi, who has shunned the limelight and decided to live a quiet, peaceful life as a 'revert to God.' Hamdi's decision to quit the music industry was the result of a battle between two extremes — an endless internal struggle that resulted in a complete moral and physical transformation.

Sahar Hamdi is not the only one who has said farewell to music. In the 1980s, a religious wave hit as several singers and actresses dropped out of the music and movie businesses and became devout Muslims. *Lâ Tazlemu An-Nisâ'* (Don't Blame the Women) star Hanna Tharwat, singer Yasmin Al-Khayyam, popular belly dancer Zizi Moustafa, along with dancers Hala Al-Safi and Sahar Hamdi, were among the women who made repentance to Allah (ﷻ) for their past.[8]

Those film actresses, singers and dancers in Egypt have made it a custom that whenever another woman from the media repents and joins them, they organize a program in honour of the newcomer, in which they recite the noble Qur'an together and welcome the new guest into their circle. All these women collectively listen to the lectures of different Islamic scholars to learn about Islamic teachings.[9] The decision of this generation of

---

[8] Summer Said, "Egyptian Celebrities Turn to Religion." *Arab News,* March 29, 2005. Accessed November 1, 2010. http://archive.arabnews.com/?page=9&section=0&article=61269&d=31&m=3&y=2005.

[9] Mâlik 'Abbâs Akhtar Awân, *Film Actresses and Singers under the Shadow of the Qur'an* (Lahore: Azaan-e-Sehr Publishers, 2006).

celebrities to abandon artistic circles and devote their lives to serving Islam was in part due to the influence of Egypt's famous shaykh, Muhammad Mutwalli Ash-Shârawi. In his lectures, Ash-Shârawi urged such women to quit their careers and focus more on worshipping God.

This phenomenon did not end in the 1980s, thanks also to two popular young preachers: Amr Khaled from Egypt and Shaykh Al-Habib ibn Ali from Yemen. It seems that many actresses were listening to the sermons of such scholars.[10] The list of stars who left the entertainment industry for a more pious life is not limited to Egyptian female singers. Lebanese female singers Arooba and Nehad Fatooha are also among those who have left the profession of music and adopted an Islamic life. Veteran singer Yasmin Al-Khayyam was asked if she was surprised that so many of them had made the decision to repent in just a short period of time. She replied, with a voice immersed in faith: "We are surprised if a child leaves its mother's lap in anger. However, if the same child returns back into its mother's lap, why would we be amazed?"[11]

Most of the celebrities who have become religious never make any more public appearances. They stay out of the spotlight, instead dedicating their lives and time to lecturing and teaching others about Islam.

Junaid Jamshed — Former pop star chooses the path of Allah

Junaid Jamshed, born in 1964, is a famous former Pakistani pop singer. He was the lead singer of the first ever Pakistani pop

---

[10] Said, "Egyptian Celebrities Turn to Religion."

[11] Awân, *Film Actresses and Singers under the Shadow of the Qur'an.*

band, Vital Signs, which peaked in 1987 with the release of their signature song *Dil Dil Pakistan*. When the group split up in 1995, Junaid went on to pursue a solo career. In fact, Junaid Jamshed was the first pop star on the Pakistani music scene. At the height of his career, he turned his back on the world of glitz and glamour and devoted himself to Islam. In the year 2003, he ended his career as a pop star to lead a more spiritual life. Junaid recalled the turning point in his life in his search for inner peace, which was in October 1997 when he went with a friend to invite others to Islam. That was the time when, in his words, he realized what a big mistake his whole life had been and that he needed to change.[12]

It took another five years before Jamshed reached the conclusion that his career was not compatible with Islam. On August 14, 2003, he finally bid farewell to the world of pop music, but it was a difficult decision for Jamshed because music was not just his passion but also his career and only source of livelihood. However, his strong faith in Allah (ﷻ) rescued him. After embarking on his journey to religious enlightenment and leaving the music business, Jamshed launched a highly successful fashion chain under his name. In ten cities across Pakistan, consumers can shop in Junaid Jamshed boutiques for traditional clothing, alcohol-free perfumes and shoes. In the very short time of two and a half years, his business grew by leaps and bounds even though Jamshed did not have a background in business.

When Jamshed announced his decision to depart from the music industry, there was a huge outcry. The music world was shocked and bemused at the news. His fans mourned the loss of

---

[12] "Biography", accessed November 23, 2010,
http://www.jjamshed.com/biography/.

their favourite singer. In Junaid Jamshed's words:

> Initially most people thought I was mad. It was hard for them
> to take, as I was telling them that everything that I had done
> was not right.[13]

Now seen with a long beard and wearing the *shalwar kameez*,
Pakistan's traditional dress, Jamshed has the appearance of an
Islamic scholar and, in fact, he is quickly progressing in that
direction. He explains why it was essential for him to leave pop
music:

> Islam does not permit music, especially the way it is done these
> days, and the money that you earn from it is ḥarâm (not
> permitted). It was not the kind of life I wanted to lead.[14]

He says of the day when he declared that his career in pop
music was over:

> I was very sad because music was in my blood and under my
> skin and the only thing I was used to. But, I also wanted to
> please Allah — I did not want to be someone who was written
> in his bad books.[15]

In another interview given to Mâlik Akhtar 'Abbâs Awân, the
editor of *Khwateen* magazine, Jamshed expressed the feelings of
guilt he used to have when he was at the peak of his musical
career. He said:

> When I was singing on the stage, I used to think that the girl
> dancing in front of me is certainly a sister or a daughter to

---

[13] Ibid.

[14] Ibid.

[15] Ibid.

someone and what am I making those daughters of the Ummah of Prophet Muhammad (ﷺ) do? Such girls will not give birth to personalities such as Muhammad ibn Qassim and Salah ud-Din Ayyubi. Today our Muslim nation does NOT need singers and musicians. Instead, our Muslim Ummah needs such great leaders as Muhammad ibn Qassim, Khalid ibn Walid, Dharâr ibn Azoor, Abu Ubaida ibn Jarrah. Such great personalities are born from the wombs of pious and God-fearing mothers who observe ḥayâ', modesty and shame.[16]

Junaid Jamshed gave up his musical career at the pinnacle of fame to pursue a new direction in life. Before, music was his passion; now Islam is his life. He is fully dedicated to spreading the message of Islam to humanity, and he has made it clear that he has no regrets over his decision:

In the early part of my life, I used to invite people to something which was against the religion of Allah, and now I call them towards Allah and ask them to fulfil what he wants them to do. I do not miss my previous lifestyle in show business. My new life is simple and pure. I have a strong conviction that if we bring into our life the commandments of Allah and the way His beloved Prophet (ﷺ) performed them, our life can become blissful even in this world. Life in this world is temporary. We all need to realize this before it is too late.[17]

---

[16] Awân, *Film Actresses and Singers under the Shadow of the Qur'an.*
[17] Ibid.

Shaykh Yusuf Estes —
From music business to Islamic preaching

American Muslim convert Shaykh Yusuf Estes was born into a very devout Christian family in the Midwest region of the United States. His family and his ancestors built many churches and schools across the U.S. In 1949, while he was in elementary school, his family relocated to Houston, Texas. During his youth, he became very interested in different types of music, especially Gospel and classical music. Because his whole family was religious and musical, it followed that he too would begin his studies in both areas. In many of the churches with which he became affiliated over the years, it was logical that he be given the role of Music Minister.

Being a talented musician due to his education and experience, Shaykh Yusuf Estes started teaching keyboard musical instruments in 1960. By the year 1963, he owned his own studios in Laurel, Maryland, called Estes Music Studios. Shaykh Estes and his father owned other businesses, including Estes Music Company and Estes Piano & Organ Co. He and his father used to establish music stores, television and radio programs and outdoor entertainment for fun and profit, but their primary target was to sell musical instruments across the country. He was also a member of the NAAMM (National Association of American Music Manufacturers).[18]

Estes was in the music industry for many years. Then, in 1991, he had the opportunity to have an Arab Muslim businessman,

---

[18] Shaykh Yusuf Estes, e-mail message to author, 2006.

Muhammad, as a guest at his home. Shaykh Estes had many doubts about Islam that he had picked up from the media, but Muhammad clarified all his doubts. Eventually, Shaykh Estes embraced Islam, along with his wife and children as well as his parents. After becoming a Muslim, he studied the Islamic sciences very diligently. Presently, he is the National Muslim Chaplain for American Muslims, sponsored by a number of organizations in Washington, DC, especially concentrating his efforts in the institutional areas such as military, universities and prisons. In addition, he travels around the world sharing the message of Islam.

Conclusion

"Oh! Music is music, and Islam is Islam,
And never the twain shall meet."

Now that this book has reached its completion, it is hoped that the arguments presented to the readers from the Qur'an, hadiths and rulings of Islamic scholars, all prove that music is prohibited in Islam except under limited circumstances. The subject of music is not a controversial issue in Islam. If there is a tiny minority of scholars who permit listening to music, this does not make this difference of opinion an acceptable one. The tolerable difference is where there is room for ijtihâd, and this occurs only when the difference of opinion is a major one. This is obviously not the case for music, as nearly all the scholars throughout the Islamic history have agreed that listening to music is forbidden. It must also be stressed here that we are discussing scholars in plural form, and Allah (ﷻ) has granted protection against errors in their collective opinion and direction.

It is also important to understand that it is possible for individual scholars to err, but not the majority of scholars together. Once we understand this fact, we should not wonder why a scholar would oppose such a vast majority of the scholars. The more important question to ask is: How can the vast majority of Islamic scholars be wrong in considering musical instruments to be forbidden?

We must know that many scholars declared a consensus on the prohibition of musical instruments. Some of the Islamic scholars believed that listening to musical instruments gives birth to hypocrisy in the heart. As noted earlier, Imam Mâlik said: "Here, in fact, that is done only by the sinful ones."

It is interesting to note that Imam Mâlik lived from the years 93 AH to 179 AH in Madinah, the abode of the Companions of the Prophet Muhammad (ﷺ). This means that Imam Mâlik's espoused opinion was in fact a Madinan opinion, which reflected a consensus among the people of Madinah, thereby being a source of legislation.[1]

It has been shown in this book that music deludes people and diverts their attention from Allah (ﷻ). For this reason, Islam has forbidden not only playing music but also listening to it. It is similar to the prohibition on alcohol and drugs, which also affect the intellect. Music acts like an intoxicant by making one forget his or her surroundings and become unaware of what is happening.

The prevalence of music and singing on such a large scale is one of the signs of the end of time. Music acts as a barrier (*rân* in the Qur'anic terminology) between Allah (ﷻ) and humans. As a consequence, people forget their Creator and the real purpose of their life in this world, which is clearly mentioned in the Qur'an:

(سورة الذَّارِيَات : ٥٦)   ﴿وَمَا خَلَقْتُ ٱلْجِنَّ وَٱلْإِنسَ إِلَّا لِيَعْبُدُونِ ۝﴾

﴿And I [Allah] did not create the *jinn* and mankind except to

---

[1] Al-Haddad, "Music: A Simple Matter of Disagreement?" Consensus is considered a source of Islamic law. In the Mâliki madh-hab, this refers to the consensus of the people of Madinah in the early years of Islam. [Editor]

worship Me [Alone].❩   *(Qur'an 51: 56)*

Hypocrisy, vice, neglect and a host of other evils can sprout in the hearts of those who listen to music and singing. This results first in a diseased heart and ultimately in a spiritually deceased heart. Music is not food for the soul; on the contrary, it is cancerous for the soul. Listening to music and singing consumes time, money and energy, and it creates *rân*, or rust, in the hearts of the listeners. Music arouses passions in its listeners, opens the door to temptations, leads them towards sin, excites their animal instincts and dulls their spirituality. Worst of all, it confuses their minds and diverts them from thinking through the really important questions about their existence — the purpose of everyone's lives: to worship the Almighty Allah (ﷻ) and to strive for our target destination after death, which is paradise.

Using scientific evidence, this book has also shown in great detail that musical lyrics do much more than go 'in one ear and out the other.' Music can take people to a stage where their intellect ceases to function altogether, where they become slaves to their emotions. It is not religion but music that is the opium of people. Music creates imbalance in human faculties, constricts spiritual development and destroys ethical values. It is among the factors that boost human emotions and arouse the sensual powers beyond their natural limit, while inducing the angelic element of the human personality to sleep. It acts as a ladder to adultery and drug abuse because it makes shame and modesty disappear in its listeners. Music can intensify and change emotional states due to its immense power, which is why it is used in the mass media as a means of mass manipulation. Nowadays there is no need for brutal force to rule people. Music alone can be utilized to create mass delusion of the worst kind.

The power of music is contained in its ability to bypass reason, penetrating straight into the emotions and the subconscious, to manipulate a person's feelings. Music makes emotions dominant over the intellect because it appears to have great emotional significance in the lives of many people. Music has the ability to influence moods, to remind us of certain moments and to create feelings. Music conveys information with semantic and emotional elements. In some cases, people claim that their relationship to music is far more important to them than their relationship with any other human being.[2]

The social scientific research presented in this book makes it clear that music has a domineering influence on the worldview and on the sexual and violent behaviour of youth. There appears to be a relationship between the messages that adolescents and young adults consume from music and the way they perceive the world around them. In fact, music can affect their lifestyles, psychosexual development, fashion, culture and relationships with their parents. In addition, the music and the artists form a consistent package with which many youth identify strongly. Music encourages young girls and boys to live in a dream world of romance, which paralyzes them and prevents them from facing the real challenges of life.

The indulgence of Muslims in music is not just a disease; it is one of the symptoms of a plague that is infecting them — a plague consisting of love of the world and love of the self. It is a consequence of the detachment of Muslims from the Qur'an and

---

[2] John A. Sloboda, "Empirical Studies of Emotional Response to Music," in *Cognitive Bases of Musical Behaviour*, edited by M. R. Jones and S. Holleran (Washington, D.C.: American Psychological Association, 1992).

Sunnah. Today, those Muslims who claim to be modernists, and who apologetically try to present a 'modern' Islam to the non-Muslims, have to reconsider their assumptions. They have to stop looking at the world through colonized eyes, in which the only form of entertainment is music and movies.

Even if the majority of people in a society are committing an evil, this does not justify and rationalize that evil act. This fact has convinced many prominent musicians and singers of the present age, who have accepted Islam, to leave this corrupt profession, as shown in the previous chapter.

As Muslims, Allah (ﷻ) has bestowed on us the recitation of the Qur'an, which is a better alternative than music. We need not stray in search of things that may soothe our hearts because we know that reading and listening to the Qur'an can pacify our hearts. When we listen to the recitation of the Qur'an, we will not have the feelings of emptiness afterwards.

The last part of this book is meant for those Muslims who are immersed in music but who may want to rectify themselves and evolve spiritually. Their condition is not hopeless. The door of repentance to Allah (ﷻ) is always open. They can sincerely repent to Allah (ﷻ) by starting to follow His commandments holistically, and eventually they may become glittering examples of piety and spirituality for the later generations. I would like to end this book with these eye-opening words from a converted Muslim sister, Yvonne Ridley:

> Quite frankly, I really don't know how anyone in the Ummah [Muslim nation] can really let go and scream and shout with joy at pleasure domes when there is so much brutality and suffering going on in the world today. The rivers of blood flow

freely from the veins of our brothers and sisters from across the Muslim world. Screaming and shouting the names of musical heroes drown out the screams coming from the dungeons of Uzbekistan where brothers and sisters are boiled alive in vats of water. How many will jump up and down and wave their arms in the air, shouting wildly for justice for our kin in Kashmir, Afghanistan, Chechnya, Palestine, and Iraq.... Oh, Muslims, wake up! The Ummah is not bleeding; it is hemorrhaging. Listen not to what is ḥarâm. Listen to the pain of your global family.[3]

---

[3] Ridley, "Pop Culture in the Name of Islam."

Bibliography

Islamic Sources

'Abdul-Ghaffar, Hasan. "Islam and Music" [in Urdu]. *Meesâq,* January 2003.

'Abdul-Ḥaqq, Mohammad Muhaddith Dehlavi. *Sharah Safr-us-Sa'adah.* India: Munshi Nol Kishore, 1875.

Abu Dâwood, Imam Sulayman as-Sijistâni. *Sunan Abu Dâwood.* Lahore: Islamic Academy Urdu Bazaar, 1984.

Aḥmad, Dr. Shabbir. *Dastak* [in Urdu]. Florida.

Al-Albâni, Muhammad Nâṣir ad-Deen. *Ṣaḥeeḥ al-Jâmi' aṣ-Ṣagheer wa Ziyâdatih.* 3rd ed. Beirut: Al-Maktab al-Islâmi, 1988.

———. *Ṣaḥeeḥ Sunan Abu Dâwood.* 1st ed. Beirut: al-Maktab al-Islâmee, 1989.

———. *Taḥreem Alât at-Tarab* (Arabic) [The Prohibition of Musical Instruments]. Egypt: Maktaba Ad-Daleel, 1996.

Al-Muttaqi, Shaykh 'Ali al-Hindi. *Kinz ul-Ummâl fee Sunan al-Aqwâl wal Af'âl.* 5th ed. Beirut: Mo'assisa ar-Risala, 1401 AH.

Aloosi, Maḥmood ibn Abdullah. *Rooḥ al-Ma'âni fee Tafseer al-Qur'ân al-'Adheem was-Sab' al-Mathâni.* Beirut: Dar al-Fikr, 1983.

Arberry, Arthur John. *The Qur'an Interpreted: A Translation.* New York: Touchstone, 1996.

Asad, Muhammad. *Islam at the Crossroads.* Lahore: Sh. Muhammad Ashraf Publishers, 1991.

Al-Attas, Muhammad Al-Naquib. *Islam and Secularism.* Delhi: New Crescent Publishing Company, 2002.

Al-Awadi, Dr. Hesham. *The Four Great Imams.* California: Awakening, 2004. 13 audio CDs.

Awân, Mâlik 'Abbâs Akhtar. *Film Actresses and Singers under the Shadow of the Qur'ân* [in Urdu]. Lahore: Azân-e-Sehr Publishers, 2006.

————. *Media Celebrities under the Shadow of the Qur'ân* [in Urdu]. Lahore: Azân-e-Sehr Publishers, 2006.

Azad, Maulana Abul-Kalâm. *Ghubâr-e-Khatir (Emotions of the Heart).* Lahore: Islamic Publishing House, 1982.

Badri, Malik. *Contemplation: An Islamic Psychospiritual Study.* London: The International Institute of Islamic Thought, 2000.

Baghawi, Imam Abu Muhammad al-Husayn. *Ma'alim at-Tanzeel.* Egypt: Mat'bâ Al-Minâr, 1347 AH.

Baig, Khalid. *Slippery Stone: an Inquiry into Islam's Stance on Music.* Garden Grove, CA: Open Mind Press, 2008.

Bayhaqi, Imam Abu Bakr Ahmad. *Sunan al-Kubrâ.* Edited by Muhammad 'Abdul-Qâdir Ata. 11 vols. Beirut: Dar al-Kutub al-'Ilmiyah, 1423 AH/2003 CE.

Bayhaqi, Imam Abu Bakr Ahmad. *Shu'ab al-Eemân.* 1ˢᵗ ed. Beirut: Dar al-Kutub al-Ilmiyah, 1415 AH.

Bennabi, Mâlik. *The Qur'ânic Phenomenon: An Essay of a Theory on the Qur'ân.* Translated by Mohamed El-Tahir El-Mesawi. Kuala Lumpur: Islamic Book Trust, 2001.

Bukhari, Imam Muḥammad Ismâ'eel. *Ṣaḥeeḥ al-Bukhari.* 8 vols. India: Markazi Jamiat Ahle Hadeeth Hind, 2004. (Urdu translation by Mohammad Dawood Râz.)

Dhahabi, Ḥâfidh Shamsud-Deen. *Mizânul E'tidâl.* Cairo: Dar al-Iḥyâ' Kutub al-'Arabiyya, 1382 AH.

Eaton, Charles Le Gai. *Islam and the Destiny of Man.* New York: The Islamic Texts Society, 1985.

Elkadi, Ahmed. "Health and Healing in the Qur'an". In *Islamic Perspectives in Medicine — A Survey of Islamic Medicine: Achievements and Contemporary Issues,* edited by Shahid Athar, M.D. Indianapolis: American Trust Publications, 1993.

Farid, Ahmad, comp. *The Purification of the Soul.* U.K.: Al-Firdous Publications Ltd., 1989.

Al-Ghazâli, Imam Abu Ḥâmid. *Iḥyâ' 'Uloom ud-Deen.* Karachi: Darul Isha'at Publishers, 1978.

Al-Haddad, Haytham bin Jawwad. "Music: A Simple Matter of Disagreement?" Accessed June 01, 2007. http://ww.islamicawakening.com <http://www.islamicawakening.com>.

Al-Hâkim, Imam. *Mustadrak.* Hyderabad (Deccan): Dairatul Ma'ârif an-Nizamiyya, 1342 AH.

Al-Haythami, Ibn Ḥajar al-Makki. *Kaff ar-Ra'â' 'an Muḥarramât al-Lahwa was-Samâ' (Prohibiting People from the Forbidden Distractions and Singing).* Egypt: Shirka' Maktaba wa Mat'ba

Mustafa Al-Bâbi al-Halabi wa Awlâduhu, 1370 AH.

Al-Haythami, Ḥâfiḏẖ Noor ad-Deen 'Ali bin Abu Bakr. (735-807 AH) *Majma az-Zawâid*. Beirut: Dar al Kitâb, 1967.

Ibn 'Abdul-Hâdi, Ḥâfiḏẖ Shams ud-Deen Abu Abdullah Al-Maqdisi Al-Ḥanbali. *Tabaqât Ulamâ al-Ḥadeeth*. Beirut: Al-Resalah Publishing House, 1996 CE/1417 AH.

Ibn Ḥajar al-'Asqalâni. *At-Talkhees al-Habeer*. Madinah: Syed Abdullah Hashim al-Yamani al-Madni, 1384 AH.

Ibn Ḥajar al-'Asqalâni. *Lisânul Mizân*. Edited by Shaykh 'Abdul Fattah Abu Ghuddah. Beirut: 1423 AH/2002 CE.

Ibn Ḥanbal, Aḥmad. *Al-Musnad*. Edited by Aḥmad Shakir and Hamza Razin. 20 vols. Cairo: Dârul Ḥadeeth, 1995.

Ibn Kathir, Ḥâfiḏẖ Abul-Fida Imad ud-Deen. *Tafsir Ibn Kathir* (English translation) (Jeddah: Darussalam Publishers, 2000)

Ibn Sa'd, Abu Abdullah Muhammad. *Kitâb at-Tabaqât al-Kabeer*. New Delhi: Kitab Bhavan.

Ibn Taymiyah, Shaykh ul-Islam. *Majmoo' al-Fatâwa*. Riyadh: Mat'ba ar-Riyadh, 1381 AH.

Ibn Taymiyah, Shaykh ul-Islam. *Risâlah Waj'd wa Samâ'*. Lahore: Al-Hilal Book Agency, 1365 AH.

Iqbal, Dr. Sir Muhammad. *Bang-e-Dara*. Lahore: Shaykh Ghulam Ali and Sons, 1987.

Iqbal, Dr. Sir Muhammad. *Islam and Ahmadism*. Lahore: Sh. Muhammad Ashraf, 1980.

Iqbal, Dr. Sir Muhammad. *The Reconstruction of Religious Thought in Islam*. New Delhi: Kitaab Bhavan, 1994.

Iyad, Qadi Ibn Moosâ al-Yahsubi. *Muhammad Messenger of Allah* (Arabic title: *Ash-Shifa*). Translated by Aisha Bewley. Scotland: Madinah Press, 1991.

Al-Jasâs, Imam Abu Bakr. *Aḥkâm ul-Qur'ân*. Egypt: Al-Mat'bâ Al-Bahia, 1347 AH.

Jilâni, 'Abdul-Qâdir. *Ghuniyatu Ṭâlibeen*. Karachi: Nafees Academy, 1989.

Al-Kanadi, Abu Bilal Mustafa. *The Islamic Ruling on Music and Singing*. Jeddah: Abul-Qasim Bookstore, 1986.

Keller, Shaykh Nuh Ha Mim. "Is Listening to the Recorded Music Permissible?" http://www.sunnipath.com/Resources/Questions/QA00004456.aspx.

Keller, Shaykh Nuh Ha Mim. *Reliance of the Traveller* Maryland: Amana Publications, 1994. (English translation of Aḥmad ibn Naqib al-Misri's *'Umdat as-Sâlik wa 'Uddat an-Nâsik*).

Mâlik, Imam. *Muwaṭṭa Imam Mâlik*. Lahore: Islamic Academy Urdu Bazaar, 1402 AH.

Al-Mas'oodi, Maḥmood ibn Abdullah. "The First Ghinâ' among the Arabs." In *Murooj adh-Dhahab*. Beirut: Dar El-Marefah, 2005.

Al-Muḥâsibi, Ḥârith ibn Asad. *Risâlah al-Mustarshideen*. Halb: Maktab al-Matboo'at al-Islamiya, 1383 AH.

Al-Munâwi, Zayn ad-Deen 'Abdur-Ra'uf ibn Taj al-Arifeen (d. 1031 AH). *Fayd al-Qadeer Sharḥ Jâmi' aṣ-Ṣagheer*. Mat'bâ Mustafa Mohammad, 1938.

Murtaza Zabidi, Syed Abul-Faidh ibn Muhammad al-Ḥussaini (d. 1205 AH). *Ithâf Sâdatul Muttaqeen*. Egypt: Al-Mat'bâ al-

Maimanah, 1311 AH.

Mushtaq, Gohar, PhD. *The Intelligent Heart, The Pure Heart: An Insight into the Heart based on Qur'ân, Sunnah and Modern Science.* London: Ta-Ha Publishers, 2006.

Muslim, Imam Abul-Ḥasan ibn al-Ḥajjâj. *Ṣaḥeeḥ Muslim.* Lahore: Khalid Ihsan Publishers, 1981.

an-Nabulsi, 'Abdul-Ghani. *Iḍâḥ ad-Dalâlat fee Samâ' al-Âlât* (Explaining the Arguments for Listening to Instruments). Damascus: 1302 AH.

Najati, Mohammad Usman. *Ḥadeeth and Ilm un-Nafs.* Lahore: Al-Faisal Publishers and Traders, n.d.

Al-Khatib, Muhammad ash-Shirbini and Imam Yahya ibn Sharaf Nawawi. *Mughni al-muhtaj ila ma'rifa ma'ani alfaz al-Minhâj* (Nawawi's *Minhâj aṭ-Ṭalibeen* with al-Khatib's commentary printed below it). 4 vols. 1933/1353 AH. Reprint. Beirut: Dar Iḥyâ' at-Turath al-'Arabi, n.d.

Philips, Dr. Bilal. *Discussion with the Youth.* Audio recording of a lecture in Riyadh, Saudi Arabia: n.d.

———. *Silence.* Audio recording of a lecture in Saudi Arabia: n.d.

———. *Usool at-Tafseer: The Methodology of Qur'aanic Explanation.* Sharjah: Dar Al Fatah, 1997.

Pickthall, Mohammad Marmaduke. *The Meaning of the Glorious Qur'an: Text and Explanatory Translation.* Edited by Arafat K. El Ash. Maryland: Amana Publications, 1996.

Puree, Abâd Shâh. *Bright Stars of Preaching and Forbearance* [in Urdu]. Lahore: Al-Badar Publications, 1991.

Qadi Abu Bakr. *Aḥkamul Qur'an*. Egypt: Al-Matbâ' al-Bahiya, 1347 AH.

Qurtubi, Imam Abu Abdullah Muhammad ibn Aḥmad al-Anṣâri. *Al-Jâmi' li-Aḥkam al-Qur'ân*. Beirut and Egypt: Darul-Kutub Al-Misriyah, 1953.

Ridley, Yvonne. "Pop Culture in the Name of Islam." Last modified April 24, 2006. http://www.islamicawakening.com/viewarticle.php?articleID=1261.

Sâd, Abu. *Playing and Listening to Music and Singing: In Light of Qur'ân and Sunnah* (in Urdu). Karachi: Dar-ut-Taqwa, 2003.

Shafee, Mufti-Mohammad. *Islam and Music*. Edited by Mohammad 'Abdul-Mu'izz. Karachi: Maktaba Darul Uloom, 2002.

Shâfi'i, Imam Mohammad ibn Idrees. *Kitâb al-Umm*. Egypt: Maktaba al-Kulliyât al-Azhar, 1381 AH.

Shawkani, Qadi Mohammad ibn Ali. *Nayl al-Awtâr*. Lahore: Dost Associate Publishers, 2000.

Sirhindi, Shaykh Aḥmad Farooqi. *Maktubât Mujaddid Alf Thâni* (Collected Letters). Translated by Syed Zawwar Hussain Shâh. Karachi: Idara Mujaddadia, n.d.

Suhrawardi, Shaykh Shahâb ud-Deen. *'Awârif al-Ma'ârif*. Beirut: Darul Kitâb Al-'Arabi, 1966.

as-Suyooṭi, Imam Jalâl ud-Deen. *Al-Khasâis ul-Kubrâ*. Lahore: Maktaba A'la Hadhrat, 2003.

as-Suyooṭi, Imam Jalâl ud-Deen. *Jâmi' aṣ-Ṣagheer*. Egypt: Shirkah Maktaba wa Mat'ba Mustafa Al-Bâbi al-Halabi wa Awlâduhu, 1358 AH.

aṭ-Ṭabari, Abu Ja'far Muhammad ibn Jarir. *Jâmi' al-Bayan Fi Ta'wil ayi'l Qur'an.* Beirut: Dar al-Kutub al-'Ilmiyah, 1992.

Tirmidhi, Imam Abu 'Iesa. *At-Tirmidhi.* Lahore: Zia ul Ihsan Publishers, 1988.

Usmani, Justice Muhammad Taqi. *Islâh-e-Muashara* (in Urdu) (Reform of Society). Karachi: Maktaba Dar ul-'Uloom, 1998.

Waliullah, Shâh Muhaddith Dehlavi. *Hujjatullah al-Bâlighah.* Karachi: Darul Isha'at, n.d.

General Sources

Ankenberg, Frank and John Weldon. *The Facts on Rock Music.* Eugene, Oregon: Harvest House Publishers, 1992.

Baxter, R.L., C. De Riemer, A. Landani. "A Content Analysis of Music Videos." *Journal of Broadcasting and Electronic Media* 29 (1985): 333-340.

Beck, A.T., R.A. Steer, M. Kovacs and B. Garrison. "Hopelessness and Eventual Suicide." *American Journal of Psychiatry* 142 (1985): 559-563.

Bloom, Allan. *The Closing of the American Mind.* New York: Simon and Schuster, 1987.

Bly, Robert. *The Sibling Society.* New York: Addison-Wesley Publishing Company, 1996.

Brand, E.A. *Modern Supermarket Operation.* New York: Fairchild Publications, 1963.

Brown, E.F. and W.R. Hendee. "Adolescents and their Music: Insights into the Health of Adolescents." *The Journal of the American Medical Association* 262 (1989): 1659-1663.

Bryden, P., R. Ley and J. Sugerman. "A Left-ear Advantage for Identifying the Emotional Quality of Tonal Sequences." *Neuropsychologia* 20 (1982): 83-87.

Bullerjahn, C. and M. Guldenring. "An Empirical Investigation of Effects of Film Music using Qualitative Content Analysis." *Psychomusicology* 13 (1994): 99-118.

Cacioppo, J. T. and W. L. Gardner. "Emotion." *Annual Review of Psychology* 50 (1999): 191-214.

Capps, Pamela Marsden. "Rock on Trial: Subliminal Message Liability." *Columbia Business Law Review 27 (1991).*

Chalfant, Paul, and Robert Beckley. "Beguiling and Betraying: The Image of Alcohol Use in Country Music." *Journal of Studies on Alcohol* 38 (1977): 1428-1433.

Chepesiuk, Ron. "Decibel Hell: The Effects of Living in a Noisy World." *Environmental Health Perspectives* 113, no. 1 (January 2005): A35-A41.

Christenson, Peter G. and P. DeBenedittis. "Eavesdropping on the FM Band: Children's Use of Radio." *Journal of Communication* 36, no. 2 (1986): 27-38.

Christenson, P.G., and Donald F. Roberts. *It's Not Only Rock and Roll: Popular Music in the Lives of Adolescents.* Cresskill, NJ: Hampton Press, 1998.

Clayman, Charles B., MD, ed. *The American Medical Association Home Medical Encyclopedia: An A-Z Reference Guide to over 5000 Medical Terms.* New York: Random House, 1989.

Cohen, Annabel J. "Music as a Source of Emotion in Film." In *Music and Emotion: Theory and Research,* edited by Patrik N.

Juslin and John A. Sloboda, 249-272. New York: Oxford University Press, 2001.

Cole, R. "Top Songs in the Sixties." In *Mass Communication and Youth: Some Cultural Perspectives*, edited by F. Gerald Kline and P. Clarke. Beverly Hills, CA: Sage Publications, 1971.

Damasio, Antonio. *Descartes' Error: Emotion, Reason and the Human Brain*. New York: Quill Publishers, 1994.

Darwin, Charles. *The Descent of Man, and Selection in Relation to Sex*. London: John Murray, 1871.

DuRant, R.H., E.S. Rome, M. Rich, E. Allred, S.J. Emans, and E.R. Woods. "Tobacco and Alcohol Use Behaviors Portrayed in Music Videos: A Content Analysis." *American Journal of Public Health* 87 (1997): 1131-1135.

Gabrielsson, A. "Experiencing music." *Canadian Journal of Research in Music Education* 33 (1991): 21-26.

Galizio, M. and C. Hendrick. "Effect of Musical Accompaniment on Attitude: The Guitar as a Prop for Persuasion." *Journal of Applied Social Psychology* 2 (1972): 350-359.

Geller, B. and Greydanus, D.E. "Aggression in Adolescents: Aspects of Pathogenesis." *Journal of Adolescent Health Care* 1, no. 3 (1981): 236-243.

Girardeau, John L. *Instrumental Music in the Public Worship of the Church*. Richmond, VA: Whittet and Shepp, 1888.

Goldstein, Avram. "Thrills in Response to Music and Other Stimuli." *Physiological Psychology* 8, no. 1 (1980): 126-129.

Gore, Tipper. *Raising PG Kids in an X-rated Society*. Nashville: Abingdon Press, 1987.

Gorn, Gerald J. "The Effects of Music in Advertising on Choice Behavior: A Classical Conditioning Approach." *Journal of Marketing* 46 (Winter 1982): 94-101.

Gow, J. "Reconsidering Gender Roles on MTV: Depictions in the Most Popular Music Videos of the Early 1990s." *Communication Reports* 9 (1995): 151-161.

Greenwald, A.G. "The Totalitarian Ego: Fabrication and Revision of Personal History." *American Psychologist 35, no. 7 (1980): 603-618.*

Greeson, L.E. and R.A. Williams, "Social Implications of Music Videos for Youth: an Analysis of the Contents and Effects of MTV." *Youth and Society* 18 (1986): 177-189.

Grube, J.W. and L. Wallack. "Televised Beer Advertisement and Drinking Knowledge, Beliefs, and Intentions among School Children." *American Journal of Public Health* 84 (1994): 254-259.

Guze, S.B. *Criminality and Psychiatric Disorders*. New York: Oxford University Press, 1976.

Jackson, John H. "On Affections of Speech from Disease of the Brain." *Brain* 1 (1878): 304-330.

Jameelah, Maryam. *The Generation Gap: Its Causes and Consequences*. Lahore: Mohammad Yusuf Khan and Sons, 1981.

Kalinack, K. *Settling the Score*. Madison, WI: University of Wisconsin Press, 1992.

Key, Wilson Bryan. *Media Sexploitation*. New York: Signet Books, 1976.

King, Paul M.D. "Heavy Metal Music and Drug Abuse in Adolescents." *Postgraduate Medicine* 83, no. 5 (April 1988): 295-301, 304.

Loyau, A., M. Saint Jalme and C. Cagniant. "Multiple Sexual Advertisements Honestly Reflect Health Status in Peacocks (*Pavo cristatus*)." *Behavioral Ecology and Sociobiology* 58, no. 6 (2005): 552-557.

Luther, Martin. "Liturgy and Hymns," in *Luther's Works, American Edition* (55 vols.; edited by Jaroslav Pelikan and Helmut T. Lehmann; Philadelphia: Muehlenberg and Fortress, 1965), vol. 53.

Martino, Steven C., Rebecca L. Collins, Marc N. Elliott, Amy Strachman, David E. Kanouse, Sandra H. Berry. "Exposure to Degrading Versus Nondegrading Music Lyrics and Sexual Behavior among Youth." *Pediatrics* 118, no. 2 (August 2006): 430-441.

Meyer, Leonard. *Emotion and Meaning in Music.* Chicago: University of Chicago Press, 1961.

Milliman, R.E. "The Influence of Background Music on the Behavior of Restaurant Patrons." *Journal of Consumer Research* 13 (1986): 286-289.

Münsterberg, Hugo. *The Photoplay: A Psychological Study.* New York: Arno, 1970.

Nietzsche, Friedrich. *The Birth of Tragedy and The Case of Wagner.* New York: Vintage Books, 1967.

———. *Thus Spoke Zarathustra: A Book for All and None.* New York: Modern Library, 1995.

Noebel, David A. *The Marxist Minstrels: A Handbook on Communist Subversion of Music*. American Christian College Press, 1974.

Nyklicek, I., J.F. Thayer and L.J.P. van Doornen. "Cardiorespiratory Differentiation of Musically-induced Emotions." *Journal of Psychophysiology* 11 (1997): 304-321.

Palmer, C. *The Composer in Hollywood*. New York: Marion Boyars, 1990.

Pardun, Carol J., Kelly Ladin L'Engle and Jane D. Brown. "Linking Exposure to Outcome: Early Adolescents' Consumption of Sexual Content in Six Media." *Mass Communication and Society* 8 (May 2005): 75-91.

Peck, M. Scott. *The Road Less Traveled*. New York: Simon and Schuster, 1998.

Peretz, Isabelle. "Listen to the Brain: A Biological Perspective on Musical Emotions." In *Music and Emotion: Theory and Research*, edited by Patrik N. Juslin and John A. Sloboda, 105-133. New York: Oxford University Press, 2001.

Pike, Alfred. "A Phenomenological Analysis of Emotional Experience in Music." *Journal of Research in Music Education 20 (1972)*: 262-267.

Plomp, Reinier. *The Intelligent Ear: On the Nature of Sound Perception*. Mahwah, New Jerse): Lawrence Erlbaum Associates, 2002.

Power, Roderick. "The Dominance of Touch by Vision: Occurs with Familiar Objects." *Perception* 10 (1981): 29-33.

Quinlan, Mike, J.D. and Jim Persels, J.D. "It's Not My Fault, the Devil Made Me Do It: Attempting to Impose Tort Liability on Publishers, Producers, and Artists for Injuries Allegedly 'Inspired' by Media Speech." *Southern Illinois Law Journal* 18, no. 417 (Winter 1994).

Rehman, S. and S. Reilly, "Music Videos: a New Dimension of Televised Violence." *Pennsylvania Speech Communication Annual* 41 (1985): 61-64.

Rich, C.L., D. Young and R.C. Fowler, "San Diego Suicide Study. I. Young vs. Old Subjects." *Archives of General Psychiatry* 43, no. 6 (1986): 577-582.

Roberts, Donald F., U.G. Foehr and V.J. Rideout. *Generation M2: Media in the Lives of 8- to 18-Year-Olds.* Palo Alto, CA: Kaiser Family Foundation, 2010.

Roberts, Donald F., L. Henriksen and Peter G. Christenson. *Substance Use in Popular Movies and Music.* Washington, DC: Office of National Drug Control Policy, 1999.

Roberts, Donald F. and Peter G. Christenson. *"Here's Looking at You, Kid": Alcohol, Drugs and Tobacco in Entertainment Media.* New York: Kaiser Family Foundation, 2000.

Robinson, Thomas N., Helen L. Chen and Joel D. Killen. "Television and Music Video Exposure and Risk of Adolescent Alcohol Use." *Pediatrics* 102, no. 5 (1998): e54-e59.

Rosenfeld, Anne H. "Music, The Beautiful Disturber." *Psychology Today*, December 1985.

Rubin, R.B., A.M. Rubin and E.M. Perse. "Media Use and Meaning of Music Video." *Journalism Quarterly* 63 (1986): 353-359.

Said, Summer. "Egyptian Celebrities Turn to Religion." *Arab News,* March 29, 2005. Accessed November 1, 2010. h t t p : / / a r c h i v e . a r a b n e w s . c o m / ?page=9&section=0&article=61269&d=31&m=3&y=2005.

Schaefer, James M. "Slow Country Music and Drinking." Paper presented at the annual meeting for the American Anthropological Association, Phoenix, Arizona, 1988.

Schwartz, Ted and Duane Empey. *Satanism: Is Your Family Safe?* Grand Rapids, MI: Zondervan, 1989.

Seidman, S.A. "An Investigation of Sex-role Stereotyping in Music Videos." *Journal Broadcast Electron* 36 (1992): 209-216.

Sherman, B. and J. Dominick. "Violence and Sex in Music Videos: TV and Rock 'n' Roll." *Journal of Communication* 36, no. 1 (1986): 79-93.

Sloboda, John A. "Empirical Studies of Emotional Response to Music." In *Cognitive Bases of Musical Behaviour*, edited by M. R. Jones and S. Holleran. Washington, D.C.: American Psychological Association, 1992.

Sloboda, John A. "Music Structure and Emotional Response: Some Empirical Findings." *Psychology of Music* 19 (1991): 110-120.

Sloboda, John A. and Patrik N. Juslin. "Psychological Perspectives on Music and Emotion." In *Music and Emotion: Theory and Research*, edited by John A. Sloboda and Patrik N. Juslin. New York: Oxford University Press, 2001.

Stack, Steven. "New Micro Level Data on the Impact of Divorce on Suicide, 1959-1980: A Test of Two Theories." *Journal of Marriage and the Family* 52 (1990): 119-127.

Stack, Steven and Jim Gundlach. "The Effect of Country Music on Suicide." *Social Forces* 71, no. 1 (1992): 211-218.

Ward, L. Monique. "Talking About Sex: Common Themes about Sexuality in Prime-time Television Programs Children and Adolescents View Most." *Journal of Youth and Adolescence* 24 (1995): 595-615.

Watkins, Terry. "It's Only Rock 'n' Roll... But It Kills." Accessed on November 1, 2010. http://www.av1611.org/rockm.html.

Winn, Denise. *The Manipulated Mind: Brainwashing, Conditioning, and Indoctrination*. Cambridge, MA: Marlor Books, 2000.

Young, Louisa. *The Book Of The Heart*. New York: Doubleday, 2003.

Appendix

Arabic Text of Hadiths and Quotes Cited in this Book

Introduction

تَعَلَّمْنَا الْإِيْمَانَ ثُمَّ تَعَلَّمْنَا الْقُرآنَ

*A*bdullah Ibn Mas'ood (ﷺ), a well-known Companion of Prophet Muhammad (ﷺ) said: "We were taught (by Prophet Muhammad) faith first, and then we were taught the Qur'an."

...the hadith narrated on the authority of Wabisa ibn Ma'bad (ﷺ), who went to the Messenger of Allah (ﷺ), who said:

جِئْتَ تَسْأَلُ عَنِ الْبِرِّ قُلْتُ نَعَمْ قَالَ: اَسْتَفْتِ قَلْبَكَ. الْبِرُّ مَا اطْمَأَنَّتْ إِلَيْهِ النَّفْسُ وَاطْمَأَنَّ إِلَيْهِ الْقَلْبُ. وَالْإِثْمُ مَا حَاكَ فِي النَّفْسِ وَتَرَدَّدَ فِي الصَّدْرِ وَإِنْ أَفْتَاكَ النَّاسُ وَأَفْتَوْكَ (مسند أحمد).

«You have come to ask about righteousness? I said: Yes. He (ﷺ) said: Consult your heart. Righteousness is that about which the soul feels tranquil and the heart feels tranquil, and wrongdoing is that which wavers in the soul and moves back and forth in the breast (in your heart) even though people again and again have given you their opinion in its favour.» (recorded by Aḥmad and graded as reliable by al-Albâni)

An-Nawwâs ibn Sam'an narrated that the Prophet Muhammad (ﷺ) said:

البِرُّ حُسْنُ الْخُلُقِ وَالإِثْمُ مَا حَاكَ فِي صَدْرِكَ وَكَرِهْتَ أَنْ يَطَّلِعَ عَلَيْهِ النَّاسُ (صحيح مسلم).

«Virtue is good ethics and behaviour, and wrong action is what irritates the heart and what you do not want other people to see.» (Muslim)

...we must never forget the command of our beloved Prophet (ﷺ):

مَنْ رَأَى مِنْكُمْ مُنْكَراً فَلْيُغَيِّرْهُ بِيَدِهِ فَإِنْ لَمْ يَسْتَطِعْ فَبِلِسَانِهِ فَإِنْ لَمْ يَسْتَطِعْ فَبِقَلْبِهِ وَذَلِكَ أَضْعَفُ الإِيْمَانِ (صحيح مسلم).

«Whoever among you sees an evil action, let him change it with his hand; if he is unable to do that, then let him change it by his tongue, and if he is unable to do so, let him hate it in his heart, and that is the weakest faith.» (Muslim)

Chapter 1
Music from the Sharia View

In one hadith narrated by al-Miqdâm ibn Ma'dikarib, Prophet Muhammad (ﷺ) warned us:

إلا إِنِّي أُوتِيتُ الْكِتَابَ وَمِثْلَهُ مَعَهُ أَلاَ يُوشِكُ رَجُلٌ شَبْعَانٌ عَلَى أَرِيكَتِهِ يَقُولُ عَلَيْكُمْ بِهَذَا الْقُرْآنِ فَمَا وَجَدْتُمْ فِيْهِ مِنْ حِلاَلٍ فَأَحَلُّوْهُ

وَمَا وَجَدْتُمْ فِيهِ مِنْ حَرَامٍ فَحَرِّمُوهُ (سنن أبي داؤد).

«Beware! I have been given the Qur'ân and something like it, yet the time is coming when a man replete on his couch will say: Keep to the Qur'ân; what you find in it to be permissible, treat as permissible, and what you find in it to be prohibited, treat as prohibited.» (recorded by Abu Dâwood and graded as sound by al-Albâni)

Hadith 1

لَيَكُونَنَّ مِنْ أُمَّتِي أَقْوَامٌ يَسْتَحِلُّونَ الحِرَّ والحَرِيرَ والخَمْرَ والمَعَازِفَ (صحيح البخاري، كتاب الأشربة).

«There will be people of my Ummah who will seek to make these lawful (*yastaḥilloona*): illegal sexual intercourse, the wearing of silk [by men], the drinking of alcoholic drinks, and the use of *ma'âzif* (musical instruments).» (Bukhari)

Hadith 2

يَشْرَبَنَّ نَاسٌ مِنْ أُمَّتِي الخَمْرَ يُسَمُّونَهَا بِغَيْرِ اسْمِها يُعْزَفُ عَلَى رُؤوسِهِمْ بِالمَعَازِفِ وَالْمُغَنِّيَاتِ يُخْسِفُ اللَّهُ بِهِمْ الأَرْضَ وَيَجْعَلُ مِنْهُمُ الْقِرَدَةَ وَالخَنَازِيْرَ (سنن ابن ماجه).

«Soon there will be people from my Ummah who will drink wine, calling it by other than its real name. There will be instruments of music and singing on their heads, and they will listen to female singers. Allah (ﷻ) will cleave the earth under them and turn others into apes and swine.» (recorded by Ibn Mâjah and graded as sound by al-Albâni)

Hadith 3

اللَّهَ حَرَّمَ عَلَيَّ أَوْ حُرِّمَ الْخَمْرُ وَالْمَيْسِرُ وَالْكُوبَةُ
قَالَ وَكُلُّ مُسْكِرٍ حَرَامٌ قَالَ سُفْيَانُ فَسَأَلْتُ عَلِيَّ بْنَ بَذِيمَةَ عِنِ الْكُوبَةِ
قَالَ الطَّبْلُ (سنن أبو داؤد، مسند أحمد).

«Verily, Allah (ﷺ) prohibited wine, gambling and the *kuba*, and every intoxicant is prohibited. Sufyân said: I asked the narrator, 'Ali ibn Badheemah: What is the kuba? He answered: It is the drum.» (recorded by Abu Dâwood and Aḥmad, and graded as sound by al-Albâni)

Hadith 4

إِنَّ اللَّهَ حَرَّمَ عَلَى أُمَّتِي الْخَمْرَ وَالْمِيْسِرَ وَالْمَزَرِ وَالْكُوْبَةَ
وَالْقَيْنَيْنِ وَزَادَنِيْ صَلَاةَ الْوِتْرِ (مسند أحمد).

«Verily, Allah (ﷺ) has prohibited for my Ummah wine, gambling, a drink distilled from corn, the drum and the lute...» (recorded by Aḥmad and graded as sound by al-Albâni)

Hadith 5

إِنِّيْ لَمْ أَنْهَ عَنِ الْبُكَاءِ، وَلَكِنْ نَهَيْتُ عَنْ صَوْتَيْنِ أَحْمَقَيْنِ فَاجِرَيْنِ :
صَوْتٍ عِنْدَ نِعْمَةِ لَهْوٍ وَلَعِبٍ، وَمَزَامِيْرِ شَيْطَانٍ،
وَصوْتٍ عِنْدَ مُصِيْبَةٍ لَطْمِ وُجُوْهٍ وَشَقِّ جُيُوْبٍ،
وَهَذِهِ رَحْمَةٌ، وَمَنْ لاَ يَرْحَمْ لاَ يُرْحَمْ (حاكم).

«Verily, I did not prohibit weeping, but rather I forbade two voices which are imbecilic and sinfully shameless: one a voice [singing] to the accompaniment of musical amusement (*lahwa*) and Satan's [wind] instruments; the other, a voice [wailing] due to some calamity, accompanied by striking the face and tearing the garments. This [weeping of mine] stems from compassion, and whoever does not show compassion will not receive it.» (recorded by al-Hâkim and graded as reliable by al-Albâni)

Hadith 6

Anas ibn Mâlik (ﷺ) related that the Prophet (ﷺ) said:

صَوْتَانِ مَلْعُونَانِ فِي الدُّنْيَا وَالآخِرَةِ مِزْمَارٌ عِندَ نِعْمَةٍ وَرَنَّةٌ عِندَ مُصِيبَةٍ

(مجمع الزوائد)

«Two cursed sounds are that of the [wind] instrument played on the occasion of joy and grace, and woeful wailing upon the occurrence of adversity.» (recorded by Al-Haythami, who considered it sound)

Hadith 7

عَنْ نَافِعٍ مَوْلَى ابْنِ عُمَرَ أَنَّ ابْنَ عُمَرَ سَمِعَ صَوْتَ زَمَّارَةِ رَاعٍ فَوَضَعَ أُصْبُعَيْهِ فِي أُذُنِهِ وَعَدَلَ رَاحِلَتَهُ عَنِ الطَّرِيقِ وَهُوَ يَقُولُ يَا نَافِعُ أَتَسْمَعُ فَأَقُولَ نَعْ "مْ فَيَمْضِيْ حَتَّى قُلْتُ لاَ فَوَضَعَ يَدَيْهِ وَأَعَادَ رَاحِلَتَهُ إِلَى الطَّرِيقِ وَقَالَ رَأَيْتُ رَسُولَ اللَّهِ صَلَّى اللَّهُ عَلَيْهِ وَسَلَّمَ سَمِعَ صَوْتَ زَمَّارَةِ رَاعٍ فَصَنَعَ مِثْلَ هَذَا (سنن أبو داؤد، مسند أحمد).

«Imam Nâfi‘ narrates that once when Abdullah ibn ‘Umar (ﷺ) heard the sound of a flute being played by a shepherd, he immediately put his fingers in his ears and diverted his riding animal in the other direction. Then he asked his servant Nâfi‘ (who had not reached adolescence yet): Can the sound still be heard? Nâfi‘ replied: Yes. Abdullah ibn ‘Umar (ﷺ) kept on walking until Nâfi' told him that the sound could no longer be heard. Abdullah (ﷺ) then removed his fingers from his ears and told Nâfi' that he had seen Prophet Muhammad (ﷺ) doing the same thing when he (ﷺ) heard the sound of a flute being played by a shepherd.» (a sound hadith recorded by Abu Dâwood and Aḥmad)

Hadith 8

عَنْ عِمْرَانَ بْنِ حُصَيْنٍ رَضِيَ اللَّهُ عَنْهُ أَنَّ رَسُوْلَ اللَّهِ صَلَّى اللَّهُ عَلَيْهِ وَسَلَّمَ قَالَ فِيْ هَذِهِ الأُمَّةِ خَسْفٌ وَمَسْخٌ وَقَذْفٌ فَقَالَ رَجُلٌ مِنَ الْمُسْلِمِيْنَ :

يَا رَسُوْلَ اللَّهِ وَمَتَى ذَلِكَ؟ قَالَ :

إِذَا ظَهَرَتِ الْقِيَانُ وَالْمَعَارِفُ وَشُرِبَتِ الْخُمُوْرُ (رواه الترمذي).

«'Imrân bin Ḥuṣayn (ﷺ) narrates that the Messenger of Allah (ﷺ) said: In my Ummah, there will be punishments of earthquakes, disfigurement of faces and showers of stones. A man from amongst the Muslims asked: O Prophet of Allah! When will that happen? He replied: When singing women and musical instruments become prevalent and drinking alcohol becomes common.» (a sound hadith recorded by Tirmidhi)

'Ali ibn Abi Ṭâlib (ﷺ) said that he heard the Prophet Muhammad (ﷺ) say:

ما هممت بقبيح مما كان أهل الجاهلية يهمون به إلا مرتين من الدهر، كلتيهما يعصمني اللَّه – تعالى – منهما، قلت ليلة لفتى كان معي من قريش بأعلى مكة في أغنام لأهله يرعاها : أبصر إلى غنمي حتى أسمر هذه الليلة بمكة كما يسمر الفتيان، قال : نعم، فخرجت [فجئت] أدنى دار من دور مكة، سمعت غناء وضرب دفوف ومزامير فقلت :

ما هذا ؟ ! قالوا : فلان تزوج فلانة ، لرجل من قريش تزوج امرأة
من قريش ، فلهوت بذلك الغناء وبذلك الصوت حتى غلبتني عيني ،
فما أيقظني إلا مس الشمس فرجعت إلى صاحبي قال : ما فعلت ؟
فأخبرته ، ثم قلت له ليلة أخرى مثل ذلك ففعل ،
فخرجت فسمعت مثل ذلكن فقيل لي مثل ما قيل لي ،
فلهوت بما سمعت حتى غلبتني عيني ، فما أيقظني إلا مس الشمس ،
ثم رجعت إلى صاحبي فقال : ما فعلت ؟ قلت : ما فعلت شيئا ،
قال رسول الله صلى الله عليه وسلم : فوالله ما هممت بعدها بسوء مما
يعمل أهل الجاهلية حتى أكرمني الله – عز وجل – بنبوته

«I was never attracted to the bad customs and amusements and entertainments of *jâhiliyah* (the age of spiritual darkness before the dawn of Islam) except on two nights, when Allah (ﷺ) protected me from any sin and kept me innocent.

One night, I was with a few of my young friends in Makkah, taking care of our herd of goats, when I heard the sounds of musical instruments and singing. I asked them: What is that? They told me that a marriage was taking place there. Allah (ﷺ) covered up my sense of hearing, and I went to sleep for so long that the rays of sun on the next morning woke me up.

On the next night, I went again towards that place and heard the same sounds of music and singing that I had heard the night before. Again, Allah (ﷺ) covered up my sense of hearing. I went to sleep, and only the heat of the sun woke me up the next morning. After that, I neither intended nor was curious for such a thing until Allah (ﷺ) granted me prophethood.» (a reliable hadith recorded by Ibn Ḥajar, Ibn Is-ḥâq, Bazzâr, Bayhaqi, Abu Nu'aym and Ibn Asâkir)

Chapter 2
Scientific Research about the Effects of Music on the Body

Moreover, Prophet Muhammad (ﷺ) used to make the following supplication to Allah (ﷻ) in the morning and in the evening, in which he mentioned the sense of hearing before the sense of seeing:

اللَّهُمَّ عَافِنِي فِي بَدَنِي، اللَّهُمَّ عَافِنِي فِي سَمْعِي،
اللَّهُمَّ عَافِنِي فِي بَصَرِيْ، لاَ إِلهَ إِلاَّ أَنْتَ (ثلاثاً).

«O Allah, grant my body health, O Allah, grant my hearing health, O Allah, grant my sight health. None has the right to be worshipped except You.» (Bukhari, Abu Dâwood and Nisâ'i)

Chapter 3
Sex, Drugs and Rock and Roll

The Prophet's Companion Ibn 'Umar (ﷺ) narrated this hadith in which Allah's Messenger (ﷺ) said:

كُلُّ مُسْكِرٍ خَمْرٌ وَكُلُّ مسْكِرٍ حَرَامٌ مَنْ شَرِبَ الْخَمْرَ فِي الدُّنْيَا فَمَاتَ وَهُوَ
يُدْمِنُهَا لَمْ يَتُبْ لَمْ يَشْرَبْهَا فِي الآخِرَةِ (صحيح مسلم).

«Every intoxicant is khamr (alcohol), and all alcohol is unlawful. He who drinks alcohol in this world and dies while he is addicted to it, not having repented, will not drink it in the hereafter.» (Muslim)

Chapter 4
Music Made Me Do It

Abu Hurayrah (رضي الله عنه) narrated that the Prophet (ﷺ) said:

الإيمان ستون أو سبعون أو أحد العددين، أعلاها شهادة أن لا إله إلا الله، وأدناها إماطة الأذى عن الطريق، والحياء شعبة من الإيمان

«Faith has seventy-something or sixty-something branches. The highest of them is testifying that there is none worthy of worship other than Allah, while the lowest of them is removing something harmful from the road, and ḥayâ' is a branch of faith.» (recorded by Ibn Abi Shaybah; al-Albani graded it sound with a good chain of narration)

'Imrân bin Ḥuṣayn said that the Prophet (ﷺ) said:

الحياء لا يأتي إلا بخير

«Ḥayâ' does not bring anything except good.» (Muslim)

Narrated Abdullah ibn 'Umar:

مر النبي صلى الله عليه وسلم على رجل،
وهو يعاتب أخاه في الحياء، يقول : إنك لتستحيي،
حتى كأنه يقول : قد أضر بك، فقال رسول الله صلى الله عليه وسلم :
(دعه ، فإن الحياء من الإيمان).

«The Prophet (ﷺ) passed by a man who was admonishing his brother regarding ḥayâ' and was saying: You are very shy, and I am afraid that might harm you. Hearing that, Allah's Apostle (ﷺ) said: Leave him, for ḥayâ' is (a part) of faith.» (Bukhari)

$$جَاءَ رَجُلٌ إِلَى رُسُوْلِ اللّٰهِ صَلَّى للهُ عَلَيْهِ وَسَلَّمَ قَالَ :$$

$$مَنْ أَحَقُّ النَّاسِ بِحُسْنِ صَحَابَتِيْ قَالَ : أُمُّكَ قَالَ : ثُمَّ مَنْ قَالَ :$$

$$ثُمَّ أُمُّكَ قَالَ : ثُمَّ مَنْ قَالَ : ثُمَّ أُمُّكَ قَالَ : ثُمَّ مَنْ قَالَ :$$

$$ثُمَّ أَبُوْكَ (صحيح مسلم).$$

«A man came to the Prophet Muhammad (ﷺ) asking: O Messenger of Allah, who among people is the most worthy of my good companionship? The Prophet said: Your mother. The man said: Then who is next? The Prophet said: Your mother. The man further asked: Then who is next? Only then did the Prophet say: Your father.» (Muslim)

$$مَنْ عَالَ جَارِيَتَيْنِ حَتَّى تَبْلُغَا جَاءَ يَوْمَ الْقِيَامَةِ أَنَا وَهُوَ وَضَمَّ أَصَابِعَهُ$$

$$(صحيح مسلم).$$

«Whoever supports two daughters until they mature, he and I will come on the Day of Judgment like this (and he pointed with his two fingers held together).» (Muslim)

$$طَلَبُ الْعِلْمِ فَرِيْضَةٌ عَلَى كُلِّ مُسْلِمٍ (سنن ابن ماجه).$$

«Seeking knowledge is mandatory for every Muslim [male and female].» (recorded by Ibn Mâjah and graded as sound by al-Albâni)

Chapter 5
Positions of the Companions, the Four Imams and other Islamic Scholars

...when Is-hâq ibn Moosâ asked Imam Mâlik about the view of people of Madinah regarding singing, Imam Mâlik replied:

إِنَّمَا يَفْعَلُهُ عِنْدَنَا الفُسَّاق

"Here, in fact, that is done only by the sinful ones."

We find this in the following hadiths:

عَنْ عَائِشَةَ رَضِيَ اللَّهُ عَنْهَا دَخَلَ عَلَيَّ رَسُولُ اللَّهِ صَلَّى اللَّهُ عَلَيْهِ وَسَلَّمَ
وَعِنْدِيْ جَارِيَتَانِ تَغْنِيَانِ بِغِنَاءِ بُعَاثَ فَاضْطَجَعَ عَلَى الْفِرَاشِ وَحَوَّلَ
وَجْهَهُ فَدَخَلَ أَبُو بَكْرٍ فَانْتَهَرَنِي وَقَالَ : مِزْمَارَةُ الشَّيْطَانِ عِنْدَ رَسُولِ اللَّهِ
صَلَّى اللَّهُ عَلَيْهِ وَسَلَّمَ فَأَقْبَلَ عَلَيْهِ رَسُولُ اللَّهِ صَلَّى اللَّهُ عَلَيْهِ وَسَلَّمَ فَقَالَ :
دَعْهُمَا فَلَمَّا غَفَلَ غَمَزْتُهُمَا فَخَرَجَتَا قَالَتْ : وَكَانَ يَوْمُ عِيْدٍ يَلْعَبُ السُّودَانُ
بِالدَّرَقِ وَالحِرَابِ فَإِمَّا سَأَلْتُ رَسُولَ اللَّهِ صَلَّى اللَّهُ عَلَيْهِ وَسَلَّمَ وَإِمَّا قَالَ :
تَشْتَهِيْنَ تَنْظُرِينَ فَقُلْتُ : نَعَمْ فَأَقَامَنِيْ وَرَاءَهُ خَدِّيْ عَلَى خَدِّهِ وَيَقُولُ :
دُونَكُمْ يَا بَنِي أَرْفِدَةَ حَتَّى إِذَا مَلِلْتُ قَالَ : حَسْبُكِ قُلْتُ :
نَعَمْ قَالَ فَاذْهَبِيْ (صحيح البخاري، كتاب العيدَين).

«It has been narrated by 'Â'ishah (رضى), the wife of the Prophet, that once the Prophet Muhammad (ﷺ) came home, and at that time, two little girls were singing songs about the battle of Buath. The Prophet (ﷺ) lay down on the bed and turned his face away. Then Abu Bakr came and scolded her, saying: These musical instruments of Satan in the house of the Prophet of Allah (ﷺ)! Prophet Muhammad turned to him and said: Leave them. In the words of 'Â'ishah (رضى): When Abu Bakr got busy in other matters, I told the two girls to leave, and they left. That was the day of Eid. The Abyssinians were playing in the mosque with shields and lances. Then either I asked the Messenger (ﷺ), or he himself said: Do you want to have a look? I said yes, so he let me stand behind him, with my cheek against his cheek, and said: Carry on, Banu Arfidah. When I became bored, he asked: Is that enough for you? I said yes. He said: Then you may leave.» (Bukhari)

Muhammad ibn Hâtib al-Jumahi relates that the Messenger of Allah (ﷺ) said:

$$فَضْلُ مَا بَيْنَ الْحَلَالِ والْحَرَام الدُّفُ وَالصَّوْتُ وَرَفْعُ الصَّوْتِ فِي النِّكَاحِ$$

$$(رواه ابن ماجه).$$

«The difference between the unlawful and the lawful (in marriage celebrations) is the duff and the voice.» (recorded by Ibn Mâjah and Tirmidhi, who considered its chain of narration reliable)

$$عَنْ عَائِشَةَ أَنَّهَا زَفَّتِ امْرَأَةٍ إِلَى رَجُلٍ مِنَ الْأَنْصَارِ فَقَالَ نَبِيُّ اللَّهِ صَلَّى اللَّهُ$$

$$عَلَيْهِ وَسَلَّمَ : يَا عَائِشَةَ مَا كَانَ مَعَكُمْ لَهْوٌ فَإِنَّ الْأَنْصَارَ يُعْجِبُهُمُ اللَّهْوُ$$

$$(صحيح بخاري، كتاب النكاح).$$

«It was narrated by 'Â'ishah (ﷺ) that when she prepared a lady as a bride for a man from the Anşâr [the Muslim citizens of Madinah who gave refuge to the Prophet (ﷺ) and the other Muslim emigrants from Makkah], the Prophet (ﷺ) said: O 'Â'ishah! Haven't you got any amusement (for the wedding), as the Anşâr like amusement?» (Bukhari)

Chapter 6
Critical Analysis of Arguments used in Favour of 'Islamic' Music

This axiom is agreed upon among the jurists, and this becomes apparent when they discuss the principle that states:

لاَ يُنْكَرْ الْمُخْتَلِفِ فِيهِ وَإِنَّمَا يُنْكَرُ الْمُجْمَعُ عَلَيْهِ

"There is NO censure in issues of disagreement, while the censure is only in issues of consensus."

It is precisely for this reason that the scholars would often say:

مَنْ تَتَبَّعَ الرُّخَصْ فَقَدْ تَزَنْدَقَ

"One who deliberately seeks out religious allowances becomes a heretic."

One hadith narrated by Abu Rafi' goes as follows:

لالفين احدكم متكئا على اريكته يأتيه الأمر من أمري مما امرت به
أو نهيت عنه فيقول لا ندري ما وجدنا في كتاب اللَّه فاتبعناه
(سنن ابي داؤد)

«Let me not find one of you reclining on his couch when he hears something regarding me, which I have commanded or forbidden, saying: We do not know. What we found in Allah's Book, we have followed only that.» (recorded by Abu Dâwood and graded as sound by al-Albâni)

In another hadith narrated by al-Miqdam ibn Ma'dikarib, Prophet Muhammad (ﷺ) warned us:

أَلا إِنِّي أُوتِيتُ الْكِتَابَ وَمِثْلَهُ مَعَهُ أَلاَ يُوْشِكُ رَجُلٌ شَبْعَانٌ عَلَى أَرِيْكَتِهِ
يَقُوْلُ عَلَيْكُمْ بِهَذَا الْقُرْآنِ فَمَا وَجَدْتُمْ فِيهِ مِنْ حِلالٍ فَأَحَلُّوْهُ
وَمَا وَجَدْتُمْ فِيهِ مِنْ حَرَامٍ فَحَرِّمُوْهُ (سنن أبي داؤد).

«Beware! I have been given the Qur'ân and something like it, yet the time is coming when a man replete on his couch will say: Keep to the Qur'ân; what you find in it to be permissible, treat as permissible, and what you find in it to be prohibited, treat as prohibited.» (recorded by Abu Dâwood and graded as sound by al-Albâni)

The Prophet (ﷺ) spoke to us about how much we lose when we waste our time, saying:

نِعْمَتَانِ مَغْبُوْنٌ فِيهَا كَثِيْرٌ مِنَ النَّاسِ : الصِّحَةُ وَالفَرَاغُ (صحيح بخاري).

«There are two blessings that many people squander: health and time.» (Bukhari)

Abi Barza Aslami narrated that Prophet Muhammad (ﷺ) said:

تَزُوْلُ قَدَمَا عَبْدٍ حَتَّى يُسْأَلُ عَنْ عُمْرِهِ فِيْمَا أَفْتَاهُ وَعَنْ عِلْمِهِ فِيْمَا فَعَلَ وَعَنْ
مَالِهِ مِنْ أَيْنَ اكْتَسَبَهُ وَفِيْمَا أَنْفَقَهُ وَعَنْ جِسْمِهِ فِيْهَا أَبْلَاهُ (ترمذي).

«No one will be permitted to turn his two feet away on the Day of Resurrection until he is questioned about the following: about his life, how he spent it; his knowledge, how much he acted upon it; his wealth, how he earned it and spent it; and his body, how he employed it.» (a reliable hadith recorded by Tirmidhi)

who try to make music permissible quote the hadith of 'Â'ishah (ﷺ), which is as follows:

عَنْ عَائِشَةَ رَضِيَ اللَّهُ عَنْهَا قَالَتْ دَخَلَ أَبُو بَكْرٍ وَعِنْدِيْ جَارِيَتَانِ مِنْ
جَوَارِي الأَنْصَارِ تَغَنَّيَانِ بِمَا تَقَاوَلَتِ الأَنْصَارُ يَوْمَ بُعَاثَ قَالَتْ وَلَيْسَتَا
بِمُغَنِّيَتَيْنِ فَقَالَ أَبُو بَكْرٍ أَمَزَامِيرُ الشَّيْطَانِ فِي بَيْتِ رَسُولِ اللَّهِ صَلَّى للهُ عَلَيْهِ
وَسَلَّمَ وَذَلِكَ فِي يَوْمِ عِيْدٍ فَقَالَ رَسُولُ اللَّهِ صَلَّى اللَّهُ عَلَيْهِ وَسَلَّمَ : يَا أَبَا
بَكْرٍ إِنَّ لِكُلِّ قَوْمٍ عِيداً، وَهَذَا عِيدُنَا (صحيح البخاري، كتاب العيدين).

«It has been narrated by 'Â'ishah (رضي الله عنها), the wife of the Prophet (ﷺ), that once Abu Bakr (رضي الله عنه) came to her home, and at that time, two Anṣâri girls were singing songs about the battle of Buath. They were not professional singers. Abu Bakr scolded her, saying: These musical instruments of Satan in the house of the Prophet of Allah (ﷺ)! It was the day of Eid, so Allah's Messenger said to him: O Abu Bakr, there is an Eid for every people, and this is our Eid day.» (Bukhari)

Another version of this hadith provides additional details about this incident:

عَنْ عَائِشَةَ رَضِيَ اللَّهُ عَنْهَا دَخَلَ عَلَيَّ رَسُولُ اللَّهِ صَلَّى اللَّهُ عَلَيْهِ وَسَلَّمَ وَعِنْدِيْ جَارِيَتَانِ تَغَنِّيَانِ بِغِنَاءِ بُعَاثَ فَاضْطَجَعَ عَلَى الْفِرَاشِ وَحَوَّلَ وَجْهَهُ فَدَخَلَ أَبُو بَكْرٍ فَانْتَهَرَنِي وَقَالَ: مِزْمَارَةُ الشَّيْطَانِ عِنْدَ رَسُولِ اللَّهِ صَلَّى اللَّهُ عَلَيْهِ وَسَلَّمَ فَأَقْبَلَ عَلَيْهِ رَسُولُ اللَّهِ صَلَّى اللَّهُ عَلَيْهِ وَسَلَّمَ فَقَالَ: دَعْهُمَا فَلَمَّا غَفَلَ غَمَزْتُهُمَا فَخَرَجَتَا قَالَتْ: وَكَانَ يَوْمُ عِيدٍ يَلْعَبُ السُّودَانُ بِالدَّرَقِ وَالْحِرَابِ فَإِمَّا سَأَلْتُ رَسُولَ اللَّهِ صَلَّى اللَّهُ عَلَيْهِ وَسَلَّمَ وَإِمَّا قَالَ: تَشْتَهِيْنَ تَنْظُرِينَ فَقُلْتُ: نَعَمْ فَأَقَامَنِيْ وَرَاءَهُ خَدِّيْ عَلَى خَدِّهِ وَيَقُولُ: دُونَكُمْ يَا بَنِي أَرْفِدَةَ حَتَّى إِذَا مَلِلْتُ قَالَ: حَسْبُكِ قُلْتُ: نَعَمْ قَالَ فَاذْهَبِيْ (صحيح البخاري، كتاب العيدَين).

«It has been narrated by 'Â'ishah (رضي الله عنها), the wife of the Prophet, that once the Prophet Muhammad (ﷺ) came home, and at that time, two little girls were singing songs about the battle of Buath. The Prophet (ﷺ) lay down on the bed and turned his face away. Then Abu Bakr came and scolded her, saying: These musical instruments of Satan in the house of the Prophet of Allah (ﷺ)!

Prophet Muhammad turned to him and said: Leave them. In the words of 'Â'ishah (﵂): When Abu Bakr got busy in other matters, I told the two girls to leave, and they left. That was the day of Eid. The Abyssinians were playing in the mosque with shields and lances. Then either I asked the Messenger (ﷺ), or he himself said: Do you want to have a look? I said yes, so he let me stand behind him, with my cheek against his cheek, and said: Carry on, Banu Arfidah. When I became bored, he asked: Is that enough for you? I said yes. He said: Then you may leave.» (Bukhari)

إِنَّ الْعُلَمَاءَ وَرَثَةُ الأَنْبِيَاءِ وَإِنَّ الأَنْبِيَاءَ لَمْ يُوَرِّثُوا دِيْنَاراً وَلاَ دِرْهَماً إِنَّما وَرَّثُوا الْعِلْمَ فَمَنْ أَخَذَهُ أَخَذَ بِحَظٍّ وَافِرٍ (سنن أبي داود).

«Certainly, the scholars are the inheritors of the prophets, for indeed the prophets did not leave behind dinars (gold) or dirhams (silver), but (they left their) knowledge. Whoever accepts it receives a great fortune.» (a sound hadith recorded by Abu Dâwood)

A well-known saying describes this miraculous quality of the Qur'an:

لاَ يَشْبَعُ مِنْهُ الْعُلَمَاءُ وَلاَ يَخْلُقُ عَنْ كَثْرَةِ الرَّدِ
وَلاَ تَنْقَضِيْ عَجَائِبُهُ مَنْ قَالَ بِهِ صَدَقَ (ترمذي، عن علي ابن طالب).

Scholars are not satiated by it, repetition does not wear it out, and its wonders do not end. Whoever recites it speaks the truth.

Jubayr ibn Mut'im, a polytheist from Makkah who had not embraced Islam yet, came to visit Madinah and said:

عَنْ جُبَيْرِ بْنِ مُطْعِمٍ رضِيَ اللَّهِ عنه قال: سَمِعتُ رَسُولَ اللَّهِ

صَلَّى اللَّهُ عَلَيْهِ وَسَلَّمَ يَقْرَأُ فِي المَغْرِبِ بِالطورِ،

فَلَمَّا بَلَغَ هَذِهِ الآيَةَ كَادَ قَلْبِيْ أَنْ يَطِيْرَ (صحيح بخاري).

«I heard the Prophet (ﷺ) reciting soorat aṭ-Ṭoor (the Mount) in the sunset prayer. When he reached the verse: ﴾Or were they created out of nothing, or were they the creators? Or did they create the heavens and the earth? Rather, they are not certain. Or have they the depositories [containing the provision] of your Lord? Or are they the controllers [of them]?﴿ *(Qur'an 52: 35-37)*, my heart practically flew to Islam.» (Bukhari)

زَيِّنُوا الْقُرآنَ بِأَصْوَاتِكُم (سنن أبو داؤد).

«Beautify the Qur'ân with your voices.» (recorded by Abu Dâwood and graded as sound by al-Albâni)

لَيْسَ مِنَّا مَنْ لَمْ يَتَغَنَّ بِالْقُرْآنِ (صحيح بخاري).

«He who does not recite the Qur'ân while beautifying it with his voice is not from amongst us.» (Bukhari)

In one hadith, al-Barâ' ibn 'Âzib reported:

عَنِ الْبَرَاءِ رَضِيَ اللَّهَ عَنْهُ قَالَ: كَانَ رَجُلٌ يَقْرَأُ سُوْرَةَ الْكَهْفِ وَعِنْدَهُ فَرَسٌ مَرْبُوْطٌ بِشَطَنَيْن فَتَغَشَّتْهُ سَحَابَةٌ فَجَعَلَتْ تَدُوْرُ وَتَدْنُوْ وَجَعَلَ فَرَسُهُ يَنْفِرُ مِنْهَا فَلَمَّا أَصْبَحَ أَتَى النَّبِيَّ صَلَّى اللَّهُ عَلَيْهِ وَسَلَّمَ فَذَكَرَ ذَلِكَ لَهُ فَقَالَ: تِلْكَ السَّكِيْنَةُ نَزَلَتْ بِالْقُرْآنِ (صحيح مسلم).

«A man was reciting soorat al-Kahf (the Cave), and there was a horse beside him, tied with two ropes. As he was reciting, a cloud overshadowed him, and as it began to come nearer and nearer, the horse began to trample violently. The man came to the Messenger of Allah (ﷺ) in the morning and mentioned the incident to him.

The Prophet (ﷺ) said: That was tranquility, which descended as a result of the recitation of the Qur'ân.» (Muslim)

Chapter 7
Music and Society

إنه من كان قبلكم من بني إسرائيل إذا عمل فيهم العامل الخطيئة فنهاه الناهي تعذيرا فإذا كان من الغد جالسه وواكله وشاربه كأنه لم يره على خطيئة بالأمس فلما رأى اللَّه تعالى ذلك منهم ضرب قلوب بعضهم على بعض على لسان داود وعيسى بن مريم ﴿ذلك بما عصوا وكانوا يعتدون﴾ والذي نفسي بيده لتأمرن بالمعروف ولتنهن عن المنكر ولتأخذن على أيدي المسيء ولتأطرنه على الحق أطرا أو ليضربن اللَّه بقلوب بعضكم على بعض ويلعنكم كما لعنهم.

«There were, before you, some of the children of Israel who, if any one of them committed a sin, they would tell him to stop doing the sin and make excuses for him. The [sinner would persist, and the] next day they would sit with him, and eat and drink with him as if they had not seen him sinning the day before. When Allah (ﷺ) saw this, he sealed their hearts (and cursed them) by the tongue of David and of Jesus, son of Mary. ﴿That was because they disobeyed and [habitually] transgressed.﴾ *(Qur'an 5: 78)* By the One Who has my soul in His hand, you will enjoin what is good and right and forbid what is evil and wrong, and you must take the sinner by the hand and lead him to the truth, or Allah (ﷺ) will seal your hearts little by little and curse you like he cursed them.» (recorded by al-Haythami with a sound chain)

...the Prophet Muhammad (ﷺ) said in an authentic hadith narrated by Abu Sa'id al-Khudri:

عَنْ أَبِي سَعِيدٍ الْخُدْرِيِّ قَالَ : قَالَ رَسُولُ اللهِ صَلَّى اللهُ عَلَيْهِ وَسَلَّمَ لَتَتَّبِعُنَّ سُنَنَ الَّذِينَ مِنْ قَبْلِكُمْ شِبْراً بِشِبْرٍ وَذِرَاعاً بِذِرَاعٍ حَتَّى لَوْ دَخَلُوا فِيْ حُجْرِ ضَبٍّ لاَتَّبَعْتُمُوهُمْ قُلْنَا : يَا رَسُولَ اللهِ الْيَهُوْدُ وَالنَصَارَى قَالَ : فَمَنْ (صحيح مسلم).

«You will surely follow in the ways of those before you, inch by inch and step by step, so much so that if they were to enter the hole of a lizard, you would follow them. The Companions asked: O Messenger of Allah, (do you mean) the Jews and the Christians? He replied: Who else?» (Muslim)

Prophet Muhammad (ﷺ) warned us against the imitation of non-Muslims in the following hadith:

مَنْ تَشَبَّهَ بِقَوْمٍ فَهُوَ مِنْهُمْ (سنن أبو داؤد).

«Whoever imitates a people (nation) is one of them.» (recorded by Abu Dâwood and Ahmad, and graded as sound by al-Albâni)

An Arab poet has rightly said:

إِذَا كَانَ رَبُّ الْبَيْتِ ضَارِباً بِالْطَّبْلِ
فَلَا تَلُمِ الْأَوْلَادَ عَلَى الرَّقْصِ

When a father plays the drum,
don't blame his children for dancing.

Chapter 8
It is Never Too Late — Inspiring Stories from History

Page 217 ...The door of repentance is wide open until we are in the throes of death, as the Prophet (ﷺ) said:

إِنَّ اللَّهَ يَقْبَلُ تَوْبَةَ الْعَبْدِ مَا لَمْ يُغَرْغَرْ (ترمذي).

«Allah (ﷺ) accepts the repentance of His servant as long as death has not reached his collarbone.» (a reliable hadith recorded by Tirmidhi)

Glossary of Islamic Terms[*]

abu (or abi)   أبو، أبي   father (of)

AH   After Hijra — the designation for the Islamic lunar calendar, which began on the day of Prophet Muhammad's departure from Makkah to Madinah (equivalent to July, 622 CE).

Allah   الله   The Arabic word Allah is equivalent to 'God' in English. Linguistically, however, the word Allah is much more precise than 'God' in its meanings. There is no gender, male or female, associated with the word Allah in Arabic, whereas the term 'God' is masculine, and its feminine is 'goddess'. Similarly, there is no plural for Allah, whereas the plural for 'God' is 'gods'. The word Allah is a proper name and the true name of God, through which humanity calls upon God personally. The name Allah is not confined to Islam; it is also the name by which Arabic-speaking Christians of the

---

* The Arabic words are transliterated according to the conventions of the Transliteration Chart found in this book. If a word has become part of the English language (i.e., is found in a dictionary of Standard English), that spelling is used in this book and appears first in this Glossary, with the transliterated form in brackets after it.

		oriental churches call upon God.
âmeen	آمين	O Allah, accept our invocation; amen
angel		A being made of light who is totally obedient to Allah and has no free will; Allah has assigned some angels specific tasks, like those who record our good and bad deeds, the Angel of Death, the guardians of hell, etc.
Anṣâr	أنصار	'helpers': the Muslim citizens of Madinah who gave refuge to the Prophet (ﷺ) and the other Muslim emigrants from Makkah
banu (or bani)	بنو، بني	*lit.* 'children (of)'; *usu.* referring to a tribe that claims a common ancestor
deen	دين	religion
dhikr Allâh	ذكر الله	remembrance of Allah; specifically, remembering Allah through praising and supplicating to Him
dinar (deenâr)	دينار	originally, a gold coin; a unit of currency
dirham	درهم	a silver coin; a unit of currency
duff	دف	A hand drum. The rim, across which the skin is stretched, is carefully shaped with a tapered edge in order to produce very crisp 'tak' (treble) sounds. When there are rings or cymbals on the duff, it is called a tambourine.
Eid ('eed)	عيد	*lit.* festival; the two celebrations: one at the end of Ramadan and the other at the culmination of the hajj
fatwa (fatwah)	فتوة	religious decision or decree issued by a qualified Islamic scholar

fiqh	فقه	Islamic jurisprudence; understanding or interpreting Islamic law
fitnah	فتنة	*lit.* trial, temptation; (attempting to sow) discord between Muslims
ghinâ'	غناء	singing or raising one's voice
Hadith (*hadeeth*)	حديث	the collected statements and actions of Prophet Muhammad (ﷺ) that with the Qur'ân form the basis of Islamic law
hadith (*hadeeth*)	حديث	a statement or action of Prophet Muhammad (ﷺ) that was remembered and recorded by his Companions and followers
Al-Hâfidh	الحافظ	'the one who has memorized (the Qur'an)': an honorific title
Hajj (*hajj*)	حج	the major pilgrimage to the Sacred Mosque, site of the Ka'bah at Makkah, to be undertaken by every able Muslim once in his/her lifetime
halal (*halâl*)	حلال	permitted according to Islamic law
harâm	حرام	forbidden according to Islamic law
hayâ'	الحياء	our natural sense of modesty, bashfulness, shyness, moral conscience and self-respect
hijab (*hijâb*)	حجاب	veil ordained by Allah for believing women
ijtihâd	إجتهاد	to use one's knowledge of the Qur'an and the Sunnah to derive rulings on matters not specifically mentioned in either source of Islamic law
jâhiliyah	جاهلية	*lit.* 'ignorance'; the age of spiritual darkness before Islam

jâriyah	جارية	a young girl who has not reached the age of puberty
jihad (jihâd)	جهاد	struggle or striving (in Allah's cause)
jinn (plural of jinni)	جن	non-human, rational beings created by Allah from fire, often referred to as 'demons' or 'devils'; They have free will like humans: some are Muslims, others disbelievers; some are obedient to Allah, others disobedient. Satan is a jinni. Some people try to 'foretell' the future by contacting a jinni. Some disobedient jinn mislead people into thinking that they can tell them what will happen in the future, near or far, or that the jinn can provide people with riches or some sort of power.
Kaaba *(Ka'bah)*	الكعبة	the House of Allah in Makkah, originally built by Prophets Abraham and Ishmael, and which Muslims face wherever they pray
ma'âzif	معازف	Plural of 'azf. It refers to all types of stringed and percussion instruments used to create music.
madh-hab	مذهب	school of juristic thought
makrooh	مكروه	disliked, hated or detested according to Islamic teachings
malâhi	ملاهي	instruments of distraction; musical instruments
musnad	مسند	a compilation (made by his student) of the hadiths related by an Imam
nasheed	نشيد	songs containing Islamic themes or poetry

'oud	عود	a pear-shaped Middle Eastern stringed instrument
prophethood		The term 'prophethood' is not in the English dictionary, but is an invented term, formed along the pattern of 'childhood' and 'motherhood,' as a noun reflecting a particular state of being. It is meant to translate the meaning of the Arabic word nubuwwah, which has no one-word equivalent in English, but which could be translated as meaning 'the state of being a prophet,' and is also used to refer to 'all things that have to do with being a prophet.' The term 'prophethood' has since become common in English-language Islamic discourse.
Ramadan (Ramaḍân)	رمضان	the ninth month in the Islamic calendar; the month of obligatory fasting; the month in which the first verses of the Qur'an were revealed
ṣaḥeeḥ	صحيح	a grade of hadith: sound or authentic
salâm	السلام	peace; the greeting of peace
ṣalât or ṣalâh	صلاة	formal prayer: a combination of physical postures, recitation and supplication
samâ'	سماع	Religious music and singing. Specifically, it refers to Sufi spiritual songs and their singing, which is most often accompanied by musical instruments.
Sharia (shari'ah)	شرعة	Islamic law derived from the Qur'an and the Sunnah

shaykh	شيخ	teacher, mentor; scholar
shirk	الشرك	associating partners with Allah
soorah or soorat	سورة	chapter of the Qur'ân
Sunnah	سنَة	the practice and collected sayings of Prophet Muhammad (ﷺ) that together with the Qur'ân forms the basis of Islamic law
tâbi'oon (*sg. tâbi'i*)	التابعون	'Successors'; those who knew or met any of the Companions and transmitted hadiths from them
tafseer	تفسير	exegesis: commentary, or explanation of the meanings (usu. of Qur'ânic verses)
taghbeer	تغبير	A practice invented in Baghdad in the second century AH, by deviant Sufis, in which people would gather and a singer would sing poems stressing the importance of the hereafter and disliking this world. This singing was accompanied by musical instruments and sometimes by dancing.
ṭawâf	طواف	circumambulation of the Ka'bah
tawḥeed	التوحيد	the Oneness of Allah: that He alone deserves to be worshipped and that He has no partners
Ummah	أمَة	community or nation: usu. used to refer to the entire global community of Muslims
'umrah	عمرة	a minor, non-obligatory pilgrimage to Makkah
zinâ	زنى	adultery or fornication

Notes

....

....

....

....

....

....

....

....

....

....

Notes

....

....

....

....

....

....

....

....

....

....

Notes

Notes

Notes

....

....

....

....

....

....

....

....

....

....

Notes

....

....

....

....

....

....

....

....

....

....

....